S.R. Bissette's Blur
(Complete Edition)
Volume 2: Video Views
(2000)

S. R. Bissette's Blur
Volume 2: Video Views
(2000)

by

Stephen R. Bissette

A Black Coat Press Book

Cover design: Jon-Mikel Gates
Packaged by SpiderBaby Grafix & Publications.

To contact the author, please write to:
Stephen R. Bissette, PO Box 157, Windsor, VT 05089,
or visit:
www.srbissette.com

A complete set of the original *Brattleboro Reformer Arts & Entertainment* sections, featuring *Video Views* and miscellaneous articles, and an almost-complete set of *VMag* are preserved in the Stephen R. Bissette Collection in the HUIE Library at Henderson State University in Arkadelphia, Arkansas. *The Reformer* is also accessible via microfiche at the Brooks Memorial Library in Brattleboro, VT.

Visit our website at www.blackcoatpress.com

For Maia Rose and Daniel Luke;
Forever first in my heart

Acknowledgements:

These reviews and essays were originally published in *The Brattleboro Reformer*, *VMag*, *The Chicopee Herald* and *The Reminder*. Some were also presented, in revised and expanded form, in *The Video Watchdog*.

My thanks to my various editors and publishers, particularly Chris Nixon (my first *Brattleboro Reformer Arts & Entertainment* editor), Willow Dannible (my second), and Jon Potter (the current *Reformer A&E* editor); Steve Murphy (*VMag* and a comrade-in-arms from my comics days/daze); G. Michael Dobbs (*The Chicopee Herald*, *The Reminder*, and the dearest and closest friend of 'em all), and Lynne Winter (editor of *Rampage* magazine).

Special thanks, too, to Tim and Donna Lucas, who accepted expanded versions of some of these reviews for inclusion in the pages of *The Video Watchdog*, beginning with the *Princess Mononoke* review which appears in this volume. Whenever possible, I have included those revised versions herein, as they were always superior to the *Video Views* versions, if only for the gift of a bit more time for one more polish, and Tim's invaluable editorial insights and guidance.

Thanks to Alan Goldstein for asking me to tackle the column back in '99. Thanks to everyone at First Run Video, including our customers. Thanks most of all to April Stage — now April Anderson — then-manager at First Run and beloved fellow employee. April "kept me honest" in this process, insisting that I do not ignore the latest Julia Roberts or Sandra Bullock opus, try as I might. Thanks, too, to the many fellow independent video store owners, members of the New England Buying Group, and the various studio reps who provided insights, opinions, and screeners whenever necessary, and often when they weren't necessary.

Special thanks to Jon-Mikel Gates for his considerable assistance with computer and information retrieval/rescue aid provided, and for his excellent cover design work. Thanks, too, to Steven Twiss for an eleventh-hour fact check.

Thanks to then-Marjory Bleier — now Marjory Bissette — who put up with me throughout this manic two year-plus saga and opened my eyes to the pleasures of films (and life) I might otherwise have skirted.

Thanks to my then-teenage offspring Maia Rose and Daniel, to whom this volume is dedicated, and who also made sure I stay tuned to many movies I might have otherwise passed over or missed altogether. You may have given me many gray hairs, but through this stretch, you kept me young.

Finally, thanks to Jean-Marc and Randy Lofficier, who made these collections possible.

SRB

Introduction

FOCUS

It's sad to note how many newspapers have eliminated critics and reviewers from their content mix. It's pandemic as of 2008, and part and parcel of the many changes shaking the marketplace of ideas and newspaper business in general.

I'll not get into the specifics here, save to note I feel luckier than ever that I had a chance, for over two years, to write *Video Views* at a time when local newspapers still cultivated such columns.

My passion for writing, and particularly for writing about cinema, dates back to my childhood. As an adult, this seemed an unnecessary and rather childish diversion to my friends, peers, and fellow pros in the comics field. Simply put, they would have much rather seen me drawing more comics, and considered anything outside that vocation a squandering of my life, time, and talents.

It was, in fact, a lifeline back to something that had always been vital and dear to me, as central to my life as my art and comics had always been. It was part and parcel of who I was, who I am, and as vital to me as my comics work, illustrations, and fiction writing.

The weekly column for *The Brattleboro Reformer* grew out of my job at First Run Video (where, at my own insistence, I began as a minimum-wage clerk like everyone else, working my way up to management within a year — hey, it isn't rocket science). First Run

Video was and is owned by my friend Alan B. Goldstein, who I'd first met in 1982 when he ran the only comic book shop and mail-order business in southern Vermont, Moondance Comics. Alan had long since left comics retailing and launched First Run Video as the area's first video superstore in November of 1991. When Chris Nixon of the *Brattleboro Reformer* approached Alan in the summer of 1999 about First Run possibly providing the paper with a weekly video column for their new weekly *Arts & Entertainment* section (incorporated into the *Reformer* every Thursday to cover the coming week and weekend), Alan naturally turned to me. So began *Video Views*, my weekly column for the *Brattleboro Reformer*.

By 1999 (when the *Video Views* column began), I had accumulated a reputation for stretching and/or missing deadlines with my comics work, but I somehow made or beat all my writing deadlines.

Writing came easy for me. It wasn't the agonizing struggle that drawing comics (as opposed to single illustrations or sketches) was, became, and remained. So, writing — particularly writing about film — was unencumbered pleasure, blighted with none of the depressing personal baggage drawing and comics were increasingly burdened with. As I made my way toward the fateful decision to retire from the comics industry at the close of 1999, my writing became more and more important to my well-being. None of this paid much of anything, but it was enormously satisfying, and kept me sane through stretches of initially depressing life changes.

The column took on another vital dimension for me: having earned a poor reputation with deadlines in the comics industry, I was determined to run the one-year gauntlet (I originally committed to one year) and never miss a weekly deadline for the *Reformer*. That I managed this feat for a little over *two* years without misstep was and is a point of accomplishment and pride, as vital to me as my having completed the world's second *24-Hour Comic* on a dare from Scott McCloud.[1] I managed all this while writing additional articles for the *A&E* editor and for other zines, completing a couple of books, writing or drawing my final professional comics work, *and* working full-time at First Run Video (not to mention raising two teenagers, among other things).

So, it seemed high time I finally gather together the *Video Views* columns, for posterity and as the vainest of vanity projects. This four-volume book series provides a permanent record of what has been (particularly to my peers in the comics industry) a limbo period in my career, the "lost years" when my comics work disappeared and it was presumed I had simply ceased to be productive in any manner.

As I hope *Blur* demonstrates, I was plenty productive, and hopefully the fruits of those years of labor will still provide some entertainment value and enlightenment to someone, somewhere.

A note on the format: This book series, to the best of my abilities, includes every *Video Views* column I wrote between 1999 and 2001. A few of these were articles, but most were the regular weekly column. Supplementing my digital files may, upon occasion, mean including work in later volumes that belonged, chronologically, in earlier volumes. In the end, in any case, *Blur* will indeed encompass my entire body of video re-

---

[1] See *24 Hour Comics*, edited by Scott McCloud (About Comics, 2004), available from www.AboutComics.com

view work, with the exception of pieces I choose to reserve for inclusion in the upcoming *Gooseflesh* volumes.

Blur, Volume 1 included capsule reviews for *VMag*, edited and published by my friend Stephen Murphy, which debuted in November 1997; a few of those capsule reviews also appear herein, when chronologically relevant and/or differing from the *Reformer* columns. For its first year of publication, *VMag* published a number of my articles (some of which will be reprinted in *Gooseflesh*), but by 1999 my submissions had narrowed to a trickle of capsule video reviews. Unlike the *Reformer*, *VMag* did not cater to a family audience — hence the more adult orientation of some of the material written for that zine.[2]

The Reformer columns began on September 9, 1999, and continued weekly thereafter through October of 2001; *Blur, Volume 1* collected every *Reformer Video View* column from that first entry to March 30, 2000.

This collection continues that chronology, beginning in April and concluding with my Halloween, 2000 column, and includes one review that was also published in revised and expanded form in the *Video Watchdog* magazine (special thanks to my *VW* editors and longtime friends Tim and Donna Lucas; please, see the acknowledgements), and another that appeared revised and expanded in the wrestling magazine *Rampage* (special thanks to my *Rampage* editor Lynne Winter, and to her

---

[2] Despite my best efforts, the lack of original digital files and/or a complete set of *VMag* (neither I nor Steve Murphy have yet found a copy of the November 2000 issue) mean a definitive inventory of my *VMag* work was inconclusive at this writing. If further material surfaces, I will incorporate it into future volumes of *Blur* for the sake of completion.

hubby Douglas E. Winter, who knows what to do with ears).

Please note that the *Video Watchdog* rewrites often included historical, industry-oriented, and/or technical information that did not appear in the original *Reformer* columns, and that Tim and Donna demanded a more rigorous attention to detail than the Reformer *Video Views* column permitted. In all cases, the *VW* versions were superior, hence those are the drafts included in these collections.

My editors at the *Reformer Arts & Entertainment* section were Chris Nixon and Willow Dannible, and I thank them again for the ongoing good relations and indulging my occasionally page-stretching extravaganzas.

The dates given before each column cite the original date of publication; on those occasions when unforeseen editorial decisions resulted in a column being 'bumped' to the following week or otherwise revised, I have preserved the chronology in which the columns were written (corresponding, by and large, with the respective video release dates), incorporating editorial alterations only when they improved or significantly altered the context of the published review. Longer columns were sometimes run as two-part pieces; those columns are specified as such with their respective publication dates, and annotated as necessary. As *Video Views* grew and reader response proved favorable, my editors seemed happy to indulge even my wildest schemes.

Unlike my ongoing writing for the horror film fan magazines (which will be collected in the book series *Gooseflesh*, also from Black Coat Press), I could not presume my readers knew anything about films or filmmakers. There was no communal shorthand I could rely upon. I was writing for an audience that *might* know who Alfred Hitchcock, Steven Spielberg, and George Lucas were, but maybe not. For most *Reformer* readers, only the big movie stars had any name value or instantly identifiable celebrity. So I took it upon myself to remind readers in almost every column that individuals — artists — indeed made these movies, these videos, that filled the new release wall at First Run Video. I hoped to elevate the interest level in the medium by doing much more than write capsule reviews, but in doing so always had to be sure I provided constant reference points. Thus, I would cite other works by the same filmmakers, other films performers had appeared in, specify cinematic precursors and sources.

In the disposable forum of a weekly newspaper column, this wasn't intrusive, but once those columns are collected, the repetition of certain filmographies or references can seem rather dreary. Still, I have decided to run the columns as they originally were published. This may make these collections more useful for younger readers and neophyte film buffs, but I hope this aspect of the columns collected in this series won't prove too exasperating to the knowledgeable film aficionados who deign to dig into these writings.

As in *Blur Volume 1*, I have provided footnotes to cite relevant reviews published earlier, the occasional source reference (which was discouraged in the original weekly newspaper format), and more current information and/or updates if I thought it important in either the February 2006 or July 2008 edit of this manuscript.

A final note, for those curious about the mid-1990s collapse of the comics direct sales market, the video business, and my own career arc during this unusual period: The review of Oliver Stone's *Any Given Sunday* (see pp. 178-180) doesn't mention it, but that video release was what I came to regard as a sort of video industry "Pearl Harbor." It was comparable to what Larry Marder (creator of *Beanworld*) called the comic book direct sales market "Pearl Harbor," the historic moment when Marvel Comics' went exclusive with their own distribution firm, Heroes World. *Any Given Sunday*'s September 1, 2000 street date (Fridays are unusual street dates in the video market; Tuesdays remain the norm) marked Warner Home Video's identical tactical move, and like almost all major upheavals in the entertainment industries, the moment and its repercussions were invisible to the customers and consumers, save for their occasional confusion over these unexpected Friday street dates.

Any Given Sunday was Warner's first exclusive title: Warner bypassed the traditional video distribution methods, refusing their product to distributors save the delegated few Warner singled out as "authorized" Warner distributors. Furthermore, those distributors were facilitators only: the "New Deal" required that video retailers deal directly with Warner to purchase *Any Given Sunday* and all future titles. This was a major blow, and began (as Marvel's decision had in the comics direct sale market) a scramble among other major studios (Universal and Columbia prominent among them) to likewise establish exclusive distribution venues.

Without going into particulars, suffice to say in the short-term, only Warner thrived, while the others who followed suit stumbled and/or suffered in various ways. Independent video retailers suffered even more. In the long-term, the exclusivity era was relatively short-lived, though it encompassed a (failed) class action lawsuit by independent video retailers against two major video chains and the major studios, and the launch and astonishingly rapid mainstream adoption of DVD as the format of choice for sales and rental (due, in no small part, to Warners' hyper-aggressive promotion of the new format as "sell-through" priced product). By the time I left the video retail business in the spring of 2005, most of the hubbub was over, but it made for a memorable five years, to say the least (including a closed-door meeting with key area Warner reps that included a naked and abusive assertion of power that dwarfed anything I'd experienced in the comics industry). Recently, the post-Miramax incarnation of the Weinstein Company has returned to exclusivity releasing in cahoots with Block-buster Video; I've no insights to add, having left the video retail market behind me.

Fortunately, unlike the comics direct sale market, the video market was vital and diverse enough to survive such shenanigans. Also unlike the comics market, independent video retailers stood up in opposition to these practices, though many succumbed to this and other overwhelming market forces at work at the turn of the millennium. But that, bunky, is quite another story.

Looking back, through the process of compiling and polishing this series of books, I have to say I found many pleasant surprises. I'd forgotten I'd seen, much less written about, many of these movies — hence the title of this book and book series.

Thankfully, it is no longer just a blur, consigned to yellowing newspapers and scattered magazines in my collection.

Enjoy.

April 6:

George Lucas' STAR WARS Breaks Records... and Hearts.

It's too early to chart the success of this past Tuesday's video release of George Lucas' long-awaited ***STAR WARS: EPISODE 1: THE PHANTOM MENACE*** (1999), but all indications are that Lucas has done it again. 20th Century Fox Video has once again scored big, approaching (or eclipsing) sales on 1998's popular video release of James Cameron's Academy-Award winner *Titanic*. That record-breaking title brightened the usually low-activity month of September for video retailers across the country. *Star Wars: Episode 1* seems to have delivered a much-needed punch amid the often soft spring season, when the change to Daylight Savings time, increased demands of school exams and work, and the enticing warm weather may keep steady renters away from their home entertainment centers. *Star Wars: Episode 1* and other strong draws like last week's release of *The Sixth Sense* [3] have kept video customers glued to their screens. The upcoming April and May releases of *The Insider, Three Kings, Boys Don't Cry, Being John Malkovich, Galaxy Quest, Dogma, Fight Club*, the James Bond opus *The World is Not Enough*, Tim Burton's *Sleepy Hollow*, and the Academy-Award sweeper *American Beauty* promise to keep up the pace set by *Star Wars: Episode 1*'s lead.

Local sales of the new *Star Wars* epic were brisk, with almost one hundred units (of the regular version

---

[3] See *Blur, Vol. 1*, pp. 250-252.

and the special edition "widescreen" boxed set combined) sold out of Brattleboro's independent video shop First Run Video by 7 PM, though owner Alan Goldstein was prepared with a steady supply of both editions for customers eager to take the latest *Star Wars* extravaganza home for keeps. Other nearby video merchants in New Hampshire, Massachusetts, and the rest of New England reported similarly lively sales. *Star Wars: Episode 1* has also scored solid rentals, though this coming weekend will undoubtably outgun the mid-week rentals... especially with the predicted wet weather sweeping through the region.

Many shops are planning special *Star Wars*-related events, including First Run Video's scheduled appearances of local fans wearing stunning costume recreations of the film's lead heroine Queen Amidala and the imposing villain Darth Maul. The local theatrical premiere of *Star Wars: Episode 1* last May at Brattleboro's Latchis Theater proved to be an event (likewise adorned with elaborately-costumed fans), as reported here in the *Reformer*.

What is it about *Star Wars* that creates such cultural shockwaves, and is Lucas' latest effort really worthy of all the attention and adulation?

Like many of my generation, I lucked into the original *Star Wars* (1977) without expectations. With my good friend and fellow cartoonist Rick Veitch and my cartooning college roommate Jack Forcier, I stumbled into the New York City premiere. We'd spotted the eye-catching poster and lobby cards outside Loew's Astor Plaza, the Manhattan theater *Star Wars* opened in, en route to a job interview; we checked the posted schedule, and decided to catch the first matinee on our way back from our publisher's office. A short time later, we paid for our tickets, scrutinized the tantalizing photos of white-armored storm-troopers astride giant lizards and laser-blazing starships engaged in deep-space dog-fights, entered Loew's expansive underground theater (which, alas, no longer exists) and chose cherry seats, and then settled into them for the show (well, Veitch almost got us tossed out, but I'll save that tale for another time). The audience was abuzz, and the serial-like opening title crawl evoked a few chuckles, but *no one* was ready for the blast of sound which came from behind and roared overhead in unison with the jaw-dropping opening image of a starship soaring above us and *into* the screen.

In a heartbeat, our collective imaginations had been engaged as never before, and we were swept along into George Lucas' lovingly crafted science fiction adventure. When the lights came up, we couldn't wait to see it again, drag our friends to it; we had tasted the Force, and we wanted more. Clearly, the Force was with George, too: positive word of mouth spread like wildfire, and an international pop-cultural phenomenon was born.

Star Wars was only Lucas' third feature. His first, the downbeat dystopian chiller *THX-1138* (1971), had earned good reviews but lost money; his second, *American Graffiti* (1973), was adopted by a wide audience at the boxoffice and spawned a long-lasting knock-off TV series, *Happy Days*. Nevertheless, when Lucas made *Star Wars*, he was still hungry, struggling to bring an anachronistic science fiction concept to the big screen despite a relatively meager budget and unenthusiastic studio. That genuine hunger, the yearning for something better, something more, and something beyond, infused every frame of *Star Wars*.

Lucas' surrogate was his hero, young Luke Sky-walker, whose need for escape and self-fulfillment through a rigorous rite-of-passage reflected Lucas' (and a youthful audience's) own needs and desires. Luke and Lucas had a date with destiny: they knew it in their bones, just as we felt we, too, had a higher calling. *Star Wars*, silly militaristic fantasy that it was, evoked and answered that call. Despite its pastiche of World War 2 war films, Leni Riefenstahl pageantry, and Depression-era space operas and Saturday-afternoon movie serials — the venerable *Flash Gordon* primary among them both — *Star Wars* was as personal a creation for Lucas as the early-1960s reverie of *American Graffiti*.

The unprecedented marketing and merchandising success of *Star Wars* subsequently freed Lucas, and the rest is legend. Mobilizing his earnings with far more skill than predecessors like Orson Welles and Francis Ford Coppola, Lucas founded and sheltered his own production firm, special effects' studios, and creative empire. He also stepped out from behind the camera, turning the directorial reins over to others to realize the subsequent *Star Wars* entries, *The Empire Strikes Back* (1980) and *Return of the Jedi* (1983).

Thus, *Star Wars: Episode 1: The Phantom Menace* marks Lucas' return to directing (and writing) after a twenty-two year hiatus. Though Lucas has remained active as a producer, two decades is a long time for any creator to step away from his profession — and unfortunately, *Star Wars: Episode 1* suffers from Lucas' sabbatical from the director's chair. It also suffers from Lucas' lack of personal attachment: the young man's dreams implicit and explicit in *Star Wars* swept up a generation. The rich man's fantasies of *The Phantom Menace* are lumbering, sterile, and mercantile in nature, as mechanical as the Droid army at the center of its most spectacular set pieces.

Gone is the intoxicating, streamlined narrative efficiency of the original *Star Wars*, emulating the primal romance of a bygone era. Instead, *The Phantom Menace* evokes the worst archetypes of our cultural debris. Many have already cited the thinly-veiled racist stereotypes at work, too: the oily Oriental "Yellow Peril" of the Trade Federation elite, the parodistic black Jamaican speech and mannerisms of the amphibious aborigines Jar-Jar and the Gungans (which are uncomfortably close to the racist batrachians stereotypes featured in an old MGM *Bosko* cartoon, *Bosko and the Cannibals*). The shoddy storytelling is equally lamentable, and far, far more damaging.

[Spoiler warning: If you haven't yet seen the film, *STOP READING NOW!*] *The Phantom Menace* opens with a rambling text crawl at odds with John Williams' rousing score: taxation of trade routes has prompted a Trade Federation blockade of "the small planet of Naboo"; instead of responding to the threat, the Republic's Congress impotently debates the issues while the Federation mounts an illegal invasion, leaving the Supreme Chancellor to assign two Jedi Knights to intercede. Huh? Taxes? A "Greedy Trade Federation"? Republicans? *Congress*? In the theaters, you could hear a sigh of relief when the words "Jedi Knights" finally slithered up the screen: finally, the promise of action! These are adult concerns reduced to gibberish amid the juvenile thrills; even the most ardent fans of the current film admit to confusion with the plot, rife with convoluted economic boycotts, political chicanery, and Machiavellian schemes.

The Phantom Menace thereafter unfolds with little concern for the most rudimentary narrative concerns. The plot intrigues (role-playing, deceptions, and duplicity) gracelessly unfold, and characterization is sketchy at best. The only adult pleasures to be had are in Ian McDiarmid's performance as Senator Palpatine, who understates his links with the future Emperor (and present Darth Sidious) despite the transparent slight-of-hand plotting. Sadly, his is the only evocative characterization: there is no chemistry between Jedi Master Qui-Gon Jinn (Liam Neeson, who at least lends an authoritarian dignity to his role) and his apprentice Obi-Wan Kenobi (Ewan McGregor); Queen Amidala (Natalie Portman) is a cipher, interchangeable with her decoy handmaiden; there are no meaningful portents of Anakin Skywalker's future persona amid all his screentime, save for Yoda's spoken reservations. We are told by his mother that Anakin (Jason Lloyd) "knows nothing of greed," though he works as a slave for their owner Watto, a gambler who deals in metal, flesh, and profit, the very personification of greed: is Anakin blind as well as young? Anakin's touted affinity for the Force is demystified (a clinically-detectable biological agent of the Force is introduced, diminishing the spiritual aspects of Lucas' most resonant *Star Wars* concept), though, in fact, such an affinity is never demonstrated. In the final act, Anakin is reduced to a buffoonish brat, accidentally triggering the Naboo Starfighter to plunge into the Trade Federation Battleship, scoring hits by aimlessly pushing buttons like a trigger-happy video-gaming tyke while spouting *bon mots* like "This is tense!", "Take this — and this!", "Now this is pod-racing!", "Oops!", and "Wooooooo!" This dialogue is chilling, but in a way Lucas never intended.

Furthermore, the Sith menace of Darth Maul is empty, literally a mask (impressive though it is): we never once see him display the deadly prowess attributed to him. We are only *told* he is evil and to be feared, but Lucas seems to have forgotten how to tell a story: Darth Maul has no dramatic weight. Consider, for instance, Akira Kurosawa's introduction of each of *The Seven Samurai* (1957), or Sergio Leone's economic introduction of bounty hunter Lee Van Cleef in the opening scene of *For a Few Dollars More* (1967), which succinctly established his armory of weapons, his sharp-shooting skills, and ruthless efficiency — or, more to the point, Lucas' own concise, chilling introduction of Darth Vader in *Star Wars*, able to choke off an offending Federation officer's breath with a mere flex of his fingers from across the room. Like the strutting, prancing Feyd Harkonnen (Sting) of David Lynch's visually opulent but similarly clumsy *Dune* (1984) — who never seemed a threat to that film's hero because Feyd never demonstrated his fighting skills prior to their final duel — we never see Darth Maul in battle. His brief skirmish with Qui-Gon occurs almost two-thirds of the way into the film, and lasts less than a minute. His only other action scene is the final duel itself, a nicely choreographed match that fails to illicit the genuine excitement of those in *Star Wars* or *The Empire Strikes Back*. Lucas further diminishes the duel's impact by cross-cutting it with three other climaxes — Queen Amidala and her minions in the occupied Naboo palace, Anakin's scattershot battle in space, and Jar-Jar and the Gungan's terrestrial war — each narratively flawed by poor conception (Jar-Jar's pratfalls accidentally scoring against the Droid army) and execution (Anakin's embarrassing antics).

The very sterility of Lucas' war scenes has become increasingly uninvolving. The man-versus-terrifying-machine battles that were such a revelation in *The Empire Strikes Back* have continued to devolve into tinkertoy panoramas. In the clash between the Gungans and the Trade Federation's mechanized Droid armies, no battle strategy or skills are evident, just the relative merits or failures of the fire-power and force-fields. The battle's decisive moment is determined by Anakin's maladroit intervention in the depths of space, but we could care less: the implacable, schematic efficiency of the Droid army, while esthetically compelling, neither rouses nor scares us.

This is poor filmmaking by any standards, but it would be less troubling if the film's ballyhoo weren't so steeped in pompous proclamations asserting its supposed import. In *Time* magazine's pre-theatrical release coverage, Bill Moyers interviewed Lucas, and both parties shamelessly wallowed in the allusions to Joseph Campbell, Carl Jung, and mythic resonance already being spun about the film.[4] The real sources of Lucas' inspiration are apparent on the screen: the elegant cities and alien landscapes are pirated from cartoonists like Alex Raymond, Al Williamson, Roy Krenkel, and John Totleben, and painters like James Gurney (of *Dinotopia* fame); the 12-minute pod-race lifted from the silent and sound film adaptations of *Ben-Hur* (and was executed, on a cinematic level, more effectively in both versions of that Biblical epic); the Jedi Council borrows the late Gil Kane's rendition of the omnipotent Guardians of the Universe from DC Comics' early 1960s *Green Lantern* comics; Darth Maul's farewell image is lifted from the climax of a minor John Frankenheimer and John Sayles' samurai film *The Challenge* (1982); and so on. Many of these are undoubtably well-intentioned, affectionate homages, but the patchwork nature of the film, lack of

---

[4] *"Of Myth and Men,"* Time, April 26, 1999, pp. 90-94.

substance, and Lucas' public piety makes the cumulative effect of such pop-cultural appropriations less than endearing. In 1977, Lucas' unpretentious associations of the original *Star Wars* with movie serials like *Buck Rogers* and *Flash Gordon*, the pulp science fiction of Edgar Rice Burroughs, westerns like John Ford's *The Searchers*, and the Carlos Casteneda Don Juan books (source of 'The Force') was an honest articulation of a dignified lineage; the subsequent academic association of the *Star Wars* series with its deeper cultural roots has clearly gone to Lucas' head, much to the detriment of Lucas the filmmaker and storyteller. Edgar Rice Burroughs was, first and foremost, a masterful storyteller, and *The Phantom Menace* could use a whole lot more of Burroughs's no-nonsense skills and a lot less Campbell ego-boo.

In the documentary preceding the video special edition, *Filmmaking Has Turned a Corner*, Lucas says, "I'm forced to move the medium forward in order to tell my stories." Unfortunately, Lucas has forgotten how to effectively tell a story; he mistakes the virtuosity of the admittedly impressive technical wizardry at his disposal for innovation, while ignoring the most basic necessities of storytelling. The documentary goes on to show us the extensive storyboarding and "pre-visualization" process (in which entire sequences are filmed and edited via puppetry into tightly-edited simulacra of the final product) which allowed Lucas to refine the effects and specific scenes. This only intensifies one's exasperation with the emptiness of the experience: if only a fraction of the effort poured into executing Lucas' conceits had been diverted into constructing a coherent, dramatic narrative, the vast expenditure of time, effort, ingenuity, and money might have yielded a film worthy of the effort.

Despite Lucas' claims to "mov[ing] the medium forward," there is nothing progressive about the film itself: cinematically, it is a crude, incoherent affair. The most rudimentary of cross-cutting climaxes from D.W. Griffith's Biograph short films (all pre-1915) remain more effective than Lucas's ham-fisted cross-editing in his *Phantom Menace* finale. Shorn of the flashy special effects tapestry, the threadbare weave of Queens and Knights, Gungans and Droids, Sith and slaves, Lucas's opus is as clumsy as the earliest silent cinema's abbreviated adaptations of Shakespeare and Alexandre Dumas, costume melodramas shorn of context. The staggering scope and audacity of *The Phantom Menace*'s visual extravaganza doesn't offset the paucity of narrative imagination, wit, or dramatic impact.

Look at it this way: for one of the few times in history, a filmmaker had all the means, money, and time at his whim to realize his vision. Given similar indulgence, a young Orson Welles cooked up *Citizen Kane*, and George Lucas came up with... this. *Star Wars: Episode 1* will retain some stature as a digitally-animated feature film populated with a few live actors, but even that must be qualified: contemporary animated features like Brad Bird's *The Iron Giant*, Hayao Miyazaki's *Princess Mononoke*, and (speaking of Burroughs) even Walt Disney's *Tarzan* [5] are far more powerful, moving, and memorable than anything in *Star Wars: Episode 1: The Phantom Menace*.

Why, then, has such a lackluster juggernaut become such a cultural event?

---

[5] See *Blur, Vol. 1*, pp. 127-129, 194-195; see *Princess Mononoke* review in this volume, pp. 181-187.

In short, it is because George, and a new generation, *willed* it. As John Rovnak (who is in his twenties) explained to me last May, prior to his waiting in line overnight to ensure a seat at the premiere, "You don't get it. I was a baby when those films came out; I never got to experience what you did. This is my chance."

Lucas made *Star Wars: Episode 1* for the legion of fans who'd missed the original buzz, the waiting in lines, the expectation for new installments. They were finally going to get an opportunity to experience it all for themselves, for the first time. The revamped editions of the original trilogy had only whet their collective appetite: *Star Wars: Episode 1* was an event for a generation who'd only heard or read about the first *Star Wars* experience, which was ironically both romanticized out of proportion and diminished hopelessly in scope by the very home video versions they'd been weaned on.

This was their *Star Wars*, moles and all — and unlike the manufactured recreated "event" of Woodstock for the 1990s, this event (however mass-produced, orchestrated, or manipulated) wasn't going to degenerate into bonfires and riots. A new universe, more expansive than that of the first trilogy, has unfolded for a new generation, and they've evidently taken it to heart.

Others are grateful for what has been delivered after so long. "This was the first movie for me that seamlessly merged computer-generated effects and live-action characters," Yves Teleno told me. "It also helped fill a big hole in the story that has kept me at the edge of my seat since I was little. Somehow, the magic of *Star Wars* never seems to wear off."

Vital to this event was the fact that whatever the film turned out to be, it came from the original source — George Lucas — and he'd lavished all his resources into making this new *Star Wars* for the new generation. Like the first *Star Wars* series (which was indeed lambasted by many critics, including genre publications like *Cinefantastique*), the new *Star Wars: Episode 1* was critic-proof. As one of my peers, G. Michael Dobbs (author, newspaper editor, and founder/editor/publisher of *Animation Planet* magazine), put it, "I like it for what it is: Bubble-gum filmmaking." Despite poor reviews and shaky word-of-mouth, *Star Wars: Episode 1* quickly became one of the top-grossing films of all time.

George, canny business tycoon that he is, had already guaranteed his profits: the reported $2 billion Pepsi paid for the *Star Wars* licensing sponsorship had nicely offset George's comparatively frugal $115 million investment in the film itself.

The Force is clearly still with George.

And, like it or not, it's once again with you, too.

Following is my capsule review of Star Wars: The Phantom Menace *for the April, 2000 issue of* VMag *(pg. 43), included here for the sake of completion.*[6]

STAR WARS: THE PHANTOM MENACE (1999) made the bundle it was marketed to shovel into Lucasfilm's coffers, but the movie itself — apart from the media event it represented — is a stinking turd. Let's face facts, shall we? For one of the precious few times in cinema history, a director had *all* the means, money, and time necessary to bring his "vision" to fruition... and *this*

---

[6] The April 2000 issue of *VMag* (pg. 42) also featured the review for *The Insider* (abridged) and two earlier *Video Views* reviews reprinted in *Blur, Volume 1*, for *Highwayman* and *The Best Man* (see pp. 219-220, 228-229).

is what George Lucas concocted. Toho's most childish *Godzilla* movies had more narrative spine then this drivel. The screenplay, such as it is, is atrocious: characterization is utterly minimal, narrative threads lead nowhere, and even the most rudimentary "foreshadowing" of the youthful Darth Vader's future nature is scuttled. There's no sense of play or excitement: the action set pieces are unfocused shambles, conceived and staged with scatter shot computer-game kinetics. Lucas had over a decade-and-a-half to hone this tripe into shape before committing a frame (or CGI-image) to celluloid (or the digital equivalent). Couldn't he have rung up his old buddies and collaborators Lawrence Kasdan, Steven Spielberg, or, heck, any 15-year-old *Star Wars* fanatic, and crafted a real script? The eye-filling visuals are all they should be at times, but there's no heart, head, or direction to lend them drama, weight, or context. In the end, the juvenile reduction of Lucas' original themes to the mind-numbing spectacle of a reckless boy accidentally accomplishing the impossible while spouting macho "gotcha!" dialogue ridicules all the portent and pretense of "The Force," destiny, and the Joseph-Campbell-mythic-roots Lucas blathered about in the torrent of media attention *Phantom Menace* garnered prior to its release. Whatever the fans and apologists claim, *The Phantom Menace* is an over-long, over-hyped, top-heavy embarrassment and bore, and Lucas has, simply put, forgotten *how* to tell a story. *(Rated "PG-13" for mild light-saber dueling and war-movie violence.)*

[Note: For what it's worth, Star Wars: Episode 2 *and* 3 *were just as dreadful, and my observation* on Episode 1 *that the "only adult pleasures to be had are in Ian*

McDiarmid's performance as Senator Palpatine" remained true to the bitter end.]

April 6:

Though *Star Wars: Episode 1: The Phantom Menace* dominates the "New Release" wall of every video store coast to coast this week (see separate review), there's still plenty of new and recent releases to lend a lift to this wet spring week. In your rush to visit "a galaxy far, far away," don't miss:

THE MESSENGER: THE STORY OF JOAN OF ARC (1999) was pilloried and condemned by most American critics for, well, being too French (if only George Lucas could have mustered a fraction of the same passionate energy!). Luc Besson (director of gems like *The Big Blue, La Femme Nikita, The Professional*, and the romantic science fiction parable *The Fifth Element*) is French, as was Jeanne d'Arc, better known as Joan of Arc, who was burned at the stake on May 30th, 1431 at the age of 19 after her decisive role in the liberation of her mother country from British and Burgundian occupation. She was subsequently canonized by the Vatican, and has been the subject of many films, prominent among them Danish director Carl Dreyer's masterpiece *The Passion of Joan of Arc* (1928), which a few critics glibly evoked in their attacks on Besson's effort. The comparison is unfair and misleading: precious few films in history can compare to Dreyer's classic (which focused on Joan's final days), nor was Dreyer a commercial filmmaker. Besson's version of Joan's story is more compelling and compassionate than any prior version — save Dreyer's. Unlike Dreyer, Besson charts the decade of Joan's ascension, from the 9-year-old girl traumatized by the savage murder and rape (in that order) of her sister, to her brief teenage reign as a visionary leader and reluctant warrior. It is, however, a messy spectacle, eschewing the piety and pageantry usually lavished on Joan's story. The medieval battle sequences are vivid and horrific (men are crushed, impaled, immolated, dismembered, and pulped on screen), to be avoided by young or timid viewers who might instead seek the recent video release *Joan of Arc* starring Leelee Sobieski, which is suitable for all ages.[7]

Like its subject, "an illiterate peasant" who claimed divine forces guided her to victory, *The Messenger* is passionate, obsessive, flamboyant, chaotic, driven, valiant, fragile, ravishing, brutal, reckless, and brave. Among its many virtues is its marvelous cast: Besson, like Dreyer, Sergio Leone, and Terry Gilliam, casts memorable faces, visages which embody, emerge and erupt from the landscape. Among them are John Malkovich (as the callow Charles VII, the Dauphin crowned King of France thanks to Joan's miraculous victory at Orleans), Faye Dunaway (her best role in years as Charles' scheming mother), frequent Besson player Tcheky Karyo (from *La Femme Nikita*), and Besson's wife Milla Jovovich as Joan. Again, the critics savaged Jovovich's performance, though she delivers a galvanizing portrait of the young woman thrust into history by forces she barely comprehends but believes in with all her heart, even as she becomes a political obstacle, embarrassment, pawn, victim, and ultimately a martyr. Throughout, the issue of Joan's all-consuming devotion and the mystery of her visions and faith remain central, mercilessly dis-

---

[7] See *Blur, Vol. 1*, pp. 58-59.

sected in the final act via her dialogues with the dispassionate Conscience (Dustin Hoffman). Though flawed, *The Messenger* is an ambitious and worthy film, my pick of the week. Recommended! *(Rated "R" for graphic violence, strong language, adult and sexual situations, a brief but brutal necrophilia scene, and intense religious material.)* [8]

The elegiac, overblown reverie of **FOR LOVE OF THE GAME** (1999) blends baseball and banal romance, evoking *Bull Durham* (1988) and *Field of Dreams* (1989), prior Kevin Costner vehicles that tread similar turf. Sadly, *For Love of the Game* doesn't make it past second base, much less score a home run, though some might enjoy it. The credits montage of home movies, newspaper clippings, baseball cards, and ephemera charts Billy Chapel's (Costner) lifelong passion for baseball from Little to Big League sports and the World Series. As the film begins, catcher Gus (John C. Reilly, likable as ever) is nursemaiding pitcher Chapel through his autumn years and a rough season capped with the sale of the team, owner Wheeler's (Brian Cox) appeal to Chapel to retire, and Chapel's lover (and professional writer) Jane Aubrey (Kelly Preston) skipping off to London — all before the last game of the season. It's Chapel's last game, we are led to believe. Wheeler bemoans "the players, the fans, TV rights, arbitrations: it isn't the same... The game stinks"; soft-spoken Chapel replies, "The game doesn't stink — it's a great game."

---

[8] An abridged version of this review of *The Messenger* was also published in *VMag* #30, May 2000, pg. 48. There were no video reviews in *VMag* #31 (June/July 2000).

And so it is, whenever director Sam Raimi (a Detroit native obviously reveling in Chapel's Detroit Tigers affiliation) brings his talents to bear portraying Chapel's ability to shut out the clamor from the bleachers and hone in on the game. "Clear the mechanism" is Chapel's mantra, and for mesmerizing, crystalline moments, the game alone matters. Then the memories intrude — and the game, and the film, grind to a halt. Billy muses over the past: his courtship and relationship with Jane, his teammates, wins and losses, and much, much more to ever-diminishing effect. The device might have worked if Dana Stevens' adaptation of Michael Shaara's novel weren't so trite and predictable, suffocating the very skills that elevate Raimi from other Hollywood filmmakers. We're repeatedly teased by the tantalizing but all-too-brief kinetics of the final game, only to succumb to the narcoleptic seizures of the soap opera plotting.

The title of director Sam Raimi's first Hollywood exercise, the Sharon Stone western *The Quick and the Dead* (1994), succinctly summarized the pace and premiere focus of Raimi's bracing earlier work (*The Evil Dead*, 1983, and *Evil Dead II*, 1987). But at two hours and 18 minutes, there's nothing quick about *For Love of the Game*, and the only dead thing was my butt. Though I'm happy for Sam's climb to the major studios, I longed for a burst of the manic energy inherent in Raimi's maiden efforts (including his underrated 1985 Coen Brothers collaboration *Crimewave*). After exorcising more juvenile demons co-producing *The Adventures of Brisco County* and *Hercules* for television and directing the closing chapter of his *Evil Dead* trilogy *Army of Darkness* (1992), Raimi matured into the measured adult focus of *A Simple Plan* (1998), his best film to date. But

I can't find much to recommend in this latest opus; must major-league legitimacy be so tedious?

Hopefully, this is just a misstep off the mound for Sam, though Kevin continues to wear out his welcome with yet another ponderous bore. Costner's last real gamble and stretch as an actor was Clint Eastwood's *A Perfect World* in '93; c'mon, Kevin, put another one out of the field. The baseball and romance are at odds here, in more ways than one. Costner fans may find something to enjoy here, but the rest of us, alas, will be aching for the final inning and a rumble in the bleachers with the Deadites. *(Rated "PG-13" for mild language, adult and sexual situations.)*

April 13:

Michael Mann's **THE INSIDER** (1999) was, to my mind, the best film of 1999. Corporate concentration, control, and regulation of news and information is a central issue in this era of ever-growing media conglomerates, and this remarkable film offers an intensive dissection of how barely-checked corporate power in "the information age" can and does implacably target and destroy lives to protect or further their own agenda. It's a sad fact of life in the late 20th and early 21st Century that such powerful, invisible forces can and do manifest themselves to protect corporate lies, interests, and profiteering derived from deliberate and active poisoning of the public. *The Insider* demonstrates just how such corruptive forces work; that this particular narrative involves such an insidious and genuine threat to public health lends it unimpeachable power. Though it is gripping as any thriller, this is hardly an entertainment: *The Insider* is a vivid, vitally important story brilliantly told.

In this case, information — raw information, a mere scrap of knowledge — indeed threatened and toppled giants who stopped just short of murder to keep the silence. The essentials of this "David and Goliath" story are true: Tobacco-industry whistle-blower Jeffrey Wigand (Russell Crowe delivering a riveting performance, also among the best of the year) was indeed targeted for his knowledge of former-employer Brown & Williamson's culpability for medical hazards associated with cigarettes. Furthermore, the corporate interests which absorbed the once-vital CBS News division indeed scuttled the *60 Minutes* investigation and broadcast of Wigand's damning information, bringing a viable, trusted news institution to its knees.

Though CBS News' demise was imminent,[9] *The Insider* surgically pinpoints the crucial issues behind the journalistic death throes. But it's Wigand's tale that proves most devastating. It's sobering, to say the least, to vicariously experience the man's agonies for knowing and speaking a fundamental truth (in the end, all the suffering was orchestrated to prevent the uttering of a single sentence).

Precious few American filmmakers could bring such incisive intelligence and dramatic clarity to the realities of big business, closed-door power brokers, legal warfare, and the very real toll such events take upon their active participants and nominal victims. Thankfully, director Michael Mann (*Thief*, 1981; *Manhunter*,

---

[9] See *Who Killed CBS?: The Undoing of America's Number One News Network* by Peter J. Boyer, Random House, 1988, covering the events prior to the Wigand *60 Minutes* debacle.

1986; *Last of the Mohicans*, 1992; *Heat*, 1995) is up to the task, co-scripting with Eric Roth. Mann and Roth tell the tale with uncanny lucidity and skill: with an ominous private meeting at Brown & Williamson as a company executive (Michael Gambon, purring venom) paternally draws the battle lines that will consume Wigand's career, marriage, and life; in a decisive meeting at CBS, as Mike Wallace (Christopher Plummer) demolishes his long-term relationship with producer Lowell Bergman (Al Pacino) with a single statement that subsequently brings their shared legacy on *60 Minutes* crashing down around their ears. Mann's tone throughout is cool, calm, and objective, but the occasional dramatic fireworks are potent: Wigand's wife (Diane Venora) opening their email to find an anonymous death-threat; the simultaneous building and fraying of trust between Wigand and Bergman; the Mississippi courtroom confrontation between opposing attorneys (beautifully played by Bruce McGill and Wings Hauser); Mike Wallace's all-too-brief cornering of a scheming CBS legal counsel (Gina Gershon). Nevertheless, it's the film's calculated orchestration of mounting, justified paranoia that coils like a serpent and fixes our attention throughout.

Mann and Roth detail the shock waves through the intimate nooks and crannies of the lives caught up in the maelstrom, tracing the invasive erosion of Wigand's dignity, sanity, and his relationship with his wife and family. They also chronicle the tentative promise Wigand seeks and finds in his new career as a teacher, providing a necessary balance to the relentless malice at work here. The fragile moment between father and daughter when Wigand's testimony is finally broadcast is heartbreaking; personal redemption has rarely been so eloquently portrayed. Wigand's Jobian trials and tribulations, and Bergman's crisis of conscience, offer a coherent arena for contemporary issues that touch or consume us all. The struggle pitting the most fundamental of individual human needs — health, sanity, dignity, safety, family, the ability to work and earn a living — against the voracious appetites and interests of the ever-growing multi-national corporations is among the most frightening facing us in this new Millennium.

By addressing this subject with such clarity and candor, *The Insider* stands tall. This cautionary tale is necessary viewing, a story well worth the telling... and it's hard to imagine how Mann's telling might be improved upon. My highest recommendation. *(Rated "R" for — well, I'm not sure what; maybe Brown & Williamson rated the film. There's no nudity, graphic violence, or sexual situations whatsoever; the language is strong. Period. I object to the MPAA rating on this film, which can and should be shared with older children — after all, it's their futures at stake.)*

David O. Russell's biting, bracing, absurdist epic **THREE KINGS** (1999) was also one of the top films of the year. Though it's deceptively energetic, spry, and often wickedly funny, the film quickly transcends its *Kelly's Heroes*-like caper comedy premise to join the ranks of genuinely subversive war classics like *Paths of Glory, M*A*S*H*, Joseph Heller's *Catch-22* (the novel, not the botched film), Francis Ford Coppola's *Apocalypse Now*, and Terrence Malick's *Thin Red Line*. Most critics and audiences failed to appreciate that *Three Kings* also owes a huge debt in content, tone, and imagery to westerns like Sam Peckinpah's classic *The Wild Bunch* (1969; in fact, *Three Kings* is almost a remake) and the political parables made in Italy in the late 1960s, from Gillo Pontecorvo's *Burn!* (1969) to many of the spaghetti westerns by Sergio Leone (particularly *Duck, You Sucker!* aka *A Fistful of Dynamite*, 1971), Sergio Corbucci, and others. Much as I enjoyed and admire Russell's prior two films (*Spanking the Monkey*, 1994, and *Flirting with Disaster*, 1995), nothing in his earlier satiric work suggested the expansive physical and political scope, much less the kinetic cinematic assurance and edge, of this masterpiece.

During the final day of the Gulf War,[10] in the immediate wake of the "cease fire" Peace Accord, a ragtag quartet of U.S. soldiers risk going A.W.O.L. (and breaking the Accord) when a map found stuffed up a military prisoner's butt reveals the locations of secret bunkers hiding booty stolen from Kuwait — including over $40 million in gold bullion. Sgt. Troy Barlow (Mark Wahlberg) is a competent, decent officer way out of his depth; Major Archie Gates (George Clooney) is an old-school soldier who's two weeks short, disenchanted with the war and his role in it, and opportunistic enough to seize the day; Chief Elgin (Ice Cube) is a devoted Christian determined to follow God's plan for him, whatever it may be; and bewildered Texan redneck Private Conrad Vig (Spike Jonze, director of *Being John Malkovich* and many innovative music videos) is along for the ride, eager to go where ever Troy goes. Together, they play off Saddam's army's preoccupation with crushing Iraqi rebellion and starving the citizenry to force the rebels out of hiding. Their amoral mercenary zeal is soon undermined as their consciences are awak-

---

[10] Younger readers please note: *Three Kings* is set during the Gulf War, not the later Iraq War waged by President George W. Bush.

ened by the first cold-blooded execution they witness. Awash in sand, blood, and milk, it becomes impossible to maintain their indifference and materialistic goals in the face of the real pain, hunger, and desperation of the innocents caught in the crossfire, and they become the reluctant protectors of a band of refugees and prisoners en route to the Iranian border.

Unlike most recent American war films, which either pick at the corpses of our past (World War 2 and Vietnam) or try to squeeze action out of covert mercenary operations or political embarrassments (as in Clint Eastwood's 1986 *Heartbreak Ridge*, which climaxed with the ignoble Grenada invasion), *Three Kings* confronts the dubious legacy of the Gulf War. Unlike Edward Zwick's *Courage Under Fire* (1996), *Three Kings* mounts a vivid and pointed attack on that shameful war: the deceptive nature of a carefully-orchestrated, government-controlled "media war"; the bodies we never saw in the military-sanctioned news coverage; the terrible consequences of President [George H.W.] Bush's appeal to the Iraqi people to rise up against Saddam Hussein sans any U.S. support; the environmental disasters, from the burning oil fields to the oil-drenched wildlife; the deserters; the torture and execution of civilians; the brutal irony of our mounting a war against an army our own government had trained and armed when Saddam was considered a political ally. Early in the film, Archie howls, "Just tell me what we *did* here!" There are no answers, save that implied by the torrent of oil poured down Troy's throat during his grueling "interrogation."

Performances, direction, production, and all technical credits are absolutely top-notch, realizing a brilliant script by Russell and John Ridley (who was sadly uncredited, though his "story by" credit remains). Newton

Thomas Sigel's vivid cinematography suffers on video; much of his imagery was deliberated manipulated, filtered, and distorted for dramatic effect, though video flattens their impact. All the more reason to check out the DVD, which is also chock-full of great extras: behind the scenes material, including deleted sequences well worth a look; *two* audio commentary tracks from Russell and his producers; and more. Be warned that the violence, when it erupts, is explicit — as it *must* be — but never gratuitous or glamorized. This grue includes harrowing, semi-impressionistic but anatomically correct 'cross sectional' views of wounds unlike anything seen before in cinema history, outside of actual autopsy footage and the most bizarre martial arts opuses (e.g., the crude 'X-ray' views of mayhem in the Sonny Chiba vehicle *The Streetfighter*, 1975).[11] Highest recommendation! (*Rated "R" for its tone, strong language, vivid violence, and torture.*)

Gavin O'Connor's **TUMBLEWEEDS** and Hampton Fancher's **THE MINUS MAN** (both 1999) are similar in their leisurely pacing, dedication to the lives of the primary characters, and their unswerving devotion to their own mesmerizing internal rhythms and logic. They are both quiet, introspective dramas which make their points with eloquent restraint, brimming with rich observations of day-to-day life, though they are light-years apart in their subjects. *Tumbleweeds* chronicles a mother and daughter's quest for a fresh start in a new community, while *The Minus Man* watches a serial killer ease his

---

[11] These then-innovative 'cross sectional' special effects were quickly absorbed into the pop culture via cable TV programs like the multiple *CSI* series.

way in and out of a community. But their spare, meditative approach to their respective stories is strikingly similar — and equally rewarding.

The titular *Tumbleweeds* are Mary Jo Walker (Janet McTeer, earning her Academy Award nomination and Golden Globe win for Best Actress) and her 12-year-old daughter Ava (Kimberley Brown delivering an equally fine performance), on the run from one soured domestic scene and sliding into another. Much to her frustration, young Ava can see the inevitable approaching, and her breakthrough bid to break the vicious cycle her mother once again tumbles into gives this moving drama its heart. (P.S.: That's writer-director Gavin O'Connor playing the truck-driving Jack, Mary Jo's latest mismatch beau.)

The Minus Man doesn't share *Tumbleweeds'* broad, easy appeal, given its autobiographical snapshot of a young serial killer named Vann (Owen Wilson) drifting into a small town with deceptive ease. Vann's modus operandi involves a fast-acting poison, skirting the bloody mayhem usual to this genre, just as its canny observations of rural Americana eschews the usual horrific hysterics. *The Minus Man* is neither a thriller nor a mystery-suspense offering; from its first frame to its last, it's as unnervingly elusive and affable as its blonde, blue-eyed killer. It creeps up on you, and stays with you long after its over. Jeanine Garofalo, Mercedes Ruehl, Dwight Yoakam, Sheryl Crow, and Brian Cox (who was, by the way, the first big-screen Hannibal Lector, in Michael Mann's excellent *Manhunter*) provide solid support. I heartily recommend both films. *(Tumbleweeds is rated "PG-13" for language, adult and sexual situations, and brief domestic violence;* The Minus Man *is rated "R" for language, adult situations, and brief violence.)*

Two of this week's three comedies (all from 1999, and all rated "PG-13") concern hetero males confused with, and assuming the guises of, gay males. ***HAPPY, TEXAS*** manages the deceit with aplomb; ***THREE TO TANGO*** is, at best, an embarrassment. ***SUPERSTAR*** is yet another spin-off from *Saturday Night Live*, inflating one of its mildly-successful sketch characters (Mary Shannon's Catholic schoolgirl Mary Katherine Gallagher) into feature length. All three comedies also reaffirm the fact that most "sitcom"-style comedy involves humiliation rather than humor, reminding me why I've hated most sitcoms since childhood.

I'll spare you the story outlines: suffice to say, *Happy, Texas* provides the liveliest entertainment of the batch, boasting a clever script, sharp direction, and two truly stellar performances (Steve Zahn's out-of-his-depth redneck Wayne Wayne Wayne, Jr., and William H. Macy's sheriff) among a great cast. I must confess, though, that the film won my heart instantly with the best on-screen use of Texan road kill in twenty-five years (since *The Texas Chainsaw Massacre* back in '74), which is no mean feat. *Happy, Texas* delivers the good time it promises in spades; recommended!

On the other hand, *Superstar* reminded me how little there is of interest in *SNL* these days, though *SNL* fans will find much to enjoy, I'm sure. I laughed twice, and my own Catholic upbringing prompted some amusement with the shrill proceedings, but none of it was as funny as the fake *Catholic High School Girls in Trouble* preview trailer in John Landis' chestnut *Kentucky Fried Movie* (1977).

I'm not sure who will enjoy *Three to Tango*, an overly contrived romantic comedy-of-manners that left me cold. The high points: Oliver Platt making the best of a sorry role; star-crossed lovers Matthew Perry and Neve Campbell bonding on a NYC street corner while vomiting up their tuna melts; Perry's wistful, nostalgic look while a wino spews on the sidewalk in the final act. The low point: the rest of the movie.

April 20, 2000:

Another one of last year's best films, **BOYS DON'T CRY** (1999), hits the video shelves this week — even as it still plays in local theaters. Kimberley Peirce's compelling, loving, and fierce feature directorial debut showcases actress Hilary Swank's riveting Academy Award-winning performance as Teena Brandon aka "Brandon Teena," the Nebraskan trans-gender whose self-transformation from young woman into young man ended in tragedy only nineteen days after his/her 21st birthday. Peirce (and co-screenwriter Andy Bienen) brilliantly weave the true story's complex emotional tapestry into a coherent, profoundly moving threnody. Though *Boys Don't Cry* is indeed tragic and often agonizing to watch, Peirce, Bienen, and Hilary Swank create an extraordinary testimonial to Brandon's quest for transformation and transcendence, true love and acceptance, and all its attendant pleasure and pain, succor and release. They capture the rush amid the risk, the joy amid the sorrow, and lend what could have been an unbearably downbeat experience considerable heart.

From its opening scene — depicting Teena's giddy first night out as Brandon, presenting herself fait accompli as a teenage boy to unsuspecting locals — we are plunged fully into Brandon's transformation. Brandon doesn't just want to look and act like a boy, she wants to embrace and own the male experience absolutely. Brandon pursues this goal with the reckless abandon of the age and gender she aspires to, but the stubborn reality of her body and gender and the inchoate tangle of desire, jealousy, homophobia, and rage Brandon illicits ultimately leads to disaster. Driven out of town, Brandon wanders to another small Nebraskan town, skirting a summons to juvenile court (she was, indeed, an incompetent petty criminal, indulging in car theft, check forgery, and shoplifting) to gravitate to another surrogate family in a chance bar encounter. There, Brandon finds true love Lana (Chloe Sevigny) and an uneasy bond with John (Peter Sarsgaard) and Tom (Brandon Sexton III), who soon become Brandon's executioners as the ruse plays itself out to its grim conclusion. Among Brandon's belongings, we glimpse a trans-gender educational flyer entitled *The Uninvited Dilemma*, and that's clearly what Brandon was to this dazed, dead-end pack of down & out losers — except for Lana, who saw in Brandon promise, escape, and redemption that was, oddly enough, only emphasized by the revelation of his/her true nature.

There's never been a film quite like this before, and I urge you to see it. Be forewarned, however, that this is a truly adult viewing experience, confronting its sexual and emotional material with unflinching clarity. The violations of Brandon's unveiling and the subsequent rape, and blunt violations of the police investigation, are forcefully conveyed. I also recommend Susan Muska and Greta Olafsdottir's documentary *The Brandon Teena*

Story (1998),[12] which details the actual case history, noting the facts *Boys Don't Cry* eschewed (including the third murder victim) while emphasizing the truth and integrity of Peirce's fictionalized portrait. The director's DVD audio commentary is sparse, but worthwhile for Peirce's occasional revelations of lines and situations lifted from its participants' accounts. Highly recommended! *(Boys Don't Cry is rated "R" for strong language, nudity, adult and sexual situations, rape, and violence.)*

Mid-town Manhattan never looked as sweet and clean as it does in **STUART LITTLE** (1999), which proves what computer-generated imagery (CGI) really can accomplish these days (only Brooklyn is portrayed as seedy, and a creepy Central-Park-by-night finale trades on the city's rep for danger). CGI also takes center stage to bring Stuart and his entourage to life, elevating the technology to a new threshold with rich, affectionate character animation that outclasses any CGI seen to date.

Adapted from E.B. White's venerable classic tale of a talkative heroic mouse named Stuart who finds love, adventure, and acceptance as the adopted son of the very human Little family, this pleasant fantasy is a satisfying blend of earnest sentimentality and arch humor. It's spry enough to blend its action setpieces (primary among them the famed boat race) and inevitable heart-tugging

---

[12] See *Blur, Vol. 1*, pp. 195-196. *"...Early in this compelling documentary, one of the many teenage girls who dated Brandon describes him as 'a woman's man, every woman's dream.' ...This deceptively straightforward chronicle negotiates a treacherous maze of emotions, gender issues, police incompetence, and irrevocable loss."*

without becoming too sticky. Thanks to the great vocal performances (led by Michael J. Fox as the utterly likable Stuart), imagination production design, and clever orchestration of live-action and CGI performances, *Stuart Little* is a charmer. Cat-lovers might find the type-casting of the feline villainy objectionable, but hey, Stuart is a mouse, after all; once again, the purr-fect vocal performances among the supporting cats — er, cast — elevate the *Tom and Jerry* setpieces (featuring Nathan Lane as the Little's jealous Snowball, Steve Zahn as flatulent Morty, and Chazz Palminteri as the sinister Smoky). Ideal family viewing, and the DVD is recommended for its sparkling transfer and loads of engaging extra features, including games and read-aloud for the kids and behind-the-scenes analysis of the cutting-edge CGI work for older viewers. *(Rated "G," suitable for all ages.)*

The "Millennium-fear" genre seems as dated as 1960s Cold War spy capers, and **END OF DAYS** (1999) remains a particularly braindead entry. Not to blame the actor, but Charlton Heston arguably paved the way for *End of Days'* hybrid brand of muscular, apocalyptic action-horror starring in films like *The Naked Jungle* (1954), *Planet of the Apes* (1968), *The Omega Man* (1971), and *Soylent Green* (1973), all of which were far better movies than this one. True to Charlton's example, *End of Days* star Arnold Scharzeneggar shares Chuck's penchant for enduring masochistic punishment, mock crucifixion, and embracing martyrdom to save mankind, while testifying to the NRA's devotion to firepower. One imagines Charlton's heart swelling with pride as Arnie snarls, "Between your faith and my Glock 9mm, I'll take my Glock!" Get thee behind me, Arnold.

Unlike Stuart Little, Schwarzeneggar inhabits a seamy, steamy film noir Manhattan; and as if there weren't already enough to dread about NYC's public bathrooms, Satan himself literally jumps into Gabriel Byrne's backside in a classy uptown restaurant restroom. After a few violent spasms on the tile floor, Byrne's up and strutting around as Hollywood's latest Lord of the Flies, in search of virginal 20-year-old Christine (Robin Tunny), who has been destined and groomed to sire his offspring and usher in a new Dark Age. En route, we learn the Devil's minions are everywhere, a lifetime of servitude will earn you a fist through the skull if you inconvenience him, his urine is an explosive flammable, incestuous "debbil sex" involves flesh fusion, and that albino street-crazies can shatter into itty-bitty pieces and still spout obscenities, just like Tex Avery cartoon characters. However, Ol' Scratch has to first bulldoze his way through New York's finest (Arnold), and conception must take place during the last hour of 1999 (in accordance with ancient Biblical prophecy that was apparently written with the Big Apple and Eastern Standard Time in mind). There's also a renegade priest hit squad out to snuff Christine before the conjugal visit can occur, while good-guy priest Rod Steiger (chewing scenery in a skinhead variation of his 1979 *The Amityville Horror* role) rants, "There are forces here at work which you couldn't possibly comprehend!"

Steiger might actually be talking about director-cinematographer Peter Hyams, who's evidently still under the spell of David Fincher's *Se7en* (1995). As in Hyams' earlier monster movie *The Relic* (1996), he's still trying to cop Fincher's look and approach without conjuring a whit of Fincher's caustic wit, style, or intelligence. Hyams can mount rousing individual action se-

47

quences and has made a few engaging movies (*The Star Chamber*, 1983; *2010: The Year We Make Contact*, 1984; *Timecop*, 1994), but horror is hardly Hyams' *forté*, and this is one of his silliest efforts (horror fans are advised to instead rent this week's *House on Haunted Hill*, which is much scarier fun). Hyams' hasn't the smarts to mount a single accent-heavy dialogue scene between Austrian Arnold and German Euro-trash co-star Udo Kier (who earned cult status starring as Andy Warhol's *Frankenstein* and *Dracula* back in '74), which would have made film history, though there's some fun to be had watching Christine's evil "big-boned" stepmother (Mariam Margoyles) toss Arnie around like a rag doll. Too bad the rest of the movie isn't half as amusing. *(Rated "R" for strong language, nudity, adult and sexual situations, blasphemous religious content, violence, gore, and casual sadism.)*

Recent & Recommended:

Hollywood comedy writer Bruce Vilanch is the subject of Andrew J. Kuehn's affectionate documentary **GET BRUCE!** (1999), and Bruce's flamboyant personality, razor-sharp banter, and troll-like physique dominate the film from beginning to end. Visible to the public primarily as a celebrity participant of the new *Hollywood Squares*, Vilanch's career is actually built upon his "invisible man" stature performing vital scripting chores for prominent comedians like Whoopi Goldberg, Robin Williams, Billy Crystal, Bette Midler, and others, all of whom lend star power to this portrait. As the behind-the-scenes footage demonstrates, Vilanch also lent (and lends) his satiric voice to the pomp and ceremony of the Academy Awards, Elizabeth Taylor's 65th Birthday,

President Clinton's 50th Birthday, AIDS fund raisers, and much, much more — including the notorious black-faced Ted Danson Friar's Roast comedy routine that earned Danson and then-partner Whoopi Goldberg such scathing press. With his humble roots in Osmonds and *Brady Bunch* arcana, Vilanch boasts credentials stretching "from Abba to [Pia] Zadora," as he puts it in his typically self-deprecating manner, making this essential viewing for any aspiring show biz or comedy aficionados. Highlights include a brief dialogue with Susan Futterman, Director of Broadcast Standards for ABC (who flatly identifies herself with, "I'm a censor") and especially Robin Williams' very, very funny improvised *X Files* parody. *(Rated "R" for language.)*

April 27, 2000:

David Fincher's ***FIGHT CLUB*** (1999) certainly isn't for everyone — its excessive mayhem, relentless kinetics, sneaky subliminals, and subversive agenda will put off many viewers — but it was one of last year's best and most under-rated films. Fincher has evolved into one of the current generation's most uncompromising visionary filmmakers, with *Se7en* (1995) his most jarring accomplishment to date. Fincher's follow-up *The Game* (1997) also garnered a following, but that contrived "trip" movie (for those who never took drugs) was just a warm-up for *Fight Club*'s genuinely heady, transformative experience.

The enigmatic relationship between Edward Norton's nervous, on-the-edge insomniac and Brad Pitt's swaggering, over-the-edge urban terrorist, the intrusive presence of parasitic Marla (Helena Bonham Carter), and the catalytic formation of the blood-drenched fraternal "Fight Club" drives this riveting satire. *Fight Club* delivers one hell of a rollercoaster ride as its lead characters pursue their obsessions to a truly cataclysmic ground zero. Personal apocalypses have rarely been rendered with such unflinching clarity, wit, or immediacy. This is also one of the most faithful film adaptations of a novel since Roman Polanski's rendition of Ira Levin's *Rosemary's Baby* (1968), bringing Chuck Palahniuk's 1996 debut novel (already an underground classic) to cinematic life with uncanny skill.

It's almost impossible to discuss the film further without giving away the essentials; I can't tell you anything more about the movie without destroying it. It must be seen and experienced on its own terms — and unless you have an aversion to the often brutal, in-your-face violence and aggression *Fight Club* necessarily revels in, I highly recommend you take the plunge. *Do not* give away the film's secret to family or friends! *(Rated a very strong "R" for harsh language, brutal interpersonal violence, gore, casual drug and alcohol abuse, adult and sexual situations.)*

NOTE: The DVD version of *Fight Club* will not be released until June 6th, so don't give the video store clerks a hard time, bub. It will be worth the wait, and no, I do *not* want to step outside.[13]

On the other hand, **MUSIC OF THE HEART** (1999) is for everyone. Director Wes Craven traded on his *Scream*

---

[13] As noted in the introduction to *Blur, Vol. 1*, the DVD format was just being launched in video stores in 1999-2000; day-and-date releases on both vhs and DVD were still relatively rare in 2000, with DVD releases usually following weeks later.

success to break out of the "horror movie director" career-strait-jacket with this fictionalized true-life story. Though he's taken a lot of critical flak for doing so, Craven nicely establishes a fresh platform for future efforts, graced with a solid script (by Pamela Gray) and top-drawer cast anchored by another fine character study from Meryl Streep, starring as Roberta Guaspari, founder of the famed East Harlem Violin Program.

Appropriately enough, Streep is the heart of the film, and she doesn't skip a beat. Drawn from the documentary *Small Wonders* (1997, also recommended), *Music of the Heart* doesn't skirt the sentimentality of similar tear-jerkers like *Mr. Holland's Opus* (1995) — the sometimes cliche melodramatics are part & parcel of Guaspari's actual trials and accomplishments — but it's Streep's absolute focus that allows the film to transcend such familiar material. Her character's strengths are the film's strengths, forced upon her by the collapse of her marriage and the necessities of reinventing herself to support her two sons. The need for steady work leads her to an East Harlem school, where she becomes an impassioned violin teacher who truly believes — and proves — that any child can learn to play the instrument.

Though the inner city school environment is initially fearsome, and the obstacles (the poverty and violence of the streets, school bureaucracy, the petty jealousy of the tenured music teacher who sees her as an adversary) daunting, Guaspari's decade of struggle and success with the program is effectively portrayed. Thanks to her efforts and the breakthrough fund-raising Carnegie Hall concert that provides the film's climax (featuring Guaspari's class with violin virtuosos Isaac Stern, Itzhak Perlman, Arnold Steinhardt, and others, here playing themselves), the East Harlem Violin Program now embraces three inner city schools. This is a story well-worth the telling well-told; the DVD provides a richer transfer of the lovely musical score, and extras including the documentary *Small Wonders*. Recommended! *(Rated "PG" for language and some adult situations.)*

Recent & Recommended:

THE ADVENTURES OF SEBASTIAN COLE (1999): Adrian Grenier of the recent teen-flick *Drive Me Crazy*[14] scores a meatier and much more rewarding role here as Sebastian in one of the season's sleepers. At the inevitable senior prom, a friend (Russell Harper) complains that their prom's "not like the movies, man, it's not," to which Sebastian replies, "I hate all those dumb high-school movies." So do I, and this one stands heads and tails above its breed. Sebastian's "adventures" — the rescue of a teenage girl from an amateur pimp (Rory Cochrane) in NYC's Chinatown, a toxic alcohol overdose, etc. — are secondary to the relationships he loses, skirts, refutes, or takes for granted at the heart of this fine film. Transgender stepfather Hank/Henrietta (Clark Gregg) is the only authority or family figure who provides an anchor for the lad as he struggles to suppress the emotional turmoil that constantly threatens to overwhelm his cool exterior. Levon Helm of The Band and Famke Janssen score in their brief cameos. *(Rated "R" for strong language, casual drug and alcohol abuse, adult and sexual situations.)*

---

[14] See *Blur, Vol. 1*, pp. 235-236.

THE HOUSE ON HAUNTED HILL (1999): William
Malone's remake of William Castle's gimmicky 1958
Vincent Price schlock classic of the same name (also
recommended!)[15] provides plenty of stylish, scary fun,
and it's waaaaaaay better than DreamWorks' wretched
remake of *The Haunting*.[16] The set-up is identical to the
original film: an effete multi-millionaire (Geoffrey Rush
in the Vincent Price role) and his venomous wife
(Famke Janssen) rent a haunted house to throw a ghoulish party, in which the survivors of the night collect $1
million each (a step up from the $10,000 offered in
1958). Who could resist? The initial back-stabbing nas-
tiness between the participants is true to Robb White's
original script, but soon gives way to a clutch of genuine
ghosts and a mercurial, Rorshachian apparition that outclasses anything Castle conjured in the original film or
his 3-D follow-up *13 Ghosts* (1960). Great cast (including Peter Gallagher, Alie Larter, Taye Diggs, and Chris
Kattan), visuals, sets, chills, and plenty of gristle for
genre buffs, including Jeffrey Combs (of *The Re-
Animator* and *The Frighteners*) as the lead revenant, and
fleeting cameos from Slavitza Jovan (who played
"Gozer" in *Ghostbusters*), makeup maestro Dick Smith's
startling ghost which was stupidly cut from *Ghost Story*
(1981), and fluttering demons *à la Jacob's Ladder*. The
DVD sports diverting extras: special-effects secrets, a
bio of William Castle, and affectionate comparison of
the two versions — an honorable acknowledgement rare
among remakes. Be sure to keep watching the video after the credits crawl to catch the creepy capper most the-

---

[15] See *Blur, Vol. 1*, pp. 66.
[16] See *Blur, Vol. 1*, pp. 130-131.

atrical audiences missed! *(Rated "R" for strong language, violence, and abundant gore.)*

May 4:

Your name is Craig (John Cusack). You have reluctantly taken a dead-end job as a file clerk on the seventh-and-a-half floor of a midtown Manhattan office building, where you have to perpetually hunch over due to the low ceilings. You discover a tiny door hidden behind a file cabinet. Entering it, you are sucked into the interior of a stranger's skull, spending 15 minutes **BEING JOHN MALKOVICH** (1999) before being unceremoniously dumped alongside the New Jersey Turnpike. Maxine (Catherine Keener), the female co-worker who fires your painfully unrequited affections, immediately sees a money-making opportunity in charging others for the privilege of seeing the world through the famous actor's eyes. Your frumpy wife Lotte (Cameron Diaz) finds other possibilities, kindling an erotic spark in Maxine — but only when she's assumed Malkovich's identity.

That's the uncanny, dreamlike premise of director Spike Jonze's surreal comedy, and the wretched lot of Cusack's struggling sadsack puppeteer Craig; to give away any more of the tale would be criminal. Charlie Kaufman's delirious, perfectly tuned screenplay is that rare item, a true original. Rarer still, Jonze (renowned for his stylish music videos for Beastie Boys, Bjork, Wax, and others, and co-star of the recent *Three Kings*) and the remarkable cast strike and sustain precisely the right chord somewhere betwixt Lewis Carroll, Preston Sturges, and David Lynch. I can honestly say you've never seen anything quite like it, nor will you soon shake its lingering aftertaste.

It's a miracle this film was made at all, given the enormous odds: it's almost inconceivable that contemporary Hollywood would fund such an underivative venture, much less that Malkovich (who soars in the difficult role of playing himself) would sanction and star in the enterprise, or that once completed, the film would secure playdates and actually find its audience. Miracles do happen, though, and *Being John Malkovich* offers an evening of giddy entertainment to those willing to take the plunge. You, too, can be John Malkovich. The doorway awaits you; a video rental provides the key. This was one of the best films of 1999; Highly recommended! *(Rated "R" for language, adult and sexual situations, and nudity.)*

Miracles of another kind are central to Kevin Smith's ***DOGMA*** (1999), an outrageous theological satire that proposes Armageddon awaits us all in Red Bank, New Jersey, when two fallen angels find a loophole in God's laws that will allow them to reenter Heaven, ending all existence. No, really; I kid you not. The thing is, Kevin Smith (writer/director of *Clerks*, 1994; *Mallrats*, 1995; and *Chasing Amy*, 1998) isn't kidding either, though *Dogma* is scathingly funny from beginning to end.

Dogma invited controversy from its inception; upon completion, the film was dumped by its original distributor, subsequently condemned and picketed by many Christian organizations (Smith joined one of the protest groups, mingling with the crowd and waving a banner while questioning his fellow protesters, none of whom had seen the film). The most perverse irony here is the fact that truly blasphemous muck like the Scharzeneggar vehicle *End of Days* has no distribution problems, attracts no protests, and seems to offend no one. Smith requires his viewing audience to look, listen, and think, which is always sure to offend. Though *Dogma* is as foul-mouthed and scatological as Smith's prior gems (at one point, a dung-demon manifests itself in the sickest toilet scene since *Trainspotting*), it offers an intensive, irreverent, and ultimately moving dissection of Christianity, faith, and religious doctrine and devotion. It truly is a more religious film than, for instance, the recent grassroots Christian hit *The Omega Code* [17] (which is, in its sanctimonious way, as lurid and risible a horror opus as *End of Days*). Monty Python's *Life of Brian* (1979) comes readily to mind, but Smith's screenplay owes a far greater debt to the novels of James Branch Cabell (such as *Jurgen*, 1919), Christian scholar C.S. Lewis' classic *The Screwtape Letters* (1942), and Neil Gaiman's contemporary fantasies (including the *Sandman* graphic novels and Gaiman and Terry Pratchett's playfully apocalyptic novel *Good Omens*, 1990). Though *Dogma* clearly isn't for everyone, those up to the cheek and challenge will find this among the season's most rewarding offerings; Smith devotees, of course, need no prompting from the likes of me.

With dialogue and characterization as razor-sharp and rich as any of Smith's prior outings, *Dogma* sends its entourage of mortals and immortals off on a four-day pilgrimage to New Jersey to intercept and stop the fallen angels, Loki the former Angel of Death (Matt Damon) and Bartleby (Ben Affleck). Lapsed Catholic Bethany (Linda Fiorentino) has lost her faith and works in an abortion clinic, but she is also "the last Scion" (a mortal descendent of Jesus Christ) according to Metatron the Seraphim (Alan Rickman), who materializes in Beth-

---

[17] See *Blur, Vol. 1*, pp. 243-250.

any's apartment offering the word of God (Alanis Morrissette — again, I kid you not) to instruct her. En route, they are pursued by the demon Azrael (Jason Lee) and his murderous street-hockey-punk minions, and joined by the 13th Apostle (Chris Rock), Serendipity the Muse (Salma Hayek), and the Prophets (and permanent fixtures of Smith's cinematic universe) Jay (Jason Mewes) and Silent Bob (Kevin Smith).

The entire cast is marvelous throughout, but Alan Rickman's obedient but put-upon seraphim anchors the often giddy proceedings. Bemused by the mortals he is forced to interact with and craving pleasures he cannot indulge (including alcohol, which angels are forbidden to drink), Rickman fends off the burdens and obligations of immortality brandishing his world-weary eyes and caustic tongue like a shield. We should all be blessed with such a guardian angel. *(Rated "R" for very strong language, adult situations, violence, some gore, one sequence awash in fecal matter, and religious satire some may consider blasphemous.)*

Alan Rickman is a delight, too, as Leonard Nimoy/Mr. Spock-surrogate "Alexander Dane/Dr. Lazarus" in *GALAXY QUEST* (1999). As the former co-star of the titular cult 1960s science fiction program, Dane is a classically-trained actor trapped in a dire career spiral defined by typecasting, reruns, and a ceaseless procession of 1990s *Galaxy Quest*-fan conventions. Rickman perfectly captures Nimoy's infamous loathing of the Vulcan stereotype: his Shakespearian background and aspirations have been dashed by the undying cult devotion attached to his TV-science fiction alien character, and he chafes at the constant contact with fellow cast members trapped in the same declining orbit (led by Tim Allen as

William Shatner/Capt. Kirk clone Jason Nesmith/Capt. Taggart and Sigourney Weaver as cheesecake yeoman Gwen DeMarco/Lt. Madison). Rickman's withering glare at fans waiting in line for autographs, begging to hear "that line" one... more... time..., sets the tone for *Galaxy Quest*'s affectionate guying of the entire *Star Trek* scene.

Co-writers David Howard and Robert Gordon and director Dean Parisot then proceed to launch cast and crew into the ultimate science fiction fan's fantasy as a clutch of real aliens, "Thermians from the Klaatu Nebula," solicit the *Galaxy Quest* crew's aid in rescuing their dying race from genocide orchestrated by reptilian warlord Sarris (Robin Sachs). The Thermians think the Galaxy Quest broadcasts they've tapped into represent genuine histories, and embrace the program's bitter, washed-up cast as the real McCoys (pun intended) — and so the saga begins. When one of the snubbed convention fans (Justin Long) plays a decisive role in the climactic battle with Sarris, *Galaxy Quest* becomes a heart-felt valentine to the same Trekkies mercilessly ribbed in the opening scene. While hilariously skewering the multi-generational *Star Trek* phenomenon, convention scene, and the wear, tear, and ego battles plaguing its original cast members, *Galaxy Quest* indeed honors and elevates the ideals, heart and soul of Gene Roddenberry's brainchild. Simply put, this is the best *Star Trek* movie ever made.

A pretty mean feat, that, and *Galaxy Quest* is great fun for Trekkies and non-Trekkies alike, showcasing marvelous imagery and effects matched by the precision comedic timing of Tim Allen and the entire cast (the aliens, led by Enrico Colantoni, are particularly amusing). Sigourney Weaver (who previously demonstrated her comedic talents in *Ghostbusters*) revels in the opportunity to lampoon the busty '60s *Star Trek-*"babe" stereotype and her own association with the *Aliens* franchise. Having crawled through countless slime-encrusted ventilation ducts in that series since 1979, her exasperated cry of "Ducts!? Why is it *always* ducts??" when forced to crawl through yet another vent scores a quiet chuckle amid the genuine belly laughs. *(Rated "PG-13" for some language, mild violence, and satiric inter-species sexual situations.)*

Recent & Recommended:

THE DINNER GAME (***LE DÎNER DE CONS***, 1998): French farce isn't everyone's cup of tea, but if you have a passion for the genre don't miss the latest from writer-director Francis Veber, author of the cult favorite *La Cage aux Folles* (1978), here adapting his own stage play. Arrogant, affluent Parisian yuppie Pierre (Thierry Lhermitte) and his smug upper-crust cronies entertain themselves with the titular "Dinner Game," wherein each invites an unsuspecting eccentric — an idiot, in their eyes — for their private amusement. Pierre's latest find François (Jacques Villeret, delivering a fine-tuned comedic performance), a bumbling tax office employee who obsessively constructs matchstick replicas of national landmarks, shows up at Pierre's apartment moments after the snob has blown out his back and pissed off his girlfriend. The pot simmers amusingly until it all boils over in the giddy final act; ah, what delicious come-uppance! Rest assured that Pierre gets his just desserts in this slow-burn cause-and-effect comedy of ill-manners where nuance of character is everything. *The Dinner Game* deservedly won three Césars (the French equivalent to the Academy Awards) for Best Actor, Supporting Actor, and Veber's delightful screenplay; the Hollywood remake is already in the works, but I can't imagine them doing it justice. Veber's soufflé puts most of the current breed of Hollywood "idiot" comedies to shame. Quick, catch it before Hollywood remakes it (as they do all popular French films) and completely mucks it up (as they do with all popular French films). *(Unrated; some strong language and sexual situations, but suitable for all ages.) [Note: This title was originally scheduled for release in January, but was postponed.]*

MUMFORD (1999): The latest from writer-director Lawrence Kasdan (*Body Heat*, 1981; *The Big Chill*, 1983; *Silverado*, 1985; *I Love You to Death*, 1990; *Grand Canyon*, 1991) is his best film in years, a modest romantic comedy whose leisurely pace and affectionate perceptions of rural life arrives at something like wisdom. Affable, unflappable Dr. Mumford (Loren Dean) has a healthy psychology practice in the sleepy town of Mumford, honing his unique ability to, well, honestly listen to people. Mumford's uncommon common-sense approach to psychotherapy quietly reshapes the town and the lives of its citizens, but Mumford has a secret or two of his own: he's falling in love with his chronic fatigue patient (Hope Davis), and — ah, that would be telling. Among the film's easy virtues are the sterling cast, including Jason Lee as a skate-boarding billionaire who's a closet Frankenstein, Martin Short as the oily lawyer seeking counsel who stirs up trouble when Mumford refuses to treat him, and Alfe Woodard and Mary McDonnell (the stars of John Sayles' *Passion Fish*, 1992) as patient and landlord, respectively; they haven't any scenes together here, but it's nice to see them in the same film again. *Mumford* is a gem.

May 11:

It's another week of wonders in the video stores, as two more of 1999's top-ten movies — Academy-Award darling *AMERICAN BEAUTY* and David Lynch's jewel *THE STRAIGHT STORY* — hit the new release wall. Personal redemption is the common theme among this week's eclectic potpourri of talents and titles:

Cool as a cucumber, the aloof black comedy *AMERICAN BEAUTY* (1999) caught a bracing wave that captivated contemporary audiences, and rode it all the way to a dramatic sweep of the Academy Awards (scoring seven Oscars including best picture, actor, screenplay, and more). That such an angry, subversive, and strikingly perverse satire should reap such authoritative acclaim in the wake of the similar sweep earned by a classical Hollywood romantic epic like *Titanic* is surely an indication of national schizophrenia: we embrace and elevate our illusions, only to savor them being ground into the dirt with gleeful malevolence. *American Beauty* cuts to the core of our cultural malaise with surgical precision, dissecting the ties that bind, the desires that debase, the urges that can enlighten and destroy in the same blink of an eye. It is devastatingly funny, oddly moving, utterly mesmerizing, unshakably disturbing — and absolutely essential viewing.

Claiming center stage as narrator and the center of the film is Kevin Spacey, breathing life into another memorable character imprisoned in the underbelly of the American dream. Mired in an unwanted but hard-earned dead-end existence, 42-year-old Lester Burnham (Spacey) has somehow achieved and maintained upper-middle-class affluence while plunging to the bottom of the pecking order in his job, marriage, family, and neighborhood. Unloved by his wife Carolyn (Annette Bening), inspiring only pity and shame in his daughter Jane (Thora Birch), Lester finds succor in his unhealthy sexual fixation with Jane's cheerleader classmate Angela (Mena Suvari) and an unexpected reintroduction to marijuana's illicit bliss thanks to the brooding boy next door, Ricky Fitz (Wes Bentley). Soon after, Lester bares his teeth and begins to bite back, lashing out with a ferocity borne by a lifetime of bottled-up frustration, anger, and unrequited passion. But as he mobilizes his mid-life crisis to ruthlessly carve out a new life, Lester becomes both the eye and focus of a storm gathering around him — one which ultimately consumes him as it unleashes the furies of the inchoate, repressed rage and desires of his wife, his homophobic neighbor (Chris Cooper), and their children.

For all its irony and ire, *American Beauty*'s heart beats fierce and true. For me, that heart lies bared in a curious and sublime sequence in which the somber Ricky shows one of his private videos to Jane, eloquently rhapsodizing over a glimpse of the infinite perceived in the quiet spectacle of a plastic bag caught in the wind. Amid the suffocating spiritual and emotional vacuum of suburbia, they recognize and ponder nothing less than God dancing in the most banal of wonders: *American Beauty*, indeed. While Alan Ball's script, Sam Mendes' direction, the ensemble performances, and Thomas Newman's score are inspired, Conrad Hall's marvelous cinematography is a revelation (and deservedly won an Oscar, too). This is a rare, remarkable film, highly recommended for mature and adult viewers. *(Rated "R" for strong language, adult and sexual situations, nudity, casual alcohol and drug use and abuse, and often harrowing domestic violence.)*

A heartfelt warning to survivors of child abuse: *American Beauty* is the most prominent entry in the recent procession of films featuring Lolita-like ingenues and patriarchal predators (including *Freeway, Lolita, Election*, etc.). It is also among the most disturbing of its ilk given the first-person narration and dramatic context that arguably lionizes Kevin Spacey's pedophile character. Though the film does not ultimately condone his sexual obsession (he is, in fact, punished severely, though inadvertently), the screen time dedicated to an adult male's fixation on an underage teenage girl, and film's amoral tone and subjective depiction of this volatile element, may be painful and/or highly objectionable to survivors. Please, approach this film with caution, or avoid it altogether.

Director Martin Scorsese and screenwriter Paul Schrader, auteurs of the caustic classic *Taxi Driver* (1976), paint another painfully vivid portrait of New York's City's walking wounded in ***BRINGING OUT THE DEAD*** (1999). However, *Taxi Driver*, this isn't. Many of you won't "like" this movie — it's a messy, driven, desperate emotional experience — but Scorsese and Schrader aren't out to make "likable" movies. Like *Taxi Driver*, the film is hardly an entertainment (though it is engaging, harrowing, and often quite funny): it's an unflinching chronicle of purgatory, tracing a loner's spiritual crisis and reckless quest for release and redemption. Adapting Joe Connelly's novel (based on the author's own experiences as a paramedic) with a confrontational intensity and an eye and ear for the city's strange beauty, overwhelming delirium, and languid horrors, *Bringing Out the Dead* sends us hurtling into the twilight existence of paramedic Frank Pierce (Nicolas Cage). Five years into his job, unable to sleep, and dangerously close to madness, Pierce's days and nights are shaped by the city's victims, living and dead.

In a year punctuated by great ghost stories (*The Sixth Sense*, *A Stir of Echoes*, etc.), *Bringing Out the Dead* is most definitely a ghost tale, too. Frank is haunted by the specters of those he cannot save, primary among them a homeless teenage girl named Rose (Cynthia Roman). Lingering and staring from every sidewalk and alley, they are his demons and redeemers, his only companions. As source novelist Joe Connelly points out in the DVD extras, Frank is struggling sans any human support. Save for his ghosts, he's alone outside of his job: his partners (Ving Rhames, John Goodman, Tom Sizemore) are a bit insane, and the only tentative bond he feels for a woman in his orbit (Patricia Arquette) is defined by her father's excruciating near-death stasis. Connelly also notes how the sorely-needed "high" of the profession lies in saving lives ("It's the greatest thing in the world, it's the best drug there is"), and Frank aches for another "hit," intoxicated by the sense of power over life and death, devastated by its burden and apparent futility. The recent, strikingly similar *Broken Vessels* (1998, also recommended)[18] arguably provided a more satisfyingly, self-contained narrative, but *Bringing Out the Dead* is more alive: it frays a raw, exposed nerve from its first frame, and does so with relentless purpose. Scorsese, Schrader, and Cage

---

[18] See *Blur, Vol. 1*, pp. 143.

are in near-peak form, all creative and technical credits are top-notch, and *Bringing Out the Dead* is a reckless, ragged, raging, compassionate work. *(Rated "R" for strong language, violence, gore, casual drug and alcohol abuse, adult and sexual situations.)*

By comparison, **MYSTERY, ALASKA** (1999) is a mild diversion, a formulaic "small-town-team-makes-good" sports story. The wish-fulfillment sports movie (championing the underdogs rising to the challenge of almost insurmountable odds) has been a fixture of the cinema since the silent era (Harold Lloyd's *The Freshman*, 1925), and every generation embraces its revamp (*Rocky, One on One, Breaking Away, The Karate Kid, Hoosiers, Cool Runnings*, etc.) — even with hockey pucks (*Slapshot*). But you don't have to be a hockey (or sports) enthusiast to savor the modest but genuine pleasures of *Mystery, Alaska* — and there are many, including the fine ensemble performances anchored by Russell Crowe's lead, Peter Deming's crisp cinematography, and the extraordinary musical score from Carter Burwell (who's scored all the Coen Brothers films from *Blood Simple* to *The Big Lebowski* and *Fargo*). Sure, it's formula. Screenwriters David E. Kelly (*Ally McBeal, The Practice, Lake Placid*) and Sean O'Byrne are unapologetically populist TV writers, but they're sassy, savvy, and eager to entertain. The film skates around its template with the uncanny skill of its pond-hockey savants, questioning and probing the values at its core till the final buzzer concludes its rousing climactic game.

Mystery, Alaska is a hockey town where male merit is measured almost solely by the town's obsession with the sport, leaving sheriff and vet player John Biebe (Crowe) adrift when the town patriarchs cut John from

65

the team to make way for young upstart Stevie Weeks (Ryan Northcott). When the town's estranged "prodigal son" and *Sports Illustrated* author Charlie Danner (Hank Azaria) orchestrates a match between the New York Rangers and Mystery's homegrown team, John reluctantly agrees to coach his former teammates in a fateful test of the town's "dignity and illusions." John eventually illicits the aid of veteran coach Judge Burns (Burt Reynolds, who starred in the 1970s model of the genre, *The Longest Yard*, 1974) as the clash of small-town values and big-time NHL pro-hockey hoopla rocks Mystery to its core.

From its opening moment, the film's strong language and randy sexuality exclude it from comfortable family fare, but don't let that prejudice you: the film's often-harsh dialogue and straightforward approach to sex, love, and marriage is among its greatest virtues. Town Lothario Skank Martin (Ron Eldard) is "master of the stick" in more ways than one, a source of comedy while his allure and the emotional damage he causes are frankly assessed. There's also a sweet, clumsy first-time encounter between teen-age Stevie and the Judge's daughter Marla (Rachel Wilson) that's touchingly believable in a way few such screen rites-of-passage are. Character, community, decency, and integrity remain central to what could have been a tepid retread or sentimental drek, making *Mystery, Alaska* an engaging, entertaining model of its kind. Don't pass it up. *(Rated "R" for strong language, nudity, adult and sexual situations, one scene involving firearms, and hockey roughplay and violence.)*

THE STRAIGHT STORY (1999) is a cinematic haiku: short, simple, from and to the heart. It's also the fruit of the very unlikely wedding of David Lynch and Disney Studios, a delicious "family art movie" that works despite the contrary and highly unlikely intersection of players and genres. Who would have ever imagined cult maven Lynch capable of making a "G"-rated film, much less lovingly channeling the restless spirits of American filmmaking masters John Ford and Preston Sturges? Since his evocative debut with the horrific, absurdist "midnight movie" classic *Eraserhead* (1977), director David Lynch has made his mark as one of America's most idiosyncratic, obsessive visionaries. Small-town America has been a primary landscape for Lynch's distinctive work (see *Blue Velvet*, 1986, and the entire *Twin Peaks* phenomenon), but *The Straight Story* doesn't pepper its narrative with almost unspeakable secrets, sexuality, or violence — and yet, it is absolutely true to Lynch's universe. In an era defined by ironic cynicism, Lynch's most perversely subversive attribute may be his resolute naivete and refusal to indulge in cynicism, easy distance from the heart and hurt of life.

But don't let all this highfalutin' banter confuse the issue: *The Straight Story* lives up to its title telling the true story of Alvin Straight (Richard Farnsworth), a frail old fellow who sojourns from Iowa to Wisconsin on a lawn mower in hopes of mending the fences with his brother, though they haven't spoken in years. On the way, Alvin touches many hearts and lives. The Midwestern vistas Alvin crosses are picturesque, but Alvin's face is the most riveting landscape on view. Former cowboy and veteran character actor Richard Farnsworth's only prior starring role was the charming turn-of-the-century rogue *The Grey Fox* (1983); he captures the screen with that same forthright honesty here. The tale unfolds with an unpretentious stoicism that keeps

Farnsworth's character in absolute focus. His soulful eyes brim with affection for life and people, shadowed by past scars, regrets, and the sure knowledge of his own impending death. They quietly burn with the need to make amends with those nearest and dearest to him before time runs out.

The interludes with the people Alvin meets en route wander far and wide, but Lynch's vision remains as clear and resolute as the old man's until the final, masterfully understated moment. Freddie Francis' cinematography and Angelo Badalamanti's marvelous score (both artisans integral to Lynch's creative team since the 1980s) capture and enhance the journey with resonant clarity, emulating Alvin's and Lynch's leisurely rhythms and laconic determination to follow their paths wherever they may lead. This is Lynch's most beautiful and accessible work, and one of the loveliest American films ever made. Highest recommendation! *(Rated "G", suitable for all ages.)*

May 18:

Tim Robbins' ambitious portrait of the Depression-era Federal Theater Project in **CRADLE WILL ROCK** (1999) is a politically-charged companion to Michael Leigh's exquisite Gilbert & Sullivan timepiece *Topsy-Turvy* (1999, coming to video next month).[19] Both films pinpoint dramatic turning points in theatrical history, evoking their respective cultures, characters, and concerns (the difficult marriage of art and commerce) with affectionate precision and seductive skill. *Cradle Will*

---

[19] See review, June 22, reprinted in this volume on pg. 117-119.

Rock also compliments the recent new release *RKO 281* (1999; also recommended; the title refers to the RKO Studio's internal reference code for Welles' *Citizen Kane*). Both showcase the 1930s *enfant terrible* Orson Welles; unfortunately, Angus Macfadyen's unengaging caricature of Welles in *Cradle* is the film's weakest element (decidedly inferior to Liev Schreiber's persuasive performance for *RKO 281*).

That said, *Cradle Will Rock* is a sharp, shrewdly crafted drama. As in life, art and theater are the focus of *Cradle*'s class warfare, created by idealists and dreamers who can't help but bite the hands that feed. Orson Welles, painter Diego Rivera (Ruben Blades), and their compatriots are utterly dependent upon yet scornful of their patrons which seek to co-opt and mobilize their respective muses. Inevitably, censure and censorship rears its ugly head. As contemporary conservatives and Republicans know, art is a disease, poised to infect society with dangerous ideals and insidious transformations; that dreaded power is cunningly literalized (a syphilis cell hovers amid Rivera's opulent Rockefeller Center mural) and gleefully celebrated here.

Many of the personalities and events depicted in *Cradle Will Rock* were real. As labor strikes erupted during the Depression, the art and theatrical communities of New York City harbored a growing cultural revolution mobilized in part by the short-lived Federal Theater Project, which mounted stage productions from coast-to-coast to create jobs and bring art to the masses. Orson Welles (Macfadyen) and producer John Houseman (Cary Elwes, almost unrecognizable to *The Princess Bride* fans) were active participants; they indeed mounted a federally funded production of the controversial pro-union musical parable *Cradle Will Rock* by playwright Mark Blitzstein (Hank Azaria). The debut was in fact scuttled by budget cuts prompted by a Senate Subcommittee investigation of potential communist infiltration of the project; an impromptu performance was indeed presented despite government and union objections. Furthermore, Nelson Rockefeller (John Cusack) did commission Mexican artist Diego Rivera (Blades) to create a mural for the lobby of Rockefeller Center; Italian propagandist Margherita Sarfatti (Susan Sarandon) reportedly funded Benito Mussolini's war effort by selling paintings by da Vinci and others to sympathetic American moguls. The conceit that these events actually occurred at precisely the same moment in time seems highly unlikely, but it sure makes for provocative, rousing viewing.

Intent on wringing all the juice possible from his time capsule, writer-director Tim Robbins (who helmed *Dead Man Walking*, but remains better known as the star of *Arlington Road* and others) stacks the deck further. Robbins punctuates his colorful cast with historic figures like Frida Kahlo (Corina Katt); haunts Blitzstein with the ghost of Bertolt Brecht (Steven Skybell); and traces the unrequited love an alcoholic vaudeville ventriloquist (Bill Murray) harbors for a Theater Project employee (Joan Cusack) who testifies against her fellow workers. More believably affecting are subplots involving a homeless aspiring performer (Emily Watson of *Breaking the Waves*) and fiercely independent actor (John Turturro) whose lives are irrevocably changed by their roles in the titular musical.

The often disjointed narrative emulates the fragmented, multi-layered weave of filmmakers like Robert Altman, Alan Rudolph, and Paul Thomas Anderson (*Boogie Nights, Magnolia*), an approach Robbins orchestrates with calculated skill as he crosscuts between the musical's improvised debut, a crucial Subcommittee interrogation, and Rockefeller's heartless dealings with Rivera and his completed mural. If the climactic scheming between Rockefeller and his cronies overstates the obvious, Robbins' redeems himself with the chillingly succinct final shot. All in all, *Cradle Will Rock* is a passionate and eloquent film boasting a marvelous ensemble cast, and is highly recommended. *(Rated "R" for strong language, nudity, alcohol use and abuse, and adult situations.)*

For much of its running time, ***END OF THE AFFAIR*** (1999) threatens to become mired in the tear-jerker conventions of its genre. But Graham Greene's source novel transcended its romantic derivations, and Irish screenwriter-director Neil Jordan (*Mona Lisa*, 1986; *The Crying Game*, 1992; *Interview with the Vampire*, 1994; etc.) was never the sort to indulge in such trivialities. Much like Martin Scorsese's fine adaptation of Edith Wharton's *The Age of Innocence* (1993), *End of the Affair* is a cruel love story that evocatively captures a bygone time and moral universe that seems to suffocate its characters and foil their desires at every turn. But the tale goes much, much further, mounting a potent meditation on the existence of the Divine, our perceptions of and relations with God.

Graham Greene's fictional surrogate is novelist Maurice Bendrix (Ralph Fiennes), whose post-World War 2 chance meeting with civil servant Henry Miles (Stephen Rea), husband of his ex-mistress Sarah (Julianne Moore), threatens to rekindle his torrid but abruptly terminated affair with Sarah. The film sustains a delicate narrative tapestry woven between the post-

War present — as Maurice engages a private detective (Ian Hart) and son (Samuel Bould) to investigate Sarah's mysterious comings and goings — and the past — Maurice and Sarah's affair, and its inexplicably abrupt termination. Given the sterility of Sarah's marriage, her attraction to Maurice is understandable, and the sexual heat between them is explicitly rendered from their initial, impulsive coupling. But Maurice's selfishness renders him increasingly unsympathetic; consumed by the slow burden of their illicit meetings and the painful wake of parting, troubled by his own doubt, fear, jealousy, and the certainty of their love's end, Maurice's pleasures are fleeting, his quiet agony unending. Excited by the danger, Maurice and Sarah foolishly extend their covert beddings into the Blitzkrieg bombings of the neighborhood — much to their regret.

The personal sacrifice at the core of the story may strain the sympathies and credibility of contemporary young audiences, unable or unwilling to connect with its era's British Christian morals and moors. But older viewers will find much to appreciate here, and the coda delivers a moving surprise. Jordan's direction couldn't be better, and the cast delivers beautifully measured performances; Moore deserved her Oscar nomination, and dour Rea delivers another understated character role (he's been the anchor of fellow Irishman Jordan's career since their debut feature, *Danny Boy*, in 1984). This heartbreaker is much more than just another tragic romance — its concluding miracle edges the film into the fantastique — and well worth seeing.[20] *(Rated "R" for nudity, adult and sexual situations.)*

---

[20] Though I could not say so in this review for fear of spoiling a key plot point, *End of the Affair* is also a notable entry in the

For casual renters, the latest James Bond 007 opus *THE WORLD IS NOT ENOUGH* (1999) is undoubtably this week's prime attraction, but it's a popcorn-fart of a movie. In the era of the mega-budget action movie, the Bond franchise is more than ever before a tired anachronism. Much as I wanted to enjoy the film, only it's silly pre-credit boat-chase across the Thames and the London fruit market provided fitful amusement. The rest just wasn't enough, and it wasn't the world I was after — just a pleasant evening's diversion. *The World is Not Enough* is a clanking, grinding bore, a sterile by-the-numbers jig through the usual trappings to ever-diminishing effect.

Pierce Brosnan is back as "Bond, James Bond," thrashing around the globe to defuse a nefarious bid to control the international oil supply. The dastardly villain behind the scheme is Renard (Robert Carlyle of *Train-spotting, The Full Monty*, and *Ravenous*,[21] all of which made much better use of his talents), and as Bond villains go, he's a piker. His gimmick (all Bond villains have a gimmick) is his insensitivity to pain caused by a failed assassin's bullet lodged in his brain, short-circuiting his nervous system. This would have been a novelty in Bond's 1960s prime, but in the wake of Bruce

---

Millennial streak of excellent 'ghost story' films cited earlier (*A Stir of Echoes, The Sixth Sense*, etc.), which in hindsight clearly were immediate contemporaries of the Japanese and Asian so-called 'J-horror' films soon to impact American audiences via Hollywood remakes (e.g., *The Ring, The Grudge*, etc.). There's a book to be written about this Millennial international blossoming of the ghost genre.

[21] See *Blur, Vol. 1*, pp. 56-57.

Willis' *Die Hard* masochistic persona, Renard hardly registers. His disability allows him to pick up red-hot coals with his bare hands and shrug off falls, bullet wounds, and the like — so what? So does every post-1990 action hero, rebounding like steroid refugees from the Chuck Jones and Tex Avery cartoons of yore. Carlyle (an excellent actor) is completely wasted — as are UK music star Goldie (of *B.U.S.T.E.D.*[22]) and Robbie Coltrane (of the cracker UK series *Cracker*, which also boasted a great Carlyle performance in one episode) as even lesser villains. Sophie Marceau brings some saucy panache to her role as Elektra King, daughter of a murdered oil tycoon, but Denise Richards is excruciatingly vapid and utterly unconvincing as nuclear physicist and weapons expert Dr. Christmas Jones. Aaaah.... right. At least she offers some degree of comfort to the rest of us in her role — I mean, if Richards can be a physicist, there's no telling what we lowly mortals might manage! I'll end world hunger by next week, my cat will invent waste-free nuclear fission before next Monday, and you could bring AOL/Time-Warner to its knees in the next four hours.

Desmond Llewelyn returns as Q just long enough to introduce his replacement, R (John Cleese); alas, Llewelyn died shortly after completing his role, severing the final tie with the original Bond film series. Judi Dench is back as M, Samantha Bond is Miss Moneypenny, and I'm sure the final credits' promise that "James Bond Will Be Back" isn't just an empty threat. Lest you think me a complete spoilsport, I grew up with and still savor the Sean Connery Bonds, and consider *On Her Majesty's Secret Service* (1967) one of the finest

---

[22] See *Blur, Vol. 1*, pp. 196.

action-adventure films ever made. Sorry, but by any standard this latest Bond adventure is a clinker. The DVD boasts a glitzy menu and lots of extras, but it would have been a livelier entertainment — and truer to the modus operandi of the current Bond entries — if it included a shot-by-shot rundown of the lucrative wall-to-wall product-placements. To the corporations fueling such nonsense, the world will *never* be enough. If only Bond would take on one of the multi-national corporations in his next outing... now there's a villain worthy of Bond, and an action movie I'd like to see! *(Rated "PG-13" for suggestive dialogue and sexual situations, partial nudity, violence, and some gore.)*

Recent & Recommended:

I MARRIED A STRANGE PERSON (1997): NYC animator-extraordinaire Bill Plympton's second animated feature shares the quirky humor, delightful musical numbers (by Maureen McElheron and Hank Bones), and organically surreal visual stylings of his debut feature *The Tune* (1992; also recommended) — but this time, Plympton's out to bust a few taboos. Fornicating birds crash into Grant & Keri Boyer's satellite dish, causing a magical boil to sprout on the back of Grant's neck, giving him the power to materialize his every fantasy. At first, Grant's idle daydreams and overactive libido prompt a startling (and hilarious) array of transformations, but the intrusion of a greedy TV executive from SmileCorp and his lunatic Army colonel toadie veers the delirium into a plethora of absurdist mayhem and bloodshed. Plympton is a die-hard independent, hand-drawing all 30,000+ drawings for this ambitious outing (with finishes and colors rendered by a team of fellow animators), and the exhilarating blend of fey naivete and exuberant gut-crunching dementia is infectious. Not for all tastes, the feature loses some steam as Plympton's wild invention gives way to repetitive gore gags, but those seeking something truly different shouldn't miss this one! The video is the trimmed "R" version (cutting the wilder sexual antics); the DVD features the uncut, unrated original plus extras. Go for the DVD.

THAT'S THE WAY I LIKE IT (1998): Miramax's latest "feel-good" pickup heralds from Singapore (where English is the primary language; no subtitles or dubbing here) and honorably echoes *Dirty Dancing, Strictly Ballroom*, and *Shall We Dance?*, lending a fresh infusion to the old-fashioned dance-fantasy romantic comedy. It also borrows from Buster Keaton's *Sherlock, Jr.* and Woody Allen's *Play It Again, Sam* and *Purple Rose of Cairo* as young Ah Hock (Adrian Pang) matures beyond his selfish infatuations with Bruce Lee and motorbikes to embrace disco fever and a new role model, *Saturday Night Fever*'s Tony (Dominic Pace as a surrogate John Travolta), who emerges from the screen to counsel the confused lad in the ways of love and life. As Ah Hock rises above his own petty power-fantasies and awakens to the needs, lives, and desires of those around him, Glen Goei's entertaining spin on how our adopted pop-cultural fantasies both hinder and inspire our own respective rites-of-passage gains its own voice and becomes irresistible.

May 25:

Chris Smith's often amusing documentary ***AMERICAN MOVIE*** (1999) chronicles two-and-a-half years in the life of fanatic young Wisconsin filmmaker Mark Bor-chardt and his struggle to make movies against all odds. Born, raised, and still living with his parents in Menomonee Falls during the period *American Movie* was filmed, Mark's dreams and schemes set him apart from his family and environment, but his unending problems with unpaid bills, dead-end jobs (delivering papers and janitor work at a local cemetery), estranged girlfriends, and his three young children will strike an all-too-familiar chord for most viewers. With the grudging (but reliable) help of his mother, the reluctant financial backing of 82-year old Uncle Bill, the assis-tance of neighbors and community thespians, and a steady supply of booze, Borchardt wrestles with internal demons (including alcohol) and external obstacles to achieve his goals.

The resulting documentary is surprisingly engaging and perversely entertaining. Funny and depressing as the banter, "local color," and film-making antics may be, we can't help but root for Mark. His creative aspirations and dogged determination to complete a film — *any* film! — despite meager means and considerable limitations sets him apart from the football-obsessed factory-working townies around him. This isn't *October Sky* — Mark is hardly rocket scientist material — but it is a heartfelt testimonial to his firm belief in and passionate quest for the American Dream (as such, it's closer to the affec-tionate byways of Tim Burton's *Ed Wood* and Steve Martin's *Bowfinger* [23]). Mark's relationship with his world-weary Uncle Bill becomes remarkably touching, as does the devotion of Mark's lifelong friends who have "starred" in his films since childhood. *American Movie*

---

[23] See *Blur, Vol. 1*, pp. 183.

chronicles the tabling of Mark's grandiose, still-unfinished autobiographical epic *Northwestern* to complete a 35-minute horror film entitled *Coven* (pronounced with a long "o" for no particular reason) with a little help from family and friends. Prominent among these is Mark's brain-fried, loyal, and utterly endearing amigo Mike Shank, whose music scores both *Coven* and *American Movie*.

Mark and his entourage invite ridicule as addled acid-casualties, ragtag boozehounds, bizarre eccentrics, and poor white trash. *American Movie*'s greatest virtue is its refusal to belittle the lives and dreams it showcases, accepting Mark and company on their own terms as the desperation and dignity of their often risible efforts are lovingly unveiled. The movie behind the movie charted a similar path — *American Movie* director Chris Smith also struggled with ever-diminishing funds and film stock — and no doubt accounts for the film's undying respect for Mark and his aspirations. The DVD sports almost 30 minutes of deleted footage (including more of Mike!) and a commentary track that effectively remakes *American Movie* as a second, separate, and equally rewarding film. You'll also want to check out *Coven*, which is also included on the DVD, or can be rented separately on video exclusively at First Run Video (we ordered our copies directly from Mark, doing our part to support his fund-raising efforts to complete *Northwestern*; visit the americanmovie.com website to order your own signed copy of *Coven*). Recommended! *(Rated "R" for strong language, alcohol and drug abuse, and some patently fake gore staged for* Coven.)

How, you ask, can *EYE OF THE BEHOLDER* (1998) go wrong with attractive, talented co-stars Ewan

McGregor and Ashley Judd heading the cast? Despite —
no, thanks to — its high-profile cast and pedigree, *Eye of
the Beholder* unreels in the netherworld of the late
1960s-early '70s Italian *gialli* (the Italian moniker for a
particularly violent, lurid type of thriller; derived from
"*giallo*" meaning "yellow," which was the distinctive
book-jacket color associated with the literary genre); you
may have seen one or two at the drive-ins, on late-night
television, or rented on video. The best of these imports
(Mario Bava's *Blood and Black Lace*, 1964, *Bay of
Blood*, 1970; Dario Argento's *Bird with the Crystal
Plumage*, 1969, *Deep Red*, 1973; etc.), are gripping,
sublime, and sustain their own impeccable nightmare
logic, but the weirdest and worst of them (ever seen
Death Laid an Egg or *Black Belly of the Tarantula*?) are
shrill, explicitly violent, and damn near impossible to
decipher. They almost aren't movies at all: they are like
movies you dreamed, barely comprehending their tangled narratives or lunatic character motivations, unable
to recall them upon awakening before they dissolve into
oblivion.

For some viewers, this is an attractive proposition,
and I'm the first to admit there are pleasures to be found
in this bizarre cinematic limbo (I, personally, love the
gialli — the more outrageous, the better). Kudos to the
Eye of the Beholder team for resurrecting the vintage,
but they shouldn't have ignored the *giallo*'s strengths
before adopting the genre's most infuriating weaknesses.
I suspect most of you will find *Eye of the Beholder* as
frustratingly deranged and loopy as the most obscure of
the Italian *giallos*, however enticing the cast and packaging. The trappings of an effective thriller quickly fall
into place as a savvy young intelligence agent known
only as The Eye (McGregor) becomes obsessed with

surveillance target Joanna Eris (Judd), a suspected blackmailer who turns out to be a seductive killer. But The Eye doesn't quite have all his marbles: he is a high-tech voyeur haunted by the spectral presence of his long-lost daughter, and his obsession with Eris (Get it? Eye? "Iris"?) becomes increasingly irrational. His desperate quest to catch and court Joanna, a master of disguise who periodically abandons herself to her bloodlust, becomes more ludicrous as the delirious saga unravels.

Director Stephan Elliot (*The Adventures of Priscilla, Queen of the Desert*) must have intentionally embraced this delirium. After all, he mounts a visually stylish adaptation of Marc Behm's 1980 novel, but psychological intrigue soon blurs into incoherence. The film opens with the eye-catching intensity of one of Brian DePalma's premiere 1980s thrillers, but the devil in the details takes its toll. Why, oh why, does Eye disguise his surveillance camera as a rifle, as if a rifle barrel jutting from a window would be less suspicious or alarming than a camera lens? How, pray tell, does Joanna fill a train restroom from floor to ceiling with water to submerge her kill? Are we really supposed to believe that K.D. Lang represents Eye's vaguely defined omnipotent employers? As Eye's delusional conversations with his lost daughter fade into the web of lost plot threads, Eris inexplicably marries a wealthy blind man (Patrick Bergin) one week after meeting him (huh?), Genevieve Bujold drifts in and out as Eris' enigmatic "trainer" (*à la La Femme Nikita*) and Jason Priestley pops up as a psycho. The gadgets and globe-trotting escalates as the tentatively-sketched emotional center becomes more remote. By the time Eye, Eris, and the film dead-ends in an obscure corner of Alaska, the film has entombed its silly plot in a comparable deep-freeze. You won't need alcohol or drugs to feel more than a bit stoned by the climax, and that isn't a recommendation, Bunky. Succumb if you must, but you're on your own. *(Rated "R" for adult and sexual situations, nudity, violence, and language.)*

There's much, much more fun to be had with Tim Burton's **SLEEPY HOLLOW** (1999), a ravishing adult fairy-tale that remains one of the season's most appealing visual feasts. Johnny Depp stars as the effete Ichabod Crane, an eccentric police investigator dispatched from New York City to the remote community of Sleepy Hollow in the year of our Lord 1799 to uncover the culprit responsible for a series of beheadings locals ascribe to a murderous ghost known as the Headless Horseman (Christopher Walken). The murders are indeed the work of both human and supernatural deviltry, and as the previews and posters promised, heads do roll. Christina Ricci co-stars as Katrina Van Tassel, the beautiful and mysterious girl secretly linked with the apparently supernatural assassin, and a marvelously bewigged and costumed cast joins in the fun, including Miranda Richardson (who steals the show in its final act), Michael Gambon, Casper Van Dien, Jeffrey Jones, etc.

Though the film eschews the particulars of the classic 1820 Washington Irving short story it is drawn from, *Sleepy Hollow* is literate in its genre and invigorated by a rich and genuine affection for its roots. The film lifts its period upper New York State setting, character names, and spectral menace from *"The Legend of Sleepy Hollow,"* but has little else to do with Irving's tale of a beanpole schoolmaster murdered in (or banished from) the Hollow by a midnight encounter with the fabled Headless Horseman. Burton admits he's never read the story itself, preferring to draw from pop-cultural icons of his youth: the Walt Disney cartoon adaptation of Irving's tale (on video as *Ichabod and Mr. Toad*); the full-blooded, full-color British Hammer horror films of the late 1950s and 1960s; Roger Corman's Edgar Allan Poe films starring Vincent Price, particularly *The Pit and the Pendulum* (1961); and Italian director Mario Bava's classics *Black Sunday* (1960) and *Black Sabbath* (1963).

Burton cites the influence of these seminal works (and, ahem, *Scooby-Doo!*) in his sparse but engaging DVD commentary for *Sleepy Hollow*, and horror film buffs will also savor Burton's iconographic use of a windmill in the climax (echoing the fiery finales of James Whale's 1931 *Frankenstein* and Terence Fisher's 1960 *Brides of Dracula*) while acknowledging Depp's Ichabod Crane as the most faint-hearted hero since the silent *Nosferatu* (1921). But the conceit of Crane-as-detective works well, wielding his esoteric 18th Century forensic gadgetry and incorporating elements of Edgar Allan Poe (founder of the detective genre) and *Weird Tales* pulp author Seabury Quinn, whose fictional occult detective Jules de Grandin was the grandfather of Scooby-Doo, Carl Kolchak, and *The X-Files'* Scully and Mulder. A certain familiarity with these touchstones certainly adds to the pleasures the film offers — includ-ing the casting of Hammer vets Christopher Lee and Mi-chael Gough — but you needn't share such baggage to savor the splendid entertainment *Sleepy Hollow* offers.

This is among Burton's best films to date, as his gravest vulnerabilities as a filmmaker are admirably ad-dressed. The screenplay by Andrew Kevin Walker (*Se7en; 8MM*) is rich in character, incident, and mounts an engaging mystery; the action sequences, usually the weakest aspect of Burton's productions (see *Batman* and *Batman Returns*), are rousingly choreographed, staged, and executed. *Star Wars: The Phantom Menace* aficionados should note that Ray Park, Darth Maul himself, was the stunt player for many of the Headless Horseman's most energetic scenes. Winner of an Academy Award for its enchanting Art Direction (and nominated for Best Cinematography and Costume Design), *Sleepy Hollow* also boasts one of the most imaginative physical productions in ages, constructed and filmed in England's Hertsfordshire and the venerable Shepperton Studios' sound stages using forced perspective, fog cover, and inventive design to create its believable netherworld. It's a brilliant piece of work, evoking the similarly-accomplished sound-stage fantasy realms of Fritz Lang's *Siegfried* (1922), Max Reinhardt and William Dieterle's adaptation of Shakespeare's *A Midsummer Night's Dream* (1935), and, more recently, Ridley Scott's *Legend* (1986) and Neil Jordan's *The Company of Wolves* (1985; also drawn from the Hammer Film legacy).

"Murder begets murder," and despite the enchantments, the film revels in the most creative plethora of on-screen beheadings in cinematic history, along with vivid dismemberments, stakings, bisection, autopsies, and all manner of witchcraft. Burton and his cast & crew indulge in such blood and thunder with gleeful abandon, though some of the splashy gore is played for comedic effect (often at Depp's expense). Hence, it's deserved "R" rating — but only the most timid or squeamish should deprive themselves of *Sleepy Hollow*'s atmospheric fun. Recommended!

June 1:

Armed with the commercial clout of stars Susan Sarandon and Natalie Portman and a major Hollywood studio,

ANYWHERE BUT HERE (1999) swept the strikingly similar, independently-produced mother-and-daughter drama *Tumbleweeds* (1999, also recommended) [24] out of theaters. To my mind, *Tumbleweeds* is the better film, but that's neither here nor there: *Anywhere But Here* holds its own.

The narrative springboards of the two films are indeed alike, but their emotional landscapes and destinations detour to completely different ends... as mothers and daughters often do. While *Tumbleweeds* traced an arc in which a younger daughter played a vital role in her mother breaking her self-destructive cycles of courtship, breakdown, and escape, *Anywhere But Here* chronicles a more disturbed and disturbing rootlessness. Adele August (Sarandon) flees home and hearth in Bay City, Wisconsin seeking a clean slate in California, dragging her 16-year old daughter Ann (Portman) along for the duration. "This is like being kidnapped," Ann complains; "You don't understand that, do you?" When Adele retorts, "God, I wish somebody had kidnapped me when I was your age," Ann replies "So do I."

Thus, Adele follows her dreams and whims with impulsive recklessness; the necessarily pragmatic Ann suffers the consequences. The family ties Ann craves are frayed and severed, while the constant living-beyond-their-means in barren apartments and hotel rooms takes its toll. En route, Adele's procession of jobs provide little more than meager income; her desires are hardly addressed by fickle potential suitors (including Hart Bochner) or her amusingly haphazard encounters with a put-upon L.A. cop (Michael Milhoan). Ann is her albatross and anchor, but the girl is increasingly left to her

---

[24] See this volume, pp. 40-41.

own devices as Adele's lack of focus on anything other than the horizon casts them further adrift. Adele's erratic behavior and constant intrusion on Ann's almost non-existent boundaries — peeking in on a forced acting audition, opening Ann's mail, etc. — inexorably pushes Ann to the breaking point. Ann's life-long bond with cousin Benny (Shawn Hatosy of *Outside Providence*) and a tentative, tender budding relationship with class-mate Peter (Corbin Allred) provide some succor, but she knows she will only find an anchor free of Adele's orbit.

We can't wait to see her cut loose and fly.

Screenwriter Alvin Sargent's adaptation of Mona Simpson's novel and Wayne Wang's direction maintains some semblance of balance on the slippery soap-opera slopes, but it's Sarandon and Portman (who spends much of the film understandably near and in tears) who breathe life into the film. They provide the few fresh moments that make the rocky trip worthwhile, though there's little doubt where the wayward path is heading, or that they'll see their way through. *(Rated "PG-13" for language, adult and sexual situations.)*

I considered **SNOW FALLING ON CEDARS** (1999) among the decade's finest when I caught it in theaters, and this week's video re-viewing only reinforced that impression. Critical and audiences response was luke-warm at best, though I don't see why: director Scott Hicks (*Shine*) mounts an evocative adaptation of David Guterson's best-selling novel of first love, truth, racism, and tragedy set amid one of recent American history's most shameful chapters.

The framework hangs upon a mystery and a murder trial, but this is primarily a tale of the heart. In a small village in the Pacific Northwest, earnest young reporter

Ishmael Chambers (Ethan Hawke) is plagued by memories and his unrequited love for Hatsuo (Youki Kudoh of *Mystery Train*), whose husband Kazuo (Rick Yune) is accused of the murder. As teenagers, Ishmael and Hatsuo nurtured a growing passion that remained unconsummated, cut short by the brutal intervention of Pearl Harbor, World War 2, and the relocation of Hatsuo and her family to Manzanar, one of the concentration-camp-like "Relocation Centers" many Asian-Americans were exiled to during the war. While imprisoned in Manzanar, Hatsuo succumbed to her situation and tearfully renounced her love for Ishmael, marrying Kazuo, whose own family suffers an unjust loss of home and property during the war years. This tangled weave of heartbreak, history, and deceit leads inexorably to Kazuo's arrest and trial for the murder of a local fisherman (Eric Thal), and Ishmael's agonized coming-to-terms with his affections for Hatsuo as he uncovers a shred of evidence which could prove Kazuo's innocence.

True to Guterson's novel, Hicks orchestrates these elements with consummate skill and a ravishing cinematic eye and ear. The xenophobic legacy of Manzanar (Spanish for "apple blossom," a bitter irony given the camp's barren locale in a remote stretch of desert 200 miles north of Los Angeles) and its ilk was previously fictionalized in writer-director Alan Parker's *Come See the Paradise* (1990) and eloquently eulogized in Tom Russell's moving song *"Manzanar"* (1993); the true story of the Federal Government's War Location Authority and the imprisonment of over 115,000 Japanese-Americans and recent immigrants can be read in Lillian Baker's *American and Japanese Relocation in*

World War II.[25] It's extraordinary how Guterson and Hicks (who co-wrote the screenplay adaptation with Ron Bass) incorporate this potent material into the delicate fabric of their narrative without either trivializing the enormity of the real-life events, or burying the story's complex web of vulnerable, volatile human emotions beneath the daunting weight of such historical truths. Many honorable novelists and filmmakers have failed to walk such tightropes; *Snow Falling on Cedars* never misses a step, deftly drawing its threads together with grace and resonant clarity. (Guterson, Hicks, and Bass reorient one critical narrative thread quite ingeniously, in a manner those familiar with the novel simply may not appreciate; viewers experiencing the tale for the first time here, though, will respond. This is an entirely appropriate rethinking of the source novel for cinema, saving a key character point for a purely visual revelatory moment, indicative of the extraordinary care the cinematic adaptation was given.)

Though it's fashionable to belittle Ethan Hawke these days, he delivers an understated, nuanced performance amid a formidable ensemble (including Max Von Sydow as the elderly defense attorney and Sam Shepard as Ishmael's father). There is real chemistry smoldering between Hawke and Youki Kudoh — and between Kudoh and Rick Yune (in his feature debut role) — and young Reeve Carney and Anne Suzuki establish that passion with their strong playing of young Ishmael and Hatsuo. Robert Richardson's breathtaking cinematogra-

---

[25] Also see the exquisite autobiographical graphic novel *Citizen 13660* written and drawn by Miné Okubo (Columbia University Press, 1946; reprinted by University of Washington Press, 1983), which is most highly recommended.

phy and James Newton Howard's exquisite score are mesmerizing, capturing and contrasting the melancholy that drives Guterson's narrative. The seascapes, winterscapes, and locales are almost elemental in their dreamy rapture, by turns bleached by sun, suffused by fog, and suffocated by snow.

This often eerie beauty cradles and externalizes a resolute, gentle spirit which soars amid the sorrow and loss, desire and sacrifice, and emotional and physical violence that threatens to consume all. *Snow Falling* stands apart for that spirit, which quietly asserts and defines itself in the film's moving conclusion. In a culture obsessed with delineating love almost exclusively in sexualized or familial terms, it is unusual to find such an honest and uncluttered expression of the most fragile of virtues we hold dear.

Clumsy English fails me, but I have no doubt the Japanese have a word for it.

Snow Falling on Cedars is a marvelous film, and most highly recommended. *(Rated "PG-13" for adult and sexual situations, strong and racist language, violence associated with the crime and World War 2, and gruesome forensic imagery.)*

Recent & Recommended:

PROJECT A (*'A' GAI WAAK,* 1983) is vintage Jackie Chan, and as such prime viewing. Too many habitually pass up gems like *Project A* as "one of his old movies" and hence beneath notice, denying themselves rousing entertainments made during Jackie Chan's prime as an action star, comedian, filmmaker, and athlete. Forget the tired antics of the Hollywood-sanitized Chan features *Rush Hour* and *Shanghai Noon*; age, the insurance companies, and unimaginative studio execs won't *let* Jackie cut loose as he did in his native country. Set in turn-of-the-century Hong Kong, a port city torn by the rivalry between a corrupt police force and impoverished Navy and plagued by piracy, *Project A* has the weaknesses many Americans choke on, including thin and contrived plotting and corny dialogue further compromised by barely competent dubbing. But its virtues are captivating and the action often jaw-dropping, staged by Chan and fellow Peking Opera *Seven Little Fortunes* veterans Sammo Hung and Yuen Biao. The villainous pirate leader Lo is played with Manchurian zeal by Dick Wei, and his final showdown with Chan, Hung, and Biao is a corker. The dazzling bicycle chase sequence alone is worth the price of rental, climaxing with Jackie's dangle and plunge from a clock tower. Such bone-crunching setpieces offer further proof that Chan is channeling the spirits of silent era stars Douglas Fairbanks, Buster Keaton, and Harold Lloyd, and is a world treasure. Don't be foolish; take this one home and pop up a big batch of popcorn!

June 1-8:

ANDY KAUFMAN: THE MAN WHO FELL TO EARTH [26]

"Andy's an acquired taste — he was something you had to get used to over a period of time...

---

[26] Note: This was originally published as a two part article; I have slightly revised the published version to consolidate it into single essay. Only the transitional passages have been revised; this is the definitive version.

"Andy made himself the premise, and the entire world was the punch line." - Robin Williams

Last week's video release of **Man on the Moon** (1999), the major studio biography of the 1970s enfant terrible comedian Andy Kaufman, boasts a formidable roster of premiere talents, from mega-star Jim Carrey's Golden Globe Award-winning onscreen recreation of Kaufman to producer and co-star Danny DeVito and internationally-renowned director Milos Forman (*One Flew Over the Cuckoo's Nest, Amadeus*, etc.) at the helm. Those are heavyweight credentials, and the film is a compelling if somewhat muddled accomplishment that effectively immortalizes and lionizes Kaufman as a martyr to his art, an absurdist groundbreaking pioneer who endeared himself to millions only to aggressively alienate them in ruthless accord with his muse, a Dadaist Lenny Bruce for the 1970s.

The film also prompts the inevitable question, "Why?" Why dedicate so much talent, time, effort, money, and public focus to the odd career arc of one of a quirky era's quirkiest comedians? How could have Kaufman's child-like media-baby antics endured to be lionized in such a grandiose showcase? What has elevated Andy Kaufman from the mire of public loathing that shrouded his final plunge, disdain he actively cultivated and encouraged in his final years?

To those caught up in the contemporary wave of nostalgia for the decade of the 1970s, Andy now seems like the ultimate *That '70s Show*. He was, they argue, a brilliant iconoclast, a folk surrealist, a deconstructionist pioneer of "Performance Art," a near-mystic trickster, a subversive hero. This is a revisionist and arguably over-due reassessment that *Man on the Moon* (its title taken from the R.E.M. hit song, which played a vital role in the Andy Kaufman revival we're in) heartily endorses, evidenced not only by the film itself but also the interviews with cast and creative crew that peppers its DVD bonus features. Star Jim Carrey, director Forman, and producer/co-star Danny DeVito (significantly the only onscreen participant to have known Kaufman, working with him on 112 episodes of the popular 1970s TV program *Taxi*) embrace and encourage this perspective. Their dedication to Kaufman's life and art invigorates the film from first frame to last. The movie is further enriched and validated by the behind-the-scenes involvement of Kaufman's friends and associates Bob Zmuda (founder of Comic Relief, played in the film itself by actor Paul Giamatti) and Lynne Margulies (credited as "Creative Consultant" and played onscreen by Courtney Love, though the film's portrayal of Margulies as Kaufman's sexual partner doesn't jive with biographies; Margulies was a close friend and there to the end, but she reportedly wasn't Andy's girlfriend).

But to many, Kaufman was and remains an enigma unworthy of such attention. "Murder would be too gentle a fate for Andy Kaufman," a *Village Voice* review of Kaufman's 1979 Carnegie Hall concert concluded, saying he "...went beyond humor and into [the] cruel and vile...". For many, he wasn't the least bit funny then, and seems like a bad memory now; a dead horse not worth the flogging, much less deserving of a feature film biography. They considered Kaufman (if they considered him at all) a pathetic lunatic, a narcissistic eccentric, a bullying anarchist, an arrogant and abusive misanthrope who squandered and spurned the public affection he'd garnered in an interminable and all-too-public fit of hubris. He surely never endeared himself to many women, conservative or feminist, with his misogynist rants (repeatedly claiming females worthy only of kitchen duties and child-rearing, "All oatmeal north of the eyebrows") and "inter-gender" wrestling antics. The citizens of Memphis and the Deep South could hardly be fond of the pasty alien from Hollywood who invaded their wrestling arenas and — via TV — their homes to ceaselessly trick and insult them, mocking them as "hicks" who didn't know what soap was for ("This section of the country is the filthiest").

To its credit, *Man on the Moon* covers this demonic view of Kaufman — though it downplays his nastiest excesses — particularly through the portrayal of Kaufman's demonic Mr. Hyde persona "Tony Clifton." Looking like a mutated Roy Orbison, inflating the underbelly of Elvis Presley and Don Rickles to monstrously toadish proportions, "Clifton" was arguably Kaufman's most audacious creation: a grotesque Las Vegas lounge singer who couldn't sing, but didn't care; a belligerent boor who berated and abused his audiences; a misanthropic bile-spewing brute Kaufman used to unleash his venom on friends and fans alike. Engaging as Jim Carrey's performance as Andy Kaufman is throughout *Man on the Moon*, his recreation of "Tony Clifton" is positively frightening; when compared to the real item (immortalized on the archival videos discussed below), Carrey's "Clifton" is absolutely authentic, seething with the same dangerous energy.

The joke was that Kaufman was, and wasn't, "Tony Clifton," any more than he was "Foreign Man," *Taxi*'s Latka Gravas, "Conga Man," or the wanna-be wrestler who beat up on women and fanned public hatred. In fact, Kaufman's associate Bob Zmuda (and another of their mutual friends) often played "Tony Clifton," allowing the team to confound audiences with Andy's occasional live guest appearances onstage alongside Clifton. As DeVito intimates in his DVD bonus interview, there were many who knew Andy in life and attended his funeral who didn't believe he was dead, and *Man on the Moon* plays on that legend.

The film's greatest flaw — common to almost all screen biographies — is its sentimentalization of a very difficult subject. Screenwriters Scott Alexander and Larry Karaszewski have thus far in their careers traded on such controversial public figures, with Tim Burton's fond, funny portrait of the 1950s' impoverished filmmaker *Ed Wood* (1994) among their first and finest achievements (they also authored the recent comedy *Screwed*, among other films). Borrowing Kaufman's own framing device from his notorious ABC-TV special *Andy's Funhouse* (1977/79; better known as *The Andy Kaufman Special*), Alexander and Karaszewski cleverly set up their manipulation of the source material by presenting *Man on the Moon* as "Andy's movie," embracing Kaufman's trickster reputation. It's as if Andy hadn't died, as if his funeral were a ruse, and he'd emerged from self-imposed exile to craft his own feature-length eulogy (a feat fellow prankster Alfred Hitchcock would have envied and certainly have applauded).

Thus, they self-referentially acknowledge and excuse their indulgences, a post modernist conceit some critics lauded and considered absolutely appropriate to the subject matter. Other viewers (myself included) find this borrowed onscreen intro with Andy talking to the audience an amusing but flimsy pretense; despite my admiration and enjoyment of the film, I find myself in agreement with film historian (founder, editor, and publisher of *Animation Planet* magazine) G. Michael

Dobbs' assessment of the film as "spineless." After all, this is the very conceit deployed by the reviled John Belushi biopic, *Wired* (1989); *Sunset Boulevard*, it wasn't. Even within the chronology *Man in the Moon* endorses, the glib rearrangement of Kaufman's sell-out August 26th-27th, 1979 Carnegie Hall concert (a pinnacle in his career) to the end of the film to provide an upbeat finale is unconvincing. As detailed in the film, Kaufman's star had demonstratably plummeted, evidenced by the November 20th, 1982 *Saturday Night Live* telephone poll in which almost 200,000 viewers voted in one short hour to forever ban Kaufman from the program, though he'd previously held the record for the most *SNL* guest appearances (fourteen). Kaufman had brainstormed the poll after seeing *SNL* urging viewers to vote-by-phone to decide whether a lobster would be boiled and eaten or rescued; 500,000 voted to save the lobster. Andy couldn't match the crustacean's drawing power or votes, much less pack Carnegie Hall in 1983. Such "happy ending" tactics undermine the film's credibility, even within its own distorted chronology and "Andy's movie" conceit.

We are forced to question, and cease to believe in, the film's own context. Whether Kaufman was indeed "a patron saint of comedy" (as Carrey reveres him in the DVD bonus interview) or a despicable buffoon, he had far more cajones than *Man in the Moon* ultimately musters. As another 1970s-80s pop icon and public agitator, Johnny Rotten (John Lydon), shouted to the audience at the end of the final U.S. Sex Pistols concert in San Francisco, "Ah ha-ha. Ever get the feeling you've been cheated?" In the end, *Man on the Moon* is a cheat.

Though its final act is a letdown, *Man on the Moon* is certainly entertaining and engaging. While playing fast and loose with the chronology of Kaufman's bizarre career, much of what the film presents is surprisingly true to the archival materials, articles, and available biographies. Thanks to the insatiable appetite and relatively inexpensive access of the video market, interested viewers can draw their own conclusions by experiencing the Kaufman archive for themselves.

Feature films necessarily compress and distort people, places, facts, and events. It is impossible to maintain any degree of accuracy while squeezing years into two hours of screen time. Legal constraints often impose restrictions. And by their creative and collaborative nature, films impose an authorial perspective onto any recreation of a life or event. There are no objective screen biographies; all have an agenda, be it personal, political, or commercial. Indeed, anyone who takes *any* film biography or docudrama as a source of accurate information, much less definitively "factual," is (to put it bluntly) an idiot.

For those who care to indulge their curiosity further, a viewing of *Man on the Moon* needn't suffice. Here, then, is a capsule-review video guide to Andy Kaufman's legacy on home video:

* You might want to check out *Taxi* reruns on cable or Paramount's TV Classics four-volume set, **THE BEST OF ANDY KAUFMAN IN TAXI**. Each tape offers two episodes, including *"Latka the Playboy," "Mama Gravas,"* and the entire Latka marriage arc. Though Kaufman reviled *Taxi*, this was the series that made him a star, and as such rewards a return visit.

* Andy's few appearances in feature films may be of some interest, though they remain curios that never

showcased Kaufman's talents. Larry Cohen's offbeat theological science-fiction/horror film *GOD TOLD ME TO* (1977, aka *Demon*; highly recommended!) featured a short cameo from Kaufman as a killer cop, a role strangely suited to the comedian's subsequent guerrilla theater image as Cohen shot the violent scene amid NYC's real St. Patrick's Day police parade without proper notification or permission. Andy must have loved it. For Allan Arkush's fey science fiction romantic-fantasy *HEARTBEEPS* (1981), Kaufman played a love-sick robot opposite Bernadette Peters, revamping elements of his "Foreign Man"-inspired role as a robot in the unaired 1977 TV pilot *Stick Around* (not available on video); the film, though, is of little interest, at best an inoffensive misfire suitable for the kiddies. *God Told Me To* and *Heartbeeps* are readily available on home video, but his rousing turn as "Armageddon T. Thunderbird" in Marty Feldman's *IN GOD WE TRUST* (1980) — the only Kaufman feature really worth seeing — is a hard-to-see rarity; you may be able to catch it on eBay or on cable.

For the relatively undiluted Kaufman canon, here's the rundown:

* If you're seeking less fictionalized video biographies of Kaufman, Dan Dalton's *ANDY KAUFMAN: TANK YOU VEDY MUCH* (1999) may suffice. By all accounts, Andy was a pretty weird little kid, and this video provides a compact but sketchy chronology of Kaufman's life and career from his childhood years to his death on May 16th, 1984. There are a few nit-picky inaccuracies and distortions — Kaufman didn't debut on *The Dean Martin Show*, but on *Dean Martin's Comedy*

World (June 1974, appearing on the first and third shows); the Carl Reiner and Dick Van Dyke program was entitled *Van Dyke and Company* (1974); Andy was first on *The Mike Douglas Show* in 1977, not '78; etc. — but overall this is a worthwhile rental. Production quality is competent but unexceptional, punctuated with tantalizing film clips that may prompt you to seek out the meatier fare below.

*The best bio available at those video shops that carry audio books is the audio book *LOST IN THE FUNHOUSE: THE LIFE AND MIND OF ANDY KAUFMAN* by Bill Zehme (1999, three hours). An effective reading by Budd Friedman, proprietor of the New York City comedy club "The Improvisation" where Kaufman debuted in 1973, lends authenticity, warmth, and a veteran's personal touch to the enterprise; Friedman knew, loved, and supported Kaufman. If you want some real insight and a factual record, look — I mean, listen — to this gem. Highly recommended!

* *THE BEST OF SATURDAY NIGHT LIVE 1975-1980: CLASSICS, VOLUME 2* (1992) presents the historic Oct. 11, 1975 showcase of Kaufman's endearing "Mighty Mouse" sing-along routine. Andy's appearance only constitutes two minutes, but the entire program is well worth a look (and, for some of you, a return visit) as a genuinely funny, groundbreaking slice of the mid-'70s live comedy renaissance. Kaufman also appears on other volumes in the *SNL* video library, so check 'em out.

* If you only want to see one Andy Kaufman video, *THE ANDY KAUFMAN SPECIAL* (onscreen title:

Andy's Funhouse) is *the* one to pick. This is the remarkable special portrayed in *Man on the Moon* that ABC-TV was contractually obligated to allow Kaufman relative creative freedom to produce (within the parameters of Standards & Practices restrictions). It indeed befuddled and infuriated TV executives: though completed in 1977, ABC head honcho Fred Silverman so despised the program that he banned it from broadcast; rival network NBC pursued broadcast rights, only to drop the ball when Silverman moved to NBC. Upon Silverman's departure, ABC finally aired the special once on August 28, 1979, scoring high ratings. The onscreen title is derived from Andy's closed circuit TV show *Uncle Andy's Funhouse* (1970), which he produced while a student at Graham Junior College in Boston. *The Andy Kaufman Special* provides an ideal showcase of Kaufman's prime material at this stage in his career, from his childhood "The Cow Goes Moo" song, a clever Brechtian framing device, the classic stand-up "Foreign Man" routine and Elvis impression, subversive deconstruction of TV variety and talk show fixtures (including the "Has Been" spot, a hilariously embarrassing "guest interview" with Laverne and Shirley star Cindy Williams, and on-camera capture of supposedly off-camera "slips of the mask"), the Howdy Doody interview, and more. The notorious deliberate scrambling of the image (causing home audiences to think their TV sets needed adjustment) is indeed here. The climactic singing of the Fabian Forte song "This Friendly World" (written by K.L. Darby in 1959) is touching in hindsight, as this tune was actually sung by Andy on film at his own funeral, as depicted in *Man on the Moon*. Highly recommended!

* The next-best offering for those seeking a peek at Kaufman in his prime is Burt Sugarman's *MIDNIGHT SPECIAL* (first broadcast January 23rd, 1981), aka *ANDY KAUFMAN'S MIDNIGHT SPECIAL*. This offers a primo "Tony Clifton" setpiece, along with a rundown of some of Andy's by-this-time classic stand up material. Recommended.

* *ANDY KAUFMAN: I'M FROM HOLLYWOOD* (1989) offers definitive documentation of Andy's seemingly interminable career culmination, detour, or slide (depending on your personal assessment) into the guerrilla-theater arena of mainstream wrestling, which began in 1978 and lasted into the final months of his life (his final public match was November, 1983). The credits certainly reflect Andy's full involvement with this caper: written and directed by Lynne Margulies and Joe Orr, and prominently featuring Kaufman confederates Bob Zmuda (appearing as a referee and attorney) and Jerry "The King" Lawler, who was at that time the Southern heavyweight champion wrestler. Perhaps the reckless, ugly, volatile energy on display here was drawn in part from Kaufman's planned feature film screenplay *The Tony Clifton Story* (first draft written 1979; plug pulled 1981), which reportedly cast the misanthropic Clifton as hero pitched against Kaufman's portrayal of himself as a despicable villain. Well, he made sure he became one in life with this severe career turn, spouting misogynist rants, ridiculing and wrestling over 60 women to become the self-proclaimed "Inter-Gender Wrestling Champion of the World," slandering the South, and generally carrying on with as much abusive, malicious intent as he could manage. This video isn't for all tastes by any means — it will bore and/or piss off many, which was evidently the intention — but it does feature Lawler's devastating Memphis match pile-driver attack and the historic July 28th *Late Night with David Letterman* broadcast in which Lawler and Kaufman came to blows. As for Lawler's pile driver leveling of Kaufman, Andy reportedly suffered only minor neck strain and was well in three days, though he wore and exploited the neck brace for over five months! Kaufman subsequently starred in a bizarre, short-lived Broadway musical "Comedy about Love and Wrestling" entitled *Teaneck Tanzi, The Venus Flytrap*. This outrageous video is either a high point or inexcusable low in the Kaufman *ouevre*, depending on your take. I couldn't help but laugh, but approach with caution.

* *MY BREAKFAST WITH BLASSIE* (1984) was Kaufman's modest reply to the art-house hit *My Dinner with André* (1981), a politically-incorrect breakfast at a Los Angeles "Sambo's" restaurant (ah, the 1970s!) with veteran wrestling star Freddie Blassie, self-proclaimed "King of Men." This is slow going by any standard: wry, dry, peppered with Blassie's old-school patriarchal attitudes (rubbing the pregnant waitress' belly, calling her to the table with "Hey, Buddha!") and borderline misogyny coupled with Kaufman's "does he really mean it?" put-ons and eccentricities. The meditations on the bane of celebrity (Blassie won't sign autographs; Andy does, only to anger, then hit on, the women at a table nearby), cleanliness (ah, wetnaps!), and more is capped by an eruption of adolescent gross-out humor introduced by interloper Bob Zmuda, up to his old tricks. Notable, sadly, for the introductory footage of the premiere of the film at the NuArt Theater in Los Angeles (March 1984), where Kaufman made his final public appearance just

weeks away from his death. Already ravaged by cancer, he looks ashen gray and sports a Travis Bickle-like Mohawk that only emphasizes his condition. Again, approach with caution; necessary viewing for Kaufman devotees, but casual viewers beware.

The unanswerable question about Kaufman's final couple of years, dedicated to baiting, abusing, and galling the public via his wrestling obsession, will always remain: Why did Andy do it?

The only explanation may reside in last words of the killer cop Kaufman played in Larry Cohen's offbeat science fiction-horror gem *God Told Me To*:

"God told me to."

R.I.P., Andy Kaufman.

June 8:

Writer/director James Mangold's film adaptation of Susanna Kaysen's autobiographical work **GIRL, INTERRUPTED** (1999) chronicles the true-life story of 17-year old Kaysen's incarceration in a psychiatric hospital during the tumultuous 1960s. When Susanna's (Winona Ryder) increasingly erratic behavior leads to a reckless suicide attempt (a bottle of aspirin chased with a fifth of vodka), her affluent parents bundle her off to the famed Claymoore institute, where Susanna is diagnosed with 'borderline personality disorder.' Pitching herself against the well-intentioned professional staff (lead by Vanessa Redgrave, Jeffrey Tambor, and Whoopi Goldberg), Susanna soon bonds with the troubled young women of Claymoore, prominent among them the confrontational, impulsive, rebellious, and beguiling Lisa (Angelina Jolie delivering a Golden Globe and Academy

Award-winning performance). Lisa's caustic wit and rage unerringly targets her ward mates' vulnerabilities. Her undeniable charisma and occasional tenderness (demonstrated in Susanna and Lisa's empathy for self-immolation survivor Polly, played by Elizabeth Moss) can turn in a heartbeat, which only enhances the dangerous attraction Susanna feels. Lisa's sociopathic edge cuts deepest during a cruel encounter with Daisy (Brittany Murphy) in the "outside," a toxic turn of events that pushes Susanna to finally confront her own inner demons.

Mangold (writer/director of two excellent films, *Heavy*, 1996, and *Copland*, 1997) and co-screenwriters Lisa Loomer and Anna Hamilton Phelan clearly attempted to capture the strengths of Kaysen's compelling memoir, but the film itself is oddly conventional. Kaysen acknowledges (during the DVD bonus materials) that *Girl, Interrupted* was "sketchy in a way... kind of open and bare," challenging the transition from page to screen. Check out the deleted scenes on the DVD's bonus chapters, which considerably enrich the film. Too bad they had to go: among the casualties were vivid flashbacks of Susanna's disturbing hallucinations that culminated in her breakdown (including a shadowy bedtime vision, and a startling eruption of blood in a supermarket meat aisle), and a museum trip introducing the Vemeer painting *"Girl, Interrupted [at her music]"* that lends the book and film its title.

For some viewers, the casting of Winona Ryder as Susanna, once again in the waif role (as in *Little Women*, *Age of Innocence*, etc.) though she is at least a decade beyond Kaysen's age during the events depicted in the film, may be a liability. As demonstrated in *South Park: Bigger, Longer and Uncut* (1999), Ryder's stature has become a joke to many young viewers tired of seeing Ryder constantly cast as a representative Generation 'X' role model, but the film would never have been made without her. Jolie steals the show, but Ryder provides its anchor and focus amid a lively ensemble cast. Despite its flaws, *Girl, Interrupted* is still raw and potent enough to capture the essence of Kaysen's book, delivering a touching, often funny coming-of-age drama.

As a parent, I'd suggest adults reluctant to bring "R"-rated films into the home might allow their teenagers to see this one. Kaysen's source novel and the film successfully addresses volatile emotional issues faced by many teens, including those involving sexuality, identity, self-loathing, and suicide. If you've strong qualms, please, check the film out for yourself. *(Rated "R" for strong language, alcohol and drug abuse, self-destructive and suicidal behavior, adult and sexual situations.)*

Recent & Recommended:

MR. DEATH: THE RISE AND FALL OF FRED A. LEUCHTER, JR. (1999) is the latest documentary from American master-of-the-form Errol Morris (*The Thin Blue Line*, 1988; *A Brief History of Time*, 1992; *Fast, Cheap, and Out of Control*, 1998), turning his cameras onto another fascinating maverick. Massachusetts engineer Fred Leuchter, Jr. is a hands-on advocate of humane Capital Punishment whose father raised him amid the state correctional facilities (where, Fred tells us, he learned "many strange things"), putting him on the unique career path of constructing functional high-grade execution hardware — electric chairs, gallows, and lethal-injection machines — for state prisons sorely in need of revamped equipment. "It's not anything different than any competent engineer could do," Leuchter matter-of-factly explains. "The difference is, it's not a major market; a lot of people are not interested, and are morally opposed to working on an execution [device] — they think it's somehow going to change them." This career opportunism and opacity (and, some would argue, bad karma) sets Fred up as a willing patsy testifying on behalf of the notorious Ernst Zundel, a German National living in Canada who maintained the Holocaust never occurred, gathering dubious evidence from the Auschwitz camp sites to verify Zundel's stance. Ultimately, Leuchter's tragic, Faustian involvement with Zundel and various revisionist historians and Aryan nation groups cost him his marriage, livelihood, and dignity.

As in *The Thin Blue Line*, Morris meticulously dissects the evidence to arrive at the truth, crafting a compelling portrait of a rather simple, skilled *Popular Mechanics* layman (lacking any but the most rudimentary scientific, chemical, and research skills) who plunges way, way out of his moral and experiential depth and pays a terrible price for his ignorance. Caleb Sampson's marvelous musical score holds the film together. Morris peppers this portrait with evocative archival footage, including the horrific Edison short *Electrocuting an Elephant* (1903; so-called 'snuff films,' you see, are as old as the medium). The grim and often ghoulish subject matter will put off many viewers, but if you've a stomach for the deadpan verbal descriptions of executions and infuriating Holocaust-denial rhetoric, this counts among the season's strongest video fare. Highly recommended, with reservations.

June 15:

The late Isaac Asimov remains one of the world's premiere science fiction authors. Sadly, his visionary work and legacy has been ill-served by cinema, a medium and industry Asimov shunned (to date, there have been two shoddy low-budget adaptations of his marvelous 1941 short story *"Nightfall"* — a made-for-TV version in 1988, and upcoming Roger Corman direct-to-video remake starring David Carradine — and Asimov co-scripted the English-language dub of the French animated feature *Light Years*, 1988). Unfortunately, *BICENTENNIAL MAN* (1999) only confirms the disdain Asimov held for most filmed science fiction.

Drawn from Asimov's 1975 short story of the same name, and the novel *The Positronic Man* (1992) by Asimov and Robert Silverberg, *Bicentennial Man* tells the story of a futuristic "household appliance" named Andrew (Robin Williams), the first robot/android to achieve individuality, freedom, and autonomy over his 200-year life span. The downside of such virtual immortality takes its toll as Andrew suffers increasing loneliness and loss while his adopted family ages, matures, and dies, prompting a search for another of his kind.

The famous 'Three Laws of Robotics' (co-authored by Asimov and John W. Campbell, Jr. in the early 1940s) are immediately espoused, and an early sequence's nicely understated association between Andrew and his owner's car-as-robot is promising, but the valid science fiction of Asimov's source material is quickly reduced to unimaginative, sentimental treacle. The machine-to-man theme is overly familiar turf for even casual viewers: think Mary Shelley's *Frankenstein*, the Tin Man of *The Wizard of Oz*, or the children's classic *Pi-*

nocchio. Far, far better films and television productions have effectively explored the theme: *The Twilight Zone* episode *"The Lonely,"* Ray Bradbury's *"The Electric Grandmother,"* *Blade Runner, Robocop, Terminator 2*; hell, even the dirt-cheap 1962 *Creation of the Humanoids* was more fun. As science fiction, *Bicentennial Man* becomes increasingly infantile. The film's preview of the future is as vapid as the worst pulp science fiction, mixing contemporary interiors with scraps of weird costuming, bad hats, and occasional glimpses of cityscapes echoing the now-risible 1930s World Fair displays.

As an amusement, *Bicentennial Man* misfires, too: it's sluggish, unfunny, and interminable. Director Chris Columbus launched his career scribing the screenplay for *Gremlins* (1984), which despite its flaws boasted a gleeful, childish anarchy, mischief, and malice lacking in subsequent work. Columbus later scored at the boxoffice as a director with *Home Alone* (1990) — more cheerfully sadistic/anarchistic slapstick — and some of you may be fond of Columbus' prior Robin Williams collaboration *Mrs. Doubtfire* (1993), but like an android replicant cast in the worst Disney/Spielberg mold, Columbus is an utterly pedestrian filmmaker: competent and cozily domestic at best, at his worst banal. In *Bicentennial Man*, Columbus is eager-as-ever to pluck the heartstrings with Andrew's relationship with Little Miss (played as a child by the "Pepsi" kid, Hattie Kate Eisenberg), the sterile death-bed scenes, the first kiss, and the last act's glacial love story, but bathos, not pathos, reigns as the film lurches from setpiece to setpiece between twenty-year gaps. Actor Oliver Platt offers some relief when he pops up as Rupert Burns, the shaggy scientist who upgrades Andrew to humanoid status, but by the time he appears onscreen, such artificial respiration provides too little too late.

Bicentennial Man is also consistent with Robin Williams' continuing weakness for such sappy "child-man" mutant fare (*Toys, Being Human, Jack, Jakob the Liar,* etc.). In a way, the film is a perfect metaphor for his cinematic career, with the invigorating improvisational energy of Williams' live standup comedy buried beneath layers of robotic armor, struggling to break free. In the context of Williams' prior "child-man" roles, *Bicentennial Man* comes across as a lifeless reversal of *Jack* (the story of a kid who rapidly aged) that might be retitled *Not Being Human*. It's a painful spectacle, though Williams, as always, gives it his earnest "all," adding to the agonies.

Touchstone Pictures (a subsidiary of Disney) bally-hoo boasts, "Programmed for Heartwarming Fun!" Well, that was undoubtably the intention, but *Bicentennial Man* is too laborious to engage many adults, and too slow, talky, and obsessed with mortality to appeal to children past its first half hour. In the waning acts, Portia (Embeth Davidtz, delivering a credible performance in multiple roles) exclaims, "I can't invest my emotions in a machine!" Given this vehicle, I couldn't agree more. Sans humanoid robotic forms to work with, a quarter-century ago imaginative directors like Douglas Trumbull and George Lucas were able to stimulate far more audience empathy for what were, essentially, beeping and hissing basket-sized tubular batteries (respectively, Huey, Dewy and Louie in *Silent Running*, 1972, and R2-D2 in *Star Wars*, 1977); Columbus and Williams can't muster comparable sympathies with over two hours of dialogue, state-of-the-art Millennial special effects makeup, and Williams' uncanny pantomime abilities at their disposal. *Bicentennial Man* is a slow-mo *Pinocchio* that's too deliberate, mechanical, and manipulative to reward such an investment. In its relentless upgrading of Williams' character from robot to human being, *Bicentennial Man* is sorely in need of one or two of Columbus' malicious career-launching gremlins to provide some antic life — or, at least, subvert and gum up the inexorable grind of the narrative clockwork. *(Rated "PG" for some tame off-color jokes and a bit of language.)*

THE GREEN MILE (1999) is as populist a slice of contemporary filmmaking as *Bicentennial Man*, but — it works. While *Bicentennial Man* seems twice as long as it is, *The Green Mile*'s expansive running time affords its story and characters due narrative room to reveal their secrets.

Tom Hanks and David Morse lend integrity and heart to their roles as prison guards working Death Row — the titular "Green Mile" — at Louisiana's Cold Mountain Penitentiary. They are decent men who take their jobs seriously, doing their level best to lend some dignity to the last hours, days, months, years of the convicted men under their watch, despite the grueling nature of the task, sometimes volatile nature of the prisoners, and infuriating incompetence and cold-blooded sadism of one of fellow guard Percy Wetmore (played with deadpan relish by Doug Hutchison, who previously registered as the mutant liver-eating, limb-stretching serial-killer 'Tooms' during the first season of *The X-Files*). Enter John Coffey (Academy Award-nominated Michael Clarke Duncan), a seemingly gentle giant man-child (move over, Robin Williams) serving a death sentence for a savage crime involving two young children. In short order, it becomes apparent that Coffey is not what he seems, manifesting miracles that profoundly alter the lives of all those involved.

Just as he did for Stephen King's other tale of purgatory and personal redemption in a state prison, *The Shawshank Redemption* (1994), screenwriter-director Frank Darabont admirably adapts King's best-selling serialized novel with devotional attention to the author's considerable strengths as a story-teller (of course, if you've no affection or affinity for King's work, *Green Mile* isn't likely to please you in the first place). Darabont's affinity for King's writing was apparent from his 1983 "student" film adapted from King's short story *The Woman in the Room* (on video in the anthology tape *Stephen King's Nightshift Collection*, and well worth seeing). Indeed, that accomplished short film brought Darabont and King together, and few other filmmakers have demonstrated such a full grasp of the chemistry that makes King a celebrated best-selling author. Though Darabont necessarily compresses the narrative to squeeze King's novel into feature-film length, he remains utterly true to King's sense of place, time, characterization, and internal rhythms. The drive that propels King's writing survives the transition to the screen, and that (as all-too-many failed King adaptations prove) is quite an accomplishment in and of itself; happily, *The Green Mile* is one of King's better recent novels, worthy of Darabont's efforts. The compression does take a toll: gone is much of the nursing home framing story (including Percy's cruel surrogate); thus, the multiple climaxes, major and minor, which King carefully staggered apart in his novel's framing device are necessarily delivered in the film's finale and coda, piling revelation upon revelation. But these quibbles hardly cripple Darabont's masterful adaptation, the cast's fine-tuned ensemble playing, or the success of the film as a whole. Here's hoping the next King story Darabont adapts isn't set in a prison.

More troublesome, perhaps, are King's predilections for gruesome setpieces and yet-another noble African-American imbued with supernatural abilities. Fair warning on the former: there is a genuinely horrific electrocution scene (based in part on an actual occurrence, as described in Errol Morris' documentary *Mr. Death: The Rise and Fall of Fred A. Leuchter, Jr.*) calculated to have you covering your eyes. Darabont plays it for all it's worth, so be prepared. As to the latter, John Coffey is indeed another of King's mystically-empowered blacks (*à la* Mother Abagail, the one-hundred-year-old woman waiting alongside her Nebraskan cornfield to redeem what's left of mankind in *The Stand*, or the psychic Dick Hallorann in *The Shining*). It's stereotype that's arguably more desirable than the contemporary "urban menace" archetype, but a stereotype nonetheless. That said, Michael Clarke Duncan lends the role considerable strength and dignity; with this Oscar-contender performance and his recent turn as the hit man "Frankie" in *The Whole Nine Yards* (1999), Duncan has made his mark, recalling the screen presence of memorable precursors like Julius W. Harris (*Nothing But a Man*, 1964; *Superfly*, 1972; *Black Caesar* and *Live and Let Die*, 1973; *Shrunken Heads*, 1994).

Great fiction or filmmaking, this isn't — as far as miracles go, this week's *The Third Miracle* [27] is a far superior work — but *The Green Mile* is an engaging emotional experience. Recommended! *(Rated "R" for*

---

[27] Reviewed in this volume, pp. 119-121.

strong language, violence, gore, adult and sexual situations.)

PLAY IT TO THE BONE (1999) looks and sounds appealing. Writer-director Ron Shelton (*Bull Durham, White Men Can't Jump*) has concocted a winning premise for a shaggy-dog buddy-road-movie of two down-but-not-quite-out boxers, Vince (Woody Harrelson) and Cesar (Antonio Banderas), given one more shot at the big-time opening for Mike Tyson at a major bout in Las Vegas. The catch is, these friends and sparring-partners have to fight each other. Saucy Lolita Davidovich (recently seen in the fine *Mystery, Alaska*) provides the wheels to Vegas, breaking up with current beau Cesar en route and tantalizing Vince until a provocative hitchhiker (Lucy Liu of *Ally McBeal*) provides a greater diversion. In the end — well, I can't tell you, of course.

Suffice to say that the initially engaging, amusing characters are soon stripped down with nowhere to go. It's self-evident that the cast had a great time making this movie, and for a time their chemistry and enthusiasm is contagious. There is some fun to be had here with their endless bantering, bickering, and posturing, and that may be enough to carry the film for some viewers. But Shelton lets his colorful characters down: by refusing to live up to the title and honestly resolve the conflict it sets up from the first bell, *Play It to the Bone* is a disappointment. *(Rated "R" for language, adult and sexual situations, and strong language.)*

June 22:

In an era of expansive revisionist epics marked by *The Last Emperor* and *Kundun*, **ANNA AND THE KING**

(1999) is an anachronism: too old-fashioned, too domestic, too traditional in its colonial-era politics and notions of romance. Nevertheless, the film provides a fine evening's entertainment, a lavish recreation of 19th Century Siam (now Thailand), and a fresh revamp of the book by Margaret Landon.

This is at least the fourth filming of the true-life story of British Governess Anna Leonowens, who traveled with her young son in 1862 seeking gainful employment as educator of the harem and fifty-eight children of King Monjut — seeking, too, an exotic refuge from the wake of her husband's recent death, and the lowly stature Victorian England afforded its widows and single mothers. Whatever the historical truth of the relationship eventually kindled between Leonowens and King Monjut, they have certainly entered the pantheon of great romances, and *Anna and the King* offers an engaging retelling of the venerable tale. The physical production is sumptuous, Andy Tennant's direction is competent, and the tale (with the inevitable dramatic embellishments) is well told... but Jodie Foster (as Anna) and Chow Yun-Fat (as King Monjut) shine, and that is the sum and substance of the film, which is as it should be.

For Hollywood, the story has always been, and remains, a premiere star vehicle. In *Anna and the King of Siam* (1946), Irene Dunne (playing Leonowen, renamed "Anna L. Owens") and Rex Harrison (in his film debut as the King) embodied the battle of wits and conflicting cultural views that sparked passion. Rodgers and Hammerstein masterfully reorchestrated Landon's source novel into the Broadway musical hit *The King and I*, which was lavishly filmed in 1956 with Deborah Kerr (whose singing voice was dubbed by Marni Nixon) and Yul Brynner (winning an Oscar for the role) in the lead roles. Jodie Foster and Chow Yun-Fat are honorable successors, capturing the uneasy dance of respect and friction that grows into genuine affection and love. Foster struggles a bit with her accent, providing fair game for the critical drubbing the film suffered, but Chow Yun-Fat (finally, an Asian actor in the role!) is excellent in his breakthrough role for mainstream U.S. audiences after *Replacement Killers* and *The Corruptor* [28] eased him out of the Hong Kong action scene into the American mainstream. The co-stars generate an engaging chemistry, and are ably supported by the ensemble cast to breathe life into this tried-and-true tale.

Anna and the King plays up the political unrest and court intrigue that always provided a backdrop for the tale, emphasizing the very real threats to the throne Monjut successfully transcended during his reign. Thus, some of the violence inherent in Landon's source novel is realized here with more immediacy than either 1946 or 1956 Hollywood would have indulged, but don't let that put you off; the occasional mayhem (and tragic executions at the core of the story's best-known subplot) isn't overly graphic, and remains essential to the story. Nominated for two Academy Awards (Best Art Direction and Costume Design), *Anna and the King* may not be "Something Wonderful" (he said, coyly evoking the musical), but it's far superior to the embarrassing recent cartoon feature *The King and I*, and well worth the rental. *(Rated "PG-13" for adult situations and some violence.)*

Well, it's only the second day of summer, but the critic-proof Dumb Comedies have arrived. You don't really

---

[28] See *Blur, Vol. 1*, pp. 46-47.

need me to razz Rob Schneider's breakthrough comedy star vehicle, *DEUCE BIGALOW: MALE GIGOLO* (1999), do you? Who cares what I think? If you're a fan of the current *Saturday Night Live* regime of screen stars and vehicles — Adam Sandler, Schneider, *A Night at the Roxy, Superstar*, etc. — you'll love Schneider's turn as a professional fish tank cleaner who saves his bacon after he inadvertently demolishes the apartment (and kills the prize tropical fish) of a male gigolo client by taking the gigolo's calls and stumbling into the world's second-oldest profession. Schneider avoids the maudlin drivel his peer Adam Sandler mired the reprehensible *Big Daddy* with,[29] leaving *Deuce Bigalow* without any real emotional baggage to dampen the ensuing politically-incorrect sexual antics. Kids, of course, will want to see it, but I needn't elaborate on what a gigolo's job entails, do I? This dog is pretty tame, but parents might want to check it out before their kids do, if only to properly field any questions the film's silly sexual antics might prompt.

You know, one of my friends used to have a really homely but sweet mutt named Molly. She was a real rag doll of a dog: scruffy salt-and-pepper fur that looked and felt like wire bristles even after a shampoo and brushing; long feminine eyelashes framing chocolate-brown eyes that made her look forever forlorn; and a maladroit manner that created havoc, kept her constantly underfoot and inviting the boot (though she wasn't kicked around — don't get me wrong) every waking moment. Schneider and this shaggy-dog comedy reminded me of Molly time and time again, and I just haven't the heart to say an ill word toward the film. Go ahead, knock yourself out, and

---

[29] See *Blur, Vol. 1*, pp. 106-109.

have fun. *(Rated "R" for — well, you know. He's a gig-olo and cleans fish tanks. Go figure.)*

Woody Allen's ***SWEET AND LOWDOWN*** (1999) is conspicuously *not* being promoted as a Woody Allen film. Allen writes, directs, but doesn't star, though he does appear throughout as one of the musical historians relating the life story of Depression-era jazz guitarist Emmet Ray (Sean Penn). Like the central character in Allen's hilarious "mockumentary" *Zelig* (1983), Emmet Ray is a wholly invented character, and like many of Allen's films, *Sweet and Lowdown* is an oddly wistful confection, light enough on its feet to entertain, but too ephemeral to leave a lasting impression. Allen's passion for early 20th Century music is renowned, and his recent tour playing such music was lovingly recorded in *Wild Man Blues* (1998). Like underground cartoonist Robert Crumb (whose similar love for the early jazz and blues prompted his drawing numerous trading card sets, comics biographies of blues legends like Robert Johnson, and a brief tour in the 1970s playing guitar with the Cheap Suit Serenaders), Allen here molds his musical affections into a lovingly-crafted recreation of a bygone era, and those who share his interests will undoubtably find much to savor in this quirky portrait of a talented misanthrope.

Chameleon actor Sean Penn completely submerges himself in the role of Emmet, a graceless, womanizing, alcoholic stooge whose favorite offstage hobby seems to be shooting rats — but when he's onstage, playing his guitar, he plays like an angel. The first half of *Sweet and Lowdown* lays the groundwork for the fictional biographical sketch, dwelling on Emmet's rocky relationship with a mute young woman named Hattie (Samantha

Morton, delivering an Academy-Award nominated performance). This Chaplinesque romantic subplot — further sweetened by Hattie's fling as a Hollywood actress — is derailed by Emmet's relentless narcissism and abusive behavior, dragging the fake bio into his unlikely marriage to a tougher, worldly woman named Blanche (Uma Thurman), a writer who steers them both into a tangle with gangsters and the law.

Fictional as *Sweet and Lowdown* remains, it's hard not to read Emmet's climactic recognition of loss as an autobiographical touch, a moment that may be closer to Woody Allen's creative and personal life than we can ever know. Though the moral morass associated with Allen's public persona has undoubtably taken a toll,[30] and the generation that embraced his urban brand of comedy has moved on to leave the arena open to the likes of *Deuce Bigalow*, I for one am glad Woody is still making movies. He remains one of our greatest filmmakers, and certainly among the few to create a truly coherent and expansive body of work under his own terms. The musical score is the icing on the cake (check out the excellent soundtrack CD), much of it performed by genuine jazz guitar legend Django Reinhardt, who plays a pivotal role in the film. Cult director John Waters (*Pink Flamingos, Serial Mom, Pecker*, etc.) also has an

---

[30] This is a reference to the charges Allen's partner of 12 years Mia Farrow (they were never married) leveled against Allen during their 1992 seperation, claiming Allen had sexually molested their then 7-year-old adopted daughter Malone, and Allen's sexual relationship with his adoptive "step-daughter" Soon-Yi Previn (both Allen and Previn denied he was her stepfather, since she was adopted when Farrow was married to Andre Previn); at the time, Allen was 56 and Previn was 22. Allen and Previn subsequently married in 1997.

amusing cameo role as one of Emmet's frazzled employers. Such pleasures help *Sweet and Lowdown* live up — and down — to its title, making this one early summer rental well worth a look and listen. *(Rated "PG-13" for language, adult and sexual situations, casual alcohol abuse, and shooting at rodents.)*

Writer-director Mike Leigh's ode to Gilbert and Sullivan's legacy in ***TOPSY-TURVY*** (1999) rewards a look and listen, too.[31] *Topsy-Turvy* recalls Tim Robbins' recent *Cradle Will Rock* (1999), in that both films lovingly dote on fiery chapters in theatrical history, and the purgatories — and transcendental heaven — of risking all to bring a fresh play to life on the stage. Robbins chose Orson Welles and the Depression-era Federal Theater Project as his subject, while Leigh settles into a leisurely-paced recreation of 19th Century London. Unlike Leigh's utterly contemporary prior films (including *Naked*, 1993, and *Secrets and Lies*, 1998), *Topsy-Turvy* is a time machine, steeping the viewer in the pace and temper of its era's culture and people, always ready to pause over behavioral tics and nuances, or afford amusing glimpses of the emerging technologies (when phone etiquette involved shouting in code, and "reservoir" pens were a novelty).

Taken on its own terms, *Topsy-Turvy* (the title refers to a plot device Gilbert too often indulged, and evokes the impact Charles Darwin's scientific theories had on its era) is a marvelous piece of work, though some may find it slow going indeed, and too precious by

---

[31] Thanks to my wife Marjory and my friend Neil Gaiman for invaluable input on this review; both are great Gilbert & Sullivan fans.

half. But if the subject matter is your cup of tea, you'll savor every drop.

In the wake of the premature closing of one of their least-popular musical operettas, *Princess Ida* (1884), writer W.S. Gilbert (Jim Broadbent) and composer Arthur Sullivan (Allan Corduner) find themselves at an uncomfortable juncture in their collaborative career. To the growing discontent of critics, audiences, performers, the proprietors of the Savoy Theater (nicely played by Ron Cook and Wendy Nottingham), and most of all Gilbert and Sullivan themselves, Gilbert's librettos have become too formulaic, and Sullivan flatly refuses to labor over the writer's latest uninspired "souffle." Leigh succinctly sketches the polar opposition of the creative team's personalities: where Gilbert is staid, celibate, and utterly domestic, Sullivan is social, restless, and a devilish rake at home in both the finest music halls and bawdiest Parisian bordellos. In their creative and personal lives, Sullivan feels hopelessly constricted where Gilbert is most comfortable, and eager to compose at least one Grand Opera. When Gilbert's wife Lucy (Lesley Manville, in a delicately understated performance) forces her reluctant husband to accompany her to an exhibition of Japanese culture at London's Humphrey's Hall, inspiration strikes, and this unwelcome distraction proves to be the catalyst for *The Mikado*, one of the team's most enduring works. The subsequent creation, rehearsal, production, and debut of *The Mikado* constitutes the rest of the film, spiced with invention amid many historically-accurate details of the Gilbert and Sullivan entourage and canon.

Winner of two Academy Awards for Best Costume Design (an amusing turn in Leigh's film career; his films usually sport the drabbest, most lived-in attire imagin-

118

able!) and Makeup, and justifiably nominated for a third in Art Direction, *Topsy-Turvy* placed prominently in many of the year's "Best Film" lists. I wasn't similarly smitten by the film — other 1999 films had far greater impact and entertainment value, for my money — but it is a grand cinematic valentine to theater lovers and Gilbert and Sullivan aficionados, and compelling dissection of the trials and tribulations of the creative process. I must say I enjoyed it far more upon second viewing. This is a sumptuous feast, though certainly not to all tastes. Recommended! *(Rated "R" for adult and sexual situations)*

Recent & Recommended:

If it's miracles you're looking for, *The Green Mile* can't hold a candle to **THE THIRD MIRACLE** (1999), an excellent adaptation of Richard Vetere's novel (adapted by Vetere and John Romano). This is the latest American film by Polish director Agnieszka Holland (justifiably renowned for her *Europa, Europa*, 1990, as well as *Olivier, Olivier*, 1992; *The Secret Garden*, 1993; *Total Eclipse*, 1995; and *Washington Square*, 1997), and it's not to be missed.

The title refers to the three documented miracles necessary to the Roman Catholic Church's canonization of a saint. The film opens with a miracle: during the World War 2 bombing of the village of Bystrica in Slovakia, a little girl named Helena (Sofia Polanska) prays to the Virgin Mary, and the planes and bombs vanish. Jump to Chicago, 1979, as Father Frank Shore (Ed Harris) investigates miracles associated with a statue of the Virgin Mary that began to cry tears of blood in the wake of the death of the adult Helena (Barbara Sukowa). As the troubled Shore begins to believe, he is plagued by far more than his own self-doubts. There's Frank's tangled emotional attraction to Helena's adult daughter Roxanne (Anne Heche), who Helena abandoned at age 16 to devote herself wholly to the church; or the fact that the child Maria (Jade Smith) miraculously cured by exposure to the statue's sanguine tears has grown up (played by Caterina Scorsone) to be a drug-addict and prostitute; and the powerful opposition of pious German Archbishop Werner (Armin Mueller-Stahl), an Old World Catholic who immediately states his bias against America ever providing fertile soil for sainthood.

Early in the proceedings, Frank responds to Roxanne's confrontational nature saying, "You ask tough questions." *The Third Miracle* likewise asks the tough questions dross like *Stigmata* [32] and pop parables like *The Green Mile* skirt. Director Holland coaxes fine performances from her ensemble cast. Heche hasn't had this substantial a role in quite some time, and Ed Harris eloquently mounts a moving portrayal of a priest aching for affirmation of the faith he fears he's lost (note Harris' prior role under Holland's directorial helm in *To Kill a Priest*, 1988, as a terrifying police official tormenting a priest). Armin Mueller-Stahl (*Shine*) provides further gravity as the Church's "Devil's Advocate"; note, too, that his international career was launched alongside Holland's via their prior collaboration in the Academy-Award nominee *Angry Harvest* (1985). The DVD is well worth seeking out, particularly for Holland's engaging director commentary (noting, for instance, that the opening location-filming of the 1944 bombing of Slo-

---

[32] See *Blur, Vol. 1*, pp. 220-224.

vokia was filmed a mere week before the town was under fire again during the recent bombing of Yugoslavia).

The superficial similarities to the recent shocker *Stigmata* may seem daunting, but don't be fooled. Whereas *Stigmata* embraced the trappings and gory dramaturgy of the horror genre (it was, in fact, the antithesis of *The Exorcist*), *The Third Miracle* is a sober, passionate adult drama that eschews the hysteria usually brought to such heady religious content. Tackling issues of faith, human hubris and frailty, and "the caprice of God," the film indeed asks the hard questions, and earnestly seeks answers. These are high aspirations for any movie, and *The Third Miracle* succeeds admirably. Highly recommended! *(Rated "R" for language, alcohol and drug use and abuse, adult and sexual situations.)*

June 29:

Sandra Bullock tried very, very hard to keep you from seeing the Roger Corman production ***FIRE ON THE AMAZON*** (1992/1998?), a curio filmed early in the actress' career that remained unreleased until just this week, premiering direct-to-video after a lengthy shelf life. The film itself is (to be generous) unremarkable, but Bullock's determination to keep the film buried backfired. The negative publicity will only attract viewers like flies to — well, you know the old saying.

Roger Corman's reputation as America's premiere cheap jack film producer is the stuff of legend: he indeed filmed the classic *Little Shop of Horrors* (1960) in three-to-four days, and around the same time spun multiple low-budget science fiction features out of special effects footage lifted from a pair of Russian genre epics. Corman entered the industry in 1954, promptly establishing himself as one of the most prolific producer-directors in the business, filling drive-in screens with a half-a-dozen or more titles a year until slowing his pace in the early 1960s to lavish more time, money, and effort on his popular cycle of Edgar Allan Poe adaptations starring Vincent Price. As a producer, Corman provided debut venues for young directors like Francis Ford Coppola, Jonathan Demme, Ron Howard, Joe Dante, Martin Scorsese, Paul Bartel, and many, many others. Though Corman retired from directing in 1970 (breaking retirement only twice since, for *Frankenstein Unbound* in 1990 and a serialized horror parody for American Movie Classics last Halloween), he has founded no less than four companies to date (Filmgroup, New World Pictures, Concorde, and New Horizons), each single-mindedly dedicated to providing drive-ins and, more recently, video stores with energetic low-budget films. Corman's post-1970 formula was simple, delivering action, breasts, blood with a contemporary edge — a touch of politics or lip-service paid to a popular cause or trend — crammed into 90 minutes or less. That formula still applies.

Anyone who rents *Fire on the Amazon* expecting a polished Sandra Bullock vehicle is sure to be terribly disappointed. Those with base expectations or a taste for what are incorrectly referred to as "B" films (meaning exploitation, drive-in, or direct-to-video fare) — like myself — will savor a few choice moments.

The film fits the Corman production mold perfectly. There's a smattering of politics, corrupt police and corporate lackeys to hiss at, splashes of violence, and one heated bout of love-making between Bullock and co-star Craig Sheffer that remains the film's primary draw until it arrives at its stinger denouement (the sort the Hollywood majors shun, but one Corman's veteran drive-in crowd will recognize from the producer's *Big Bad Mama* era). Despite (or because of) the paucity of means and imagination, the film succeeds on its own modest terms. The destruction of the rain forest in South America is succinctly condensed into a melodramatic good guys & gals vs. corrupt bad guys & gals scenario, inexpensively shot on location by a young director and cast on their way up (or down, in Sheffer's case) the Hollywood ladder.

Given the career arcs at stake, I reckon *Fire on the Amazon* was completed between 1992-93, though the final credits post a 1998 copyright. Bullock (as environmentalist Alyssa Rothman) and Sheffer (as singularly stupid, abrasive, and opportunistic photojournalist R. J. O'Brien) are on the side of good, though both were deep into the "bad hair" phase of their careers. For Bullock, this looks like post-*Who Shot Pat?* and *Love Potion #9* (both 1992), and definitely pre-*Speed* (1994); for Sheffer, it's post-*A River Runs Through It* (1992) and before his direct-to-video limbo of the mid-1990s. Director Luis Llosa completed *800 Leagues Down the Amazon* for Corman in 1992-3 using the same South American locations; by the following year, he'd graduated to the majors directing Sylvester Stallone and Antonio Banderas in *The Specialist* (1994) and later returned to the Amazon to make the relatively extravagant *Anaconda* (1996). For the record, there's only four seconds' difference between the "R"-rated and "Unrated Director's Cut," amounting to a single non-explicit shot of the lovers in a particularly provocative position, but that four seconds (amid two minutes of nude romping under the influence of some native drug) seems to be what Bullock was adamantly opposed to. Tick, tick, tick...

Corman's been down this road before for a very different reason: in 1993, Corman happily sold off a completed feature film adaptation of Marvel Comics' *Fantastic Four* to larger studio interests intent on keeping Corman's cheap-suit superheroes off the market so as not to de-value their own (as yet unproduced) big-budget version.[33] Canny Corman reportedly pocketed a hefty sum in the bargain, far more than his *Fantastic Four* cost and undoubtably more than he would have earned off the film's release. I guess Sandra just wasn't up to the challenge. Corman has always been a shrewd businessman, and obviously felt *Fire on the Amazon* was worth more on video shelves than in Sandra's dumpster. Sure, it's an embarrassment. The film is at best an artifact — not only of a young actress' willingness to bare almost-all before the camera prior to the big-time, but of a period in Corman's career and the pop-culture ghetto that's already on its way out the door. *(Available in both "R" and "Unrated" versions, featuring nudity, sexual situations, gunplay, harsh language, alcohol and exotic drug use, and violence.)*

Before the title of screenwriter/director Anthony Minghella's fine adaptation of Patricia Highsmith's novel **THE TALENTED MR. RIPLEY** (1999) settles on the word "talented," a plethora of adjectives ripple across the screen in its place. "Innocent, mysterious, yearning, secretive, lonely, troubled, confused, loving, musical, gifted, intelligent, beautiful, tender, sensitive, haunted, passionate" — all applicable to the disturbingly charis-

---

[33] The big-budget 'remake' *Fantastic Four* was released in July 2005, followed by a sequel *4: Rise of the Silver Surfer* in June 2007.

matic title role played by Matt Damon (*Good Will Hunting, Saving Private Ryan, Dogma*). Damon is arguably one of the few contemporary young American actors capable of aligning our sympathies with as insidious and amoral a character as Tom Ripley for over two hours. To his credit, he does so without downplaying the deceit, death, and destruction Ripley leaves in his wake like a snail's slimy trail. As in Highsmith's original novel, Ripley is a crafty but covetous cipher in search of a role model and an escalator to the high life. He finds both in privileged Dickie Greenleaf (Jude Law), a spoiled young man born with a silver spoon in his mouth who savors *la dolce vita* with his fiancee Marge Sherwood (Gwyneth Paltrow) in Italy in the late 1950s. An initially harmless bit of deceit plants Ripley on a mission to bring Dickie back to his father (James Rebhorn) in America, but the web of lies becomes spidery as Ripley's desire for all Dickie has and is shifts from savoring the orbit to inhabiting its center: Ripley wants nothing less than to *be* Dickie — at any price.

Ripley insinuates himself into Dickie and Marge's world with ingratiating ease, and his scheme begins to bear its bitter fruit. Ripley is an uncanny mimic, master of forgery, and (as Freddie Miles — beautifully played by Philip Seymour Hoffman — puts it) "a quick study," but his greatest talent is the ability to think on his feet and through his mouth, deflecting, diverting, and twisting every increasingly murderous turn of the screw to his short-term advantage.

There's no denying the compelling grip and creepy nature of the material; on first viewing, *The Talented Mr. Ripley* left me shaken but cold (on second viewing, to write this review, I felt this was a nearly perfect film). The uneasy bond Minghella and Damon create between

Ripley and the audience, the empathy the film nurtures even as Ripley is driven to further extremes, is chilling — as it's meant to be. The taint of complicity that makes the first act so tantalizing and even titillating becomes stifling and eventually suffocating. For a change, the over-used term "Hitchcockian" is genuinely applicable, and not just because Hitchcock himself once adapted one of Highsmith's plum novels (*Strangers on a Train*, 1951). What set Hitchcock apart from his contemporary and posthumous imitators was the empathy and complicity he elicited between viewer and his characters. Just as Hitchcock's best work was ill-served by labels like "mystery" and "thriller," *The Talented Mr. Ripley* is neither, though it has the superficial trappings usually associated with genre and Hitchcock's repertoire, including the obsessions with identity, suspicion, guilt, voyeurism, and the inevitable eruptions of violence.

The Talented Mr. Ripley is an unnervingly introspective portrait of a personal metamorphosis that edges from dream to nightmare as Ripley's duplicity creates the kind of intimate purgatory that was the true sum and substance of Hitchcock's best work. Minghella won an Oscar for his work on *The English Patient* (1996), but his skillful adaptation and direction here is even better. Minghella's deviations from Highsmith's source material (making the implicit homosexuality of the novel overt; overlaying a strong jazz motif; inventing wholly new but key characters played by Cate Blanchett and Jack Davenport) are interwoven with its narrative particulars with remarkable fidelity and precision, adding threads to the original tapestry to enhance, rather than dilute, its impact. *The Talented Mr. Ripley* is one of the season's best offerings; don't miss it. *(Rated "R" for strong language, nudity, adult and sexual situations, and violence.)*

Ripley & Recommended: If you enjoy *The Talented Mr. Ripley*, check out more of Ripley's adventures in Patricia Highsmith's original novels, and be sure to see:

   * ***PURPLE NOON (PLEIN SOLEIL***, 1960) was the original film version of *The Talented Mr. Ripley*. It's an effective adaptation in its own right and a fascinating companion piece to Anthony Minghella's new version. Where Minghella and Matt Damon focus on Ripley the chameleon, French director René Clément and his Ripley, the handsome young Alain Delon, fixate on Ripley the reptile: beautiful, opaque, and venomous. The incidentals are true to the novel and recent version, from Ripley's lethal envy for the wealthy young playboy (here named Philip, played by Maurice Ronet), opportunistic reach for and grasp of the moment, and cat-and-mouse deviltry with the suspicious Freddie Miles (Billy Kearns) and police (Erno Crisa), but the homoerotic subtext remains just that as Ripley sinks his talons into Marge (Marie Laforêt) as well as Philip's fortune. Clément (and co-screenwriter Paul Gégauff) also add a new twist to the climax, which sets this adaptation apart from both the novel and its recent version. Henri Decaë's cinematography and the musical score by Nino Rota (Fellini's favorite composer) are as ravishing as the sun-baked Mediterranean scenery, and Delon is mesmerizing throughout.

   Few contemporary film aficionados or scholars remember, much less appreciate, René Clément as one of the international masters of the genre for over two decades. This laconic brand of adult continental "thriller" may seem tame to many these days, but this was once a vital and somewhat risqué vein, and it still delivers. Like his fellow countrymen Henri-Georges Clouzot (*Wages of Fear*, 1954; *Les Diaboliques*, 1955) and Claude Chabrol (*Le Boucher*, 1969; *This Man Must Die*, 1970; *La Rupture*, 1970), Clément often embraced the Hitchcock tradition, refining his own unique approach that was neither as calculatingly cool as Chabrol's or coldbloodedly cruel as Clouzot's. *Purple Noon* is an ideal introduction to Clément's best work, thankfully restored and reintroduced to a new generation under Martin Scorsese's devoted sponsorship. Recommended! *(French with English subtitles; Rated "PG-13" for adult and sexual situations, partial nudity.)*

    * Dennis Hopper (in his post-*Easy Rider*, pre-*Blue Velvet* career limbo) stars as the adult expatriate Tom Ripley. Adrift in Germany, Ripley is still seeking quick scores, easy prey, and personal redemption in Wim Wenders' superb ***THE AMERICAN FRIEND (DER AMERIKANISCHE FREUND***, 1977), adapted from Patricia Highsmith's novel *Ripley's Game*. Anachronistically sporting a cowboy hat while typically trading on his affable manner, Ripley deals in suspect art and claims he will bring the Beatles back to Hamburg as he "frames" Jonathan Zimmerman (Bruno Ganz), a professional framer and former restorer of paintings.

    Drawn to Zimmerman's decency and family life while playing on the man's fears that his ongoing illness is terminal, Ripley suckers Jonathan into a pact with furtive Raoul Minot (Gerard Blain) to commit murder — twice. The second, aboard a moving train, is the film's most harrowing passage, but director Wenders (*Paris, Texas*, 1983; *Wings of Desire*, 1988) is only marginally concerned with such setpieces; the self-destructive relationship of Ripley and Zimmerman is the absolute focus here, and *The American Friend* remains one of Wenders' finest films. Note that cult American directors Nicholas Ray (as the artist 'Derwatt') and Sam Fuller (as "The American," a cigar-chewing gangster) play key roles, adding to the fun. The poor video transfer compromises Robby Muller's fine cinematography — here's a film sorely in need of remastering and a proper re-release — but that hardly diminishes the film's power.[34]

At one point, dreading the impending second murder he has been conned into perpetrating, Zimmerman contemplates his reflection in a multi-panelled mirror, echoing similar imagery and moments in *Purple Noon* and *The Talented Mr. Ripley* that succinctly tie all three "Ripley" films together.[35] Highly recommended! *(English language and German with subtitles; Unrated, with no objectionable language, graphic violence, or sexual elements, but the tone, theme, and material is for mature viewers.)*

July 6:

SCREAM 3 (1999) has drifted so far afield from the telling pleasures that made the original *Scream* (1996) such a potent "sleeper" hit, it's hard to recall what made

---

[34] Avoid the Pacific Arts vhs version reviewed here; Anchor Bay's 2002 DVD release offers a far superior widescreen transfer.

[35] Since this writing, there have been two more Ripley films: Liliana Cavani's *Ripley's Game* (2002) with John Malkovich as Ripley and Roger Spottiswoode's *Ripley Under Ground* (2005) with Barry Pepper as Ripley.

the first entry so appealing. Make no mistake: the pre-credits sequence of the original *Scream* with Drew Barrymore was a corker — bracing, chilling, and genuinely scary. It's been all downhill from there. *Scream*'s small town setting of Woodsboro, California and circle of teenage victims and survivors was indeed lifted verbatim from the 1980s "slasher" cycle, but the film's acknowledgement of (and riffs on) those roots lent it a sense of playful savvy that seemed fresh to a generation of viewers who'd grown up watching the same videos screenwriter Kevin Williamson and his cast of characters had. *Scream* wasn't as witty, original, or horrific as many made it out to be, but it was a fun horror movie with a kick-ass opening act. Its surprise boxoffice success spawned a whole new cycle of horror films, including, inevitably, the *Scream* sequels.

    Scream 3 opens with a helicopter shot over the famous "Hollywood" sign and down onto the nearby freeway as series fixture Cotton Weary (Liev Schreiber) — former patsy convict who's now the host of a fictional TV talk show entitled *100% Cotton* — is quickly put through his paces by this entry's psycho killer. This springboard pre-credits "shock" sequence promptly regurgitates the nuts-and-bolts mechanics of the original: the seductive phone call turned venomous ("let's play a little game") using the almost magical "voice modulator," the spook-masked killer turning lover against lover, false and mistaken identities, a "breathless" chase and scuffle culminating in bloody death. Sadly, that's the whole card game, though *Scream 3* stretches it beyond the breaking point.

    Survivor heroine Sidney Prescott (Neve Campbell) and the long, lingering shadow of her mother's death and dark past remain central to the narrative, once again attracting a homicidal killer trotting out the *Scream* iconography that's already become as generic as the *Halloween* and *Friday the 13th* face-masks and phallic blades. But the movie-within-a-movie conceit (via *Stab 3, Stab* being the surrogate *Scream* franchise within the *Scream* movies) usurps the small-town setting of the original, further rupturing that film's bond with its audience by supplanting its recognizable cliques of teen students with a clutch of alien, unlikable "movie people." This privileged setting even taints the sense of play that added a charge to the first *Scream*, which has degenerated into a procession of star cameos (including Carrie Fisher, Jay and Silent Bob, and Roger Corman) and indy starlet Parker Posey's turn as an actress playing Gail Weathers (Courtney Cox Arquette).

Director Wes Craven has been down this road before (in *Scream 2*'s play-within-a-play rehearsal for the theme, and more notably Wes Craven's *New Nightmare*, 1994), and the Hollywood setting clearly resonates for him — but not for us. The increasingly unpleasant characters — fat-cat producers and harried directors, bitchy actresses and hunky actors, high-profile security bodyguards and L.A. cops — are ciphers who carp and cringe and bleed amid the false Woodsboro sets and backstage debris without mustering an ounce of sympathy. Worse still, though they're all engaged with the making of *Stab 3*, they continue to fall for the killer's (and genre's) tired bag of tricks: the dubious cell phone calls, voice changes, and faked identities; the senseless divide-and-butcher "suspense" scenes; and once again, the killer is repeatedly shot only to get back up (a tactic which induced gasps when John Carpenter concocted it for *Halloween* — twenty-two years ago!).

131

Even on its own grotty terms, *Scream 3* is a cheat. For all of the film's coy references to the "Super Trilogy Rules," none of the characters seem to be familiar with one of the genre's most popular and potent trilogies, George Romero's *Night/Dawn/Day of the Dead* (and its countless zombie movie imitations), in which "shoot 'em in the head" was the survivalists mantra. *Scream 3*'s pinhead crew still shoot for the *chest* every time. *Of course* the boogeyman gets right back up.

Scream 2 and *3* have had the kind of money and studio attention lavished upon them that precious few of Wes Craven's movies enjoyed, cozily shielding him from his primal roots. Necessity is the mother of invention — and great horror movies. With a few notable exceptions (*The Bride of Frankenstein, The Birds, The Exorcist, Jaws*, and *The Sixth Sense* come to mind), the best, bravest, and most innovative horror movies have been born of low-budget desperation, invention, and, yes, necessity — launching the careers of financially impoverished filmmakers who tap cultural taboos with ruthless precision and skill. From *The Cabinet of Dr. Caligari* (1919) to *Night of the Living Dead* (1968), *The Texas Chainsaw Massacre* (1974) to *The Blair Witch Project* (1999), the truly revelatory horror films have emerged from almost nowhere. Director Wes Craven's roots lie there: his directorial debut was *Last House on the Left* (1972), an unpolished, unapologetically reprehensible shocker that plucked a real nerve in the American psyche and made millions at American drive-ins and grindhouses.

Craven is an intelligent, eloquent, well-educated man and capable storyteller, who subsequently refined his techniques, noticeably doing his most compelling horror films during the career dry spells when the genre provided an outlet for his own anger, outrage, and fear (see *The Hills Have Eyes*,1977; *A Nightmare on Elm Street*, 1984; *The People Under the Stairs*, 1990; and, of course, *Scream*). Notably, Craven's best also involve characters who have been or feel discarded, which also reflects Craven's genuine 'outsider' status during his dry spells. That necessity and hunger seems *central* to Craven's best work. Though the man deserves all the success he's earned (most recently 'elevated' to helming the true-life drama *Music of the Heart* starring Meryl Streep), he's obviously pretty comfortable these days, and *Scream 2* and *Scream 3* reflect an unfortunate laziness. Similarly, the original (over-rated) Scream script was among screenwriter Kevin Williamson's first big scores; he was hungry and needed to make his mark, and did so in spades. Now overburdened with his subsequent career ascent (the TV series *Dawson's Creek*, the sorry but very popular *I Know What You Did Last Summer* movie franchise, the unfairly reviled *Teaching Miss Tingle*, etc.), Williamson didn't have time for *Scream 3*, leaving Ehren Kruger to cobble together the final entry in his stead. The result is another vapid example of the worst kind of filmmaking by committee (a process verified by the DVD commentary, and the onscreen crediting of no less than *eleven* producers).

When Randy (Jamie Kennedy) is resurrected via videotape in *Scream 3*, he explains: "True trilogies are all about going back to the beginning and discovering something that wasn't true from the get go." True enough — *Scream 3* proves the *Scream* franchise wasn't ever out to scare its audience. *Scream 3* isn't even a horror movie: aside from the occasional spurts of gore and harsh language, it's identical to the early talkie murder mysteries from the 1930s that were set on theatrical or

Hollywood stages. They were thin gruel then, and it's a mighty tired vein seventy years later. As the trite barrage of telegraphed "shocks" and red herrings takes its toll, one fully expects Scooby-Doo and Shaggy to wander onto the scene.

The *Scream* franchise has ended up being everything the original *Scream* mocked and labored to transcend: a predictable, formulaic sequel; the tired end of a franchise; just another sorry "slasher" movie. Choose your poison. Whatever marginally satiric or subversive undercurrents fired *Scream* have long since succumbed to the mercantile urges that extended similar franchises far beyond the point of no return, save the boxoffice. With its poseur pretensions and smug contempt for the very audience that responded to Drew Barrymore's genuinely terrifying predicament in the original, *Scream 3* fails to even generate the Neanderthal charge the least of the grisly 1980s "slasher" flicks sparked. There isn't a moment of *Scream 3* that comes close to the power of the best (*Bay of Blood, Black Christmas, Halloween, Just Before Dawn*) or the grimmest, go-for-broke bargain-basement precursors of the 1970s and '80s (*Maniac, The Mutilator, Don't Go In the House, Sleepaway Camp*, the first four entries in the *Friday the 13th* series).

Though horror and its fans are reviled by many, the genre and its devotees are driven by an honest enough impulse: just as those who love comedies really want to laugh, action fans crave vicarious thrills, and devotees of love stories want their most fragile emotions stirred, horror fans want to, well, *scream*. However refined or base the films may be, horror fans continue to watch horror movies searching for the occasional film that taps their deepest fears. All *Scream 3* taps is your pocketbook and precious time. This is hardly the stuff of nightmares; just a studio accountant's wet dream. *(Rated "R" for harsh language, gore, gunplay, and violence.)*

If it's real satire, subversion, or "shock value" you seek, Baltimore's native son John Waters is the real McCoy. With his pencil-moustache, cultured pop persona, and brash love of ballyhoo and "bad taste," Waters has become an occasional fixture of the late-night talk show circuit. He comes across as a completely self-assured, self-possessed, self-effacing, affable fellow, and can be very funny. His films are an acquired taste; fair warning here and now, I love his movies. No surprise, then, that **DIVINE TRASH** (1998) is my pick of the week, and highly recommended.

Though Waters, like Craven, emerged from his down-and-dirty roots to achieve relative mainstream success, he has done so without failing his audience or muse. By any standards, Waters' most recent feature *Pecker* (1999) seemed tame in comparison with his revelatory "midnight movie" classics *Multiple Maniacs* (1970), *Pink Flamingos* (1972), and *Female Trouble* (1974), but Waters has retained his distinctive voice and vision while adjusting to the realities of studio-financed filmmaking. *Polyester* (1981) straddled both camps (pun intended), but *Hairspray* (1988), *Cry-Baby* (1990), *Serial Mom* (1994), and *Pecker* work on their own terms: Water's satire still has a real edge, his affection for his misfit characters remains genuine, and his movies are still original, insolent, joyous, and funny. Waters was sharp enough to know he would never top *Pink Flamingos'* coprophagous climax, leaving scatological gross-out comedy to a new generation of filmmakers to explore (i.e., the Farrelly Brothers of *There's Something About Mary*, etc.) while trading on his cult reputation and "trash chic" stature to write for mainstream magazines and continue making movies his own way in Baltimore.

Waters' latest satire, *Cecil B. Demented*, hits theaters next month, making the video debut of Steve Yeager's excellent documentary *Divine Trash* particularly timely. Winner of the Filmmakers Trophy for Best Documentary at the 1998 Sundance Film Festival, *Divine Trash* offers a prime introduction to the filmmaker's life and career while chronicling the production of *Pink Flamingos*. Those who were forever marked, shaken, or traumatized by *Pink Flamingos* (which, Waters cannily notes, "worked: It made hippies crazy") will savor the behind-the-scenes material. En route, Yeager also offers testimonials from Waters' frequent cast and crew, who reward Waters' own obvious affection, devotion, and loyalty for their work and friendship with sometimes hilarious reminiscing and streetwise assessments of Waters and his films, providing a hearty tonic for the usual Hollywood pretensions and back-biting usually associated with the industry. These are spiced with insightful observations from critics like John Pierson, who accurately cites the impact "the Three Johns" — John Cassavetes, John Waters, and John Sayles — have had on the American independent cinema, noting that "Waters may have been the most influential," a seemingly grandiose claim validated by on-camera comments from an impressive lineup of contemporary filmmakers (including Jim Jarmusch, Paul Morrissey, David O. Russell, Hal Hartley, Steve Buscemi, and others). There's also Mary Avara, "The Last Film Censor in America" (of the Maryland Film Board, established in 1914 and the final state film censorship body extant), whose contempt for Waters' calculated offenses prompts the statement, "I had my own rating [for his films]: 'R.T.,' Real Trash."

Ah, *Divine Trash*, indeed. There are many surprises here, even for John Waters fans: interviews with John's parents ("It wasn't in the Dr. Spock book what to do if your child was obsessed by car accidents"); the influence the Leslie Carron film *Lili* (1952) had on his formative years, and the debt Divine's makeup (created by Van Smith) owed to *The Howdy Doody Show*'s Clarabelle the Clown; words of praise from the Reverend Fred Hannah, the Baltimore priest who allowed Waters' early films to be shown in his church ("John really came across... as an energetic young man who had a lot of creativity, and creativity is in short order in this world"); ultra-rare clips from *The Diane Linkletter Story* (1969) and the unfinished *Wizard of Oz* parody *Dorothy, Kansas City Pothead*.

The documentary is also mounts a loving portrait of Harris Glenn Milstead, aka 'Divine', who starred in all of Waters' key films until the actor's death in 1988. Though Divine crafted a persona that was "an inflated, insane Jayne Mansfield," "the Godzilla of Drag Queens," and "a drag terrorist," we are given a peek at the man behind the makeup via memories from his friends and peers, his mother Frances, and Waters himself.

In the end, Waters' unpretentious assessment of his work during a 1972 interview still holds true. "I'm not trying to say anything," he concludes, "I'm just trying to give people a good time, make them laugh, and give them a little shock value for their money." Say what you will, I'll take Waters' wit and candor over bloated, tedious dross like *Scream 3, Mission Impossible 2, Hanging Up*, or the recent *Gone in 60 Seconds* remake any day of

137

the week. *(Unrated; for mature viewers only: film clips featuring violence, gore, nudity, adult and sexual material, blasphemy, and strong language; the interviews candidly discuss theft and casual drug use.)*

July 13:

Writer-director Ben Younger's debut feature ***BOILER ROOM*** (1999) lives up to its title by plunging the viewer — along with its protagonist, Seth Davis (Giovanni Ribisi) — into the pressure-cooker of a dubious high-yield brokerage firm. Merrill Lynch, Smith Barney, and J.P. Morgan this isn't: proprietor Michael (Tom Everett Scott) maintains an impeccable front to the untrained eye, while trading in phony pharmaceutical firms and keeping his parachute escape route in easy reach. All this is initially invisible to Seth, intoxicated with the fresh potential within reach as amoral mentor Jim Young (Ben Affleck) crows, coaxes, and browbeats his recruits into believing they can rake in big bucks hustling to meet sales quotas that will make them all rich. Seth indeed makes a fortune, moving into the firm under the wing of Greg (Nicky Katt) before their relationship becomes adversarial over Seth's rapid success and his budding romance with Abby (Nia Long), the firm's attractive receptionist. Bonding with his cronies (Scott Caan, Jamie Kennedy) and quickly working his way up the ropes under the tutelage of Chris (Vin Diesel), Seth thrives in this new environment where his confederates savor the high life and spout choice dialogue during repeat plays of *Glengarry Glen Ross* and Oliver Stone's *Wall Street* (just as Wesley Snipes' 'gangsta' grooved on replays of Brain DePalma's *Scarface* in *New Jack City*).

However posh the surroundings, the moral bankruptcy becomes impossible to ignore; these hustlers are getting fat by fleecing their customers. Though Seth's father (Ron Rifkin), a veteran courtroom judge, has long since given up on his son's opportunistic ethics, we are privy to the stirrings of Seth's troubled conscience as his ongoing assessment of his new environment sends off quiet alarms. Having jumped out of the piranha pit of his private blackjack mini-casino (preying on college students and playing the odds at home) into the boiler room's shark pool where a single phone call can devastate the life savings of an unwary customer, Seth is increasingly alert to the evidence of the odds stacking against the firm's smooth facade. Smelling blood, the feds move in, even as Seth's doubts and moral pangs assert themselves.

Younger's deft, high-octane filmmaking chronicles the toxic energies at ground zero and clocks the shock waves as they total the home life of one of Seth's injudicious customers (Taylor Nichols). That path of destruction, a macrocosm of personal hells which are all-too-common today as more and more individuals succumb to the temptations of playing the market, is ironically referred to by the opening notes of Pharoahe Monch's final credits tune *"Simon Says,"* which opens with Akira Ifukube's (uncredited but instantly recognizable) theme for the Japanese *Godzilla* films. The damage wrought by hucksters like Seth may be invisible, but it leaves many private savings as ravaged as monster-stomped Tokyo, and its cumulative economic impact has yet to be measured. Keep an eye on writer-director Younger in the future; this is great first effort, and bracing film by any standard. Highly recommended! *(Rated "R" for strong language, adult and sexual situations, and casual drug and alcohol abuse.)*[36]

THE HURRICANE (1999) lives up to its title, too, though much of its fascination lays the quiet eye of the storm embodied by Denzel Washington as Ruben "Hurricane" Carter, the former heavyweight-boxing champion who spent over two decades in a New Jersey prison for a crime he did not commit. Since his debut in the sorry *Carbon Copy* (1981), Washington has been an uncommonly engaging actor — alert, focused, energetic, alive, invigorating even the most paltry of projects — and he inhabits his role as Carter with the same dignity and ferocity he brings to his best work. The parallels with his titular role in Spike Lee's *Malcolm X* (1992) are striking, but Washington is too intent on inhabiting and communicating Carter's unique persona and circumstances to permit any easy blurring of the roles; Carter is and was his own man, and Washington never lets us forget it for a moment. Struggling to control, channel, and transcend his personal history of violence, incarceration, and his volatile inner demons, Carter's fight for dignity and freedom makes a powerful story.

A quick refresher: After years of incarceration as a juvenile and adult, Paterson, New Jersey citizen Rubin "Hurricane" Carter was earning a strong reputation in boxing and was well on his way to the Middleweight Championship title when his life and career was shat-

---

[36] *Boiler Room* is even *more* painfully relevant today. It's among the most essential and prescient films of its time, vividly portraying the mindset behind the willful ravaging of the US economy throughout President George W. Bush's eight years in office. *See it.*

tered by the arrest and conviction (three consecutive life sentences) for a multiple murder he did not commit. Another innocent man who was in the car with Carter during the arrest, John Artis (played in the film by Garland White), was likewise convicted. The New Jersey Supreme Court twice upheld those convictions. While in prison, Carter drew attention to his dire situation by writing his autobiography, *The Sixteenth Round*. Though many concerned citizens and celebrities (including Bob Dylan, whose potent protest song *"Hurricane"* publicized Carter's plight) petitioned and struggled on Carter's behalf, ultimately it was the intervention and active investigation of the case by an unlikely quartet of a Brooklyn-born black teenager (Lesra Martin, beautifully played by Vicellous Reon Shannon) and his three Canadian tutors (played by Lieve Schreiber, John Hannah, and Deborah Kara Unger) that led to the convictions being overturned by U.S. Supreme Court Judge Sarokin (Rod Steiger, delivering a rare measured performance),[37] freeing Carter and Artis after almost two decades in prison.

Director Norman Jewison is an utterly traditional Hollywood filmmaker, his career studded with his share of classics (*The Russians Are Coming, The Russians Are Coming*, 1966; the original *The Thomas Crown Affair*, 1968; etc.), gems (*The Cincinnati Kid*, 1965; *Rollerball*, 1975), and turkeys (*40 Pounds of Trouble*, 1962; *Bogus*, 1996). Jewison also helmed two of Hollywood's best

---

[37] No surprise: director Norman Jewison had previously helmed Steiger's Academy-Award-winning Best Actor performance for *In The Heat of the Night* – for which Jewison was also nominated as Best Director. That film won five Oscars, including Best Picture of 1967.

films about racism — *In the Heat of the Night* (1967) and the underrated *A Soldier's Story* (1984, which co-starred Denzel Washington) — which *The Hurricane* rounds out to a trilogy of sorts (capped by Rod Steiger's presence in the first and last). *The Hurricane* is one of Jewison's best films, juggling a remarkably convoluted narrative with deceptive ease and grace. Drawing from both Rubin's *The Sixteenth Round* and *Lazarus & the Hurricane* (by Sam Chaitan and Terry Swinton, two of the three Canadian educators embroiled in the story), Jewison guides us through a tapestry of flashbacks and even flashbacks-within-flashbacks while tracing two narrative threads: Rubin Carter's story, and young Lesra "Lazarus" Martin's story. By the time these story strands intersect, the film has built a lucid, solid foundation, never losing its focus or confounding ours as an audience. This is a remarkably sober feat of craftsmanship, particularly when the temptation to embrace what Jewison refers to on his DVD commentary as "tabloid" filmmaking could have quickly derailed the film. I never thought I'd be writing these words: thank God it was Norman Jewison, not Oliver Stone, who was behind the camera and editing desk.

Despite the controversy that attended the film's theatrical opening last year, I must add that director Norman Jewison and screenwriters Armyan Bernstein have done an impeccable job shaping their source material. As I've stated before (in my recent review of Milos Forman's *Man on the Moon*), only a fool accepts fictionalized motion pictures as fact; the constrictions of legal issues (i.e., use of real names and events, etc.), running times, and the need to mold raw source materials into coherent narratives require some degree of dramatic license. *The Hurricane* often deviates from the case history to streamline characters (personifying the many corrupt Paterson, N.J. and New Jersey police and court officials in the lone figure of Detective Della Pesco, played by Dan Hedaya), discard information threads that compromised traditional storytelling momentum (including the off-the-record account of a cabdriver whose recall of the fateful night Carter was arrested proved the boxer was nowhere near the scene of the crime), and reconfigure reality to serve theatrical ends (Carter wasn't in Judge Sarokin's courtroom during the Supreme Court hearing that overturned two N.J. court convictions, and thus could not have delivered the stirring speech the film presents).

For those interested in or concerned with such dramatic deviations, I highly recommend you watch *The Hurricane* on DVD with director Norman Jewison's running audio commentary (Jewison cites the film's many detours from fact, and discusses the reasons with candor and insight), deleted scenes (including the cabdriver's claims noted above), and an interview with Rubin Carter himself. This sterling DVD dissection explains and justifies the process necessary to the making of what is, after all, a Hollywood 'biopic' — and one of the best in recent memory.

In an election year wherein one of our distinguished presidential candidates is hypocritically running on a "pro-life" platform while governing a state that seems to execute a death-row prisoner every week ("late-term" abortions, perhaps?), *The Hurricane* deserves a closer look than a casual evening entertainment might afford (you might give Errol Morris' *The Thin Blue Line* a look, too; the documentary that saved a Texan death-row inmate from execution is even more relevant today). Denzel gives this film its potent heart and soul, though his fellow performers and behind-the-camera professionals provide top-drawer support, never allowing the film to waver from Carter's plight, aspirations, or unflinching gaze. Recommended! *(Rated "R" for strong language, violence, and adult situations.)*

Don't skip **MY DOG SKIP** (1999) thinking it's just a kid's movie, or typically manipulative boy-and-his-dog crap. Like many of my generation who grew up watching *Lassie* and traumatized by the Walt Disney classic *Old Yeller* (1957) at a tender age, I am both a hapless, masochistic sap and cruel cynic when it comes to this genre. This stirring coming-of-age tale embraces many of the heart-tugging staples of the boy-and-his-dog genre, including risible puppy antics, montage interludes of boy-and-dog bonding, and the inevitable "please-don't-die-yet" weepy setpiece. Happily, *My Dog Skip* succumbs to only a few of the mongrel genes, embodies many of the best aspects, and ultimately transcends its breed. Adapted from a slim tome by the late Willis Morris (1934-99; distinguished Rhodes scholar, youngest editor on record of *Harper's Magazine*, and beloved author), *My Dog Skip* is anecdotal in nature, but its strong emotional core anchors its wistful eulogy to Morris' own beloved childhood pet and his own transition from childhood to boyhood.

"The cotton grew tall that year, but I sure didn't," Morris' recollection begins (narrated by Harry Connick, Jr.) as his 8-year-old self Willie (Frankie Muniz of Fox-TV's *Malcolm in the Middle*) approaches his ninth birthday in 1942 in Yazoo, Mississippi. That fateful birthday, his mother Eileen (Diane Lane) bucked his stern war-veteran father Jack (Kevin Bacon) to give friendless, put-upon Willie a puppy, an "only dog" for an "only child." Skip (played in his prime by Enzo, and his autumn years by Moose) quickly grants Willie the keys to the community: friendship with his bully rivals (Bradley Coryell, Cody Linley, and a marvelously open, guileless performance by Daylan Honeycutt), a budding romance, and access to the segregated black community. There's also Willie's affection and hero-worship of his next-door neighbor Dink Jenkins (Luke Wilson), the town's star white athlete who goes off to war, and whose return as a shell-shocked alcoholic casts a shadow over the boy's world, evoking his own father's wartime experiences (having lost a leg in the Spanish Civil War). Willie's nighttime initiation in the local graveyard stirs more than ghosts, too, provoking the wrath of moonshiners (Peter Crombie and Clint Howard) who play a key role in the climax.

As director Jay Russell notes in his DVD commentary for *My Dog Skip*, "This is an old-fashioned movie... sentimental, yes... with the true meaning of the word: it's about sentiment and emotion... Willie was a very sentimental writer himself." Russell is true to Morris' source material, ensuring the film is seen and felt through the heightened emotional range of childhood, while maintaining the integrity of both Morris' and his own adult perceptions. Precious few family or "children" films even try to walk this tightrope, much less with the skill Russell and screenwriter Gail Gilchriest manage throughout. Their cast clearly understood the challenge, too, and good as young Frankie Munoz is, the performances Kevin Bacon, Diane Lane, and the rest of the ensemble deliver build persuasive credibility.

The emotional core of the film is laid bare in an understated, profoundly moving sequence between father and son in the forest, as they hear gunshots (Willie whispers, "Was the war like this?") and witness the final moments of the hunters' quarry. Though seen through Willie's eyes, director Russell doesn't cater to the obvious potential of the scene. The casual interaction of the hunters and Willie's father, who talk even as Jack remains sensitive to the import of this moment to his son, is as integral to the scene as Willie's first tearful brush with death. Eschewing easy melodrama, Russell demonizes neither the hunters nor death — facts of life in Willie's world he must confront — while deepening our empathy for both father and son.

Such honest, privileged moments elevate the film beyond the easy virtues of comparable coming-of-age and boy-and-his-dog fare, and define *My Dog Skip*'s stature as the season's best family film.

Upon reflection, we realize that the view of Willie's room beneath the opening credits is actually Skip's last look at his beloved master's environment — further evidence of the rare skill and heart that eased *My Dog Skip* from the printed page to the screen.

Thankfully, Willie Morris saw the completed film a mere week before he died, and enthusiastically praised the finished product; one can only imagine what it must have meant to the man. This is a modest but lovely and loving film, and highly recommended. *(Rated "PG" for some harsh language and tastefully-handled violence necessary to the story.)*

July 20:

Pedro Almodovar's best work crackles with lively, engaging characters and situations, eye-drugging set and costume designs, and inventive narrative twists that reminds one how lifeless and unimaginative most American films truly are. ***ALL ABOUT MY MOTHER (TODO SOBRE MI MADRE***, 1999) certainly ranks among Almodovar's finest efforts (which includes *Law of Desire*, 1986; *Women on the Verge of a Nervous Breakdown*, 1988, and *The Flower of My Secret*, 1995), infusing this sensual melodrama and latest cast of playful polymorphs with a fresh sense of sincerity and tenderness.

After attending a theatrical performance of *A Streetcar Named Desire* on the 17th birthday of her son Estaban, Manuela (Cecilia Roth) indulges his birthday wish to linger in hopes of getting an autograph from the play's lead actress Huma (Marisa Paredes); chasing the star's cab, Estaban is struck and killed by another vehicle. Distraught, Manuela abandons her professional life in Madrid (as a nurse and coordinator of an organ donation clinic) to travel to Barcelona in search of Estaban's long-lost father, a seductive transsexual ne'er-do-well now known as Lola. En route, Manuela rekindles relations with friends from her past, bonds with Huma (infuriating Huma's junkie lesbian lover and co-star Nina, played by Candela Pena), and takes the idealistic nun Rosa (Penelope Cruz) under her wing when she discovers Rosa has AIDS and is pregnant with Lola's child. And that, my friends, is just the beginning.

Mothers, daughters, lesbians, transsexuals, transvestites, and prostitutes: Almodovar engages with them all with an insouciant wit, vigor, and affection that is irresistible. With his cast in top form and touchstones to Tennessee Williams, Truman Capote, and *All About Eve* (thus, the title) in place, Almodovar celebrates the grace, elan, and empathy with which his characters negotiate their way through the roughest emotional seas. As the final credits announce, this is Almodovar's valentine to motherhood and women (however biologically artificial) everywhere, and well worth sharing. Highly recommended! *(Rated "R" for adult and sexual situations, language, drug abuse, and a brief but vivid bit of street violence.)*

Bill Kaye's eye-catching photograph of child actor Joe Breen as young Frank adorns the video and DVD cover art for Alan Parker's vivid cinematic adaptation of Frank McCourt's memoir ***ANGELA'S ASHES*** (1999). The boy's face is dirty, dour, and his gaze is utterly galvanizing, which pretty well sums up the film's recreation of McCourt's memories of growing up impoverished in Ireland in the 1930s and '40s. If you start watching, you can't look away — but prepare yourself for the film's unflinching gaze (if it's an amusing diversion you seek, flee while you can).

"It was, of course, a miserable childhood," the film's narrator (Andrew Bennett) intones from McCourt's autobiographical novel; "Worse than the ordinary miserable childhood is the miserable Irish childhood — and worse yet, is the miserable Irish Catholic childhood." Director Parker (*Midnight Express*, 1978; *Shoot the Moon*, 1982; *Pink Floyd: The Wall*, 1982; *Mississippi Burning*, 1988; etc.) has never been one to shy away from misery, and *Angela's Ashes* pours on the agony in spades.

The film opens with a crib death, and it's all downhill from there for the first third of the film. Along with his grieving mother Angela (Emily Watson) and alcoholic father (Robert Carlyle) and surviving brothers, little Frank (Breen) finds himself uprooted from the slums of New York City to return to the even more desperate slums of Limerick, "the holiest city in Ireland," where the soul-crushing coils of deprivation, poverty, and despair only tighten around Frank's family. I'll spare you the details, save to warn you that the gloom is punctuated with bouts of on-screen vomiting. Grim going, indeed, unless you can derive some levity from boyhood discussions of the female anatomy, the horrors of learning Irish dancing, or a Catholic schoolmaster's sobering observation that "you don't see [the Lord] hanging on the cross sporting shoes." An hour into the film, Angela finally confesses, "It's hard to hang onto your faith," and one can only wonder how much more she might have to endure before acting on the sentiment.

Only the staunchest viewers will keep watching, but stay with it: as Frank grows into his preteen (played by Ciaran Owens) and teenage (Michael Legge) years, you can taste the boy's need to escape, and *Angela's Ashes* chronicles that process with the same loving detail it brings to its harrowing first acts. "You celebrate and you grieve at the same time," the real-life Frank McCourt explains. McCourt lived it and he heartily approves of Parker's film version, which carries considerable weight for me and more than justifies the often grueling viewing experience. It's well worth the extra time and effort to re-watch the film with McCourt's running DVD commentary; "It's a strange thing to write a book and dig back into your memories," McCourt says early on, "put it on the page, and then see it transferred to the screen with this much tenderness." Watching the film again with McCourt's commentary, one awakens to the film's considerable heart beating beneath its suffocatingly gray exterior.

Precious few contemporary films address the basest issues of survival, the all-too-real life-and-death struggles with hunger, shelter, poverty, neglect, abandonment, unemployment, injury, disease, and despair that most Americans maintain a practiced distance from. *Pelle the Conqueror* (1988), *King of the Hill* (1993), and *Joe the King* (1998)[38] come readily to mind with their ironic mock-royalty titles; *Angela's Ashes* joins their ranks, buoyed by its autobiographical nature and the implicit promise of survival, success, and transcendence.

"The dead are dead, and the living are thriving," author McCourt concludes in his captivating DVD commentary, and there's not much to say in judgment beyond that. Approach with caution, but recommended for those with the heart (and stomach) for it. *(Rated "R" for strong language, domestic violence, adult and sexual situations, adolescent male sexual activity, and alcohol abuse.)*

Recent & Recommended:

Eric Roberts stars as down-and-out Walter Pool, the titular human cockroach of *LA CUCARACHA* (1998), a surprisingly entertaining "sleeper" set South of the Border. Pool "just sort of ran away [from] regular life" in New Jersey to wallow in despair in a remote corner of Mexico, drowning his dreams of writing a novel in a sea of booze until his dead-end delirium is interrupted by a suspicious American named Louis Graves (played by James McManus, who penned the script), who makes a curious offer. Seems the local wealthy village patriarch (Joaquim De Almeida) wants his rival (Victor Rivers) murdered, ostensibly for the crime of killing the patriarch's son. Pool reluctantly accepts, only to find his descent into hell-on-Earth has only begun.

---

[38] See *Blur, Vol. 1*, pg. 205.

Grim as it sounds, *La Cucaracha* is actually quite funny and beguiling, if you're in the right mood for this sort of thing. Roberts makes the most of the best role he's had in years and becomes oddly endearing as director Jack Perez wrings every venomous drop out of McManus' sidewinding script. With an overt tip of the sombrero to authors Ernest Hemingway, Malcolm Lowry, and Graham Greene, *La Cucaracha* also treads in the footsteps of Ambrose Bierce, B. Traven, and filmmakers like John Huston (who helmed classic adaptations of Traven's *The Treasure of Sierra Madre* and Lowry's *Under the Volcano*), Sam Peckinpah (particularly *Bring Me the Head of Alfredo Garcia*), and John Dahl (*Red Rock West, The Last Seduction*), and lives up (or down) to their example quite nicely.

Brightened by the presence of the lovely Lourdes Aguirre as the woman who is the apple of Pool's blood-shot eyes, intoxicating cinematography by Shawn Maurer, and Martin Davich's evocative musical score, *La Cucaracha* is a real "sleeper." Go ahead — have a shot, amigo. *(Rated "R" for strong language, alcohol abuse, nudity, adult and sexual situations, and violence.)*[39]

July 27:

Roman Polanski definitely shaped our contemporary pop cultural conception of evil when he filmed Ira Levin's *Rosemary's Baby* (1968) with such consummate skill. Thus, one can be forgiven for having such high hopes for Polanski's latest ***THE NINTH GATE*** (1998), which ends up being a lavishly produced ride to nowhere. Po-

---

[39] The reviews for *La Cucharacha* and *The Ninth Gate* were also published in *VMag* #32, August 2000, pp. 50, 52.

lanski remains a consummate filmmaker, but the razored intensity and fierce wit the director brought to his best work (*Repulsion*, 1965; *Cul-De-Sac*, 1966; *Rosemary's Baby; Macbeth*, 1971; *Chinatown*, 1974; *The Tenant*, 1976) has seemingly dimmed with age. In the wake of the traumatizing death of his wife Sharon Tate (murdered by Charles Manson's murderous family in 1969), his flight from America amid sexual scandal, and subsequent difficulty securing financing for his projects, Polanski has only made six films in twenty years: the melancholy *Tess* (1980), the muddled *Pirates* (1986) and *Frantic* (1988), the potent return-to-form of *Bitter Moon* (1992) and *Death and the Maiden* (1994), and *The Ninth Gate*. Though any Polanski film is well worth seeing, *The Ninth Gate* hardly lives up to its precursors, premise, or promise.

Adapted from the novel *El Club Dumas* by Arturo Pérez-Reverte, *The Ninth Gate* is as rich in visuals and atmosphere as all of Polanski's films, but it's an oddly listless and toothless Gothic confection. Mercenary book expert Dean Corso (Johnny Depp) is hired by multimillionaire Boris Balkan (Frank Langella) to ferret out the two surviving companion copies of Balkan's latest acquisition, an exceedingly-rare satanic tome entitled *The Nine Gates of the Shadow Kingdom*. Corso's search embroils him in an international web of intrigue, crossing paths with prior owners (prominent among them Liana Telfer, played by Lena Olin) hungry to repossess the ominous text, book dealers (James Russo, and Spanish production manager Jose Lopez Rodero in an amusing dual role), and the targeted owners (Barbara Jefford and 'Euro-Trash' horror film veteran Jack Taylor) of the rare companion volumes. Inadvertently leaving a wake of corpses behind him while aided by a mysterious, seductive young woman (Emmanuelle Seigner) who appears at the most opportune moments, Corso's dedication to the task gives way to an obsessive need to uncover the mysteries of *The Nine Gates* for himself.

Steeped in a bloody historical legacy and rumored to have been co-authored by Lucifer himself, *The Nine Gates* is a narrative conceit that evokes a rich tradition in horror literature: fictional forbidden books that bring danger, madness, and death to those unlucky enough to stumble upon them, or those foolish or power-hungry enough to seek them. Robert W. Chambers' collected *The King in Yellow* stories (1895) arguably established the "forbidden book" sub genre over a century ago, and famed New England pulp author H.P. Lovecraft's imaginary *Necronomicon* remains its most enduring and infamous entry, but the tradition also enriched the work of brilliant authors like Jorge Luis Borges and others. It's an honorable pantheon with its share of worthy contemporary cinematic incarnations: Sam Raimi's *Evil Dead* series, John Carpenter's *In the Mouth of Madness* (1995), and best of all Guillermo del Toro's stylish *Cronos* (1994), which substituted a literally bloodthirsty 14th Century device for the usual forbidden book.

Sadly, *The Ninth Gate* is content to pirate the "forbidden book" archetype without savoring or spilling any fresh blood. Like Johnny Depp's recent horror-science fiction star vehicle *The Astronaut's Wife* (1999)[40] — a patchwork grotesque which plundered Nigel Kneale's *The Quatermass Experiment* (1955) and *Rosemary's Baby* — *The Ninth Gate* is ultimately a derivative retread. Though it's far superior to *The Astronaut's Wife*, it

---

[40] See *Blur, Vol. 1*, pp. 196-197.

still comes off as a horror movie for those who don't watch or like horror movies.

There are still some pleasures to be had, as Polanski musters his customary eye for detail, character, and sly pitch-black humor, masterfully orchestrating ravishing cinematography (by Darius Khondji), picturesque locations (France, Spain, Portugal), and often subtle CGI-enhanced visuals. But the elder Polanski indulges a lassitude his younger self would have justifiably vilified, from the increasingly static, sterile setpieces to inexcusable lapses of logic (Depp slapping the rare book down on a photocopier; a canister of gasoline placed in a burning circle of flames doesn't explode; etc.) and a limp finale hardly worthy of the sumptuous buildup.

Borges once wrote, "The solution to the mystery is always inferior to the mystery itself." As Polanski notes in his DVD commentary, the sprawling source novel was difficult to adapt to the screen and lacked a real resolution only to "dissolve" — just as the film does. The enigmatic final shot will leave most viewers feeling as stranded and desolate as Donald Pleasance was at the end of *Cul-De-Sac*. Perhaps Polanski, ever the prankster, intended as much, but I suspect Borges' observation once again holds true. *(Rated "R" for language, violence, adult and sexual situations, and blasphemous religious content.)*

August 3:

THE BEACH (1999) isn't crass or shallow enough to slide into the silly surf-and-turf of *Gilligan's Island* or *The Blue Lagoon*'s titillating teen-sex; nor is it intelligent, feral, and honest enough to live up to its debt to William Golding's *Lord of the Flies*. Then again, *The*

Beach can hardly boast comparable source material, drawn as it is from Alex Garland's timely but untested novel of contemporary paradise-found-and-lost. A map to said paradise falls into the hands of Richard (Leonardo DiCaprio), a young American traveler aching for transcendental opportunity, adventure, and rite-of-passage. Richard convinces two French companions, Françoise (Virginie Ledoyen) and Etienne (Guillaume Canet), to accompany him from the urban streets of Thailand to the remote, land-locked island lagoon and hidden commune that indeed awaits them. Tolerated by the island's militia of native marijuana-farmers and supervised by an idealistic matriarch named Sal (Tilda Swinton) who rules with an iron hand, the illusory paradise is tainted by much more than the cultural baggage Richard carries with him.

Adapted to the screen by director Danny Boyle and screenwriter John Hodge, the Scottish film tyros who galvanized audiences with their debut feature *Shallow Grave* (1994) and the bracing *Trainspotting* (1995), *The Beach* promises as much as its catalytic map does, delivering a fleeting taste of its destination before it derails. The delicate fabric of the isle community frays when confronted with real violence, loss, pain, and suffering, even as Sal's opportunistic ethics and infidelities eat away at the core; but Richard becomes the scapegoat. In short order, Richard's sexual appetite, youthful vigor and pride, and weakness to the temptations of the moment (leaving a map behind for others to find; succumbing to Sal's sexual demands when they journey back to civilization for supplies) take their toll, and he is cast adrift in the jungle. Spurned by his queen bee and his lover, banished from the commune, Richard slides into madness.

As the narrative edges deeper into the darkness William Golding and Joseph Conrad so vividly explored, it, too, loses its way, unraveling as Boyle and Hodge hedge their bets and flinch, wary (or weary?) of the path ahead. Instead of capturing the suffocating despair of Richard's descent, the intoxicating cinematic virtuosity that spun *Trainspotting* into the stratosphere is reduced to risible flourishes (Richard's surrogate "video game" self; a midnight raid on the Thai farmers' stockade opens with a self-referential nod to *Apocalypse Now*). DiCaprio, Swinton, and the cast struggle valiantly, but they're cast adrift without a compass as the film fails to come to terms with the corruption it so carefully cultivates.

Every generation, it seems, must tell itself a similar tale, or live it (my own experienced and/or witnessed the descent from Woodstock to Altamont, the bloody fanaticism of Manson's "Family," the suicidal purge of Jim Jones' Guyana religious refuge). *The Beach* lacks the spine or fervor necessary to its morality play (check out the alternate ending on the DVD, abandoned, Boyle says in his commentary, for something "more hopeful"). *Shallow Grave* and *Trainspotting* had the exceptional courage to follow their characters (and convictions) all the way to hell and back; *The Beach* doesn't. Though it's initially engaging and often quite beautiful, the film hasn't the heart or guts necessary to its own agenda. *(Rated "R" for language, violence, adult and sexual situations, nudity, drug and alcohol abuse.)*

THE WHOLE NINE YARDS (1999) kicks off as mob hitman Jimmy "the Tulip" Tudeski (Bruce Willis) moves into a Montreal suburb next door to an unhappily-married dentist (Matthew Perry of *Friends*) saddled with a greedy, scheming wife (Rosanna Arquette), venomous mother-in-law, and a crippling debt left by his late father-in-law's embezzlement of the business. Seizing the opportunity, back-stabbing Arquette packs a reluctant Perry off to his home-town Chicago to rat out Tudeski's whereabouts to a mob rival (Kevin Pollak) even as she arranges to have her hubby hit. But nervous husband and the-hitman-next-door have already struck up a tentative friendship, and Tudeski's estranged wife (Natasha Henstridge) further complicates matters.

For a black comedy, *The Whole Nine Yards* isn't so much toothless as it is sweet-toothed, favoring star-crossed romance and true love despite the body count. Willis effortlessly grounds the proceedings and enjoys an engaging chemistry with twitchy Perry, who's in comparatively top form here after the recent embarrassment of *Three to Tango*. Perry's schtick is, essentially, Bob Newhart for the 1990s, and he comes across affable and baffled enough to hold his own in Willis's seasoned shadow. Able support from Michael Clarke Duncan (Academy-Award nominee from *The Green Mile*), Henstridge (far from the sexual mayhem of the *Species* series), and Arquette adds luster, but the real surprise is Amanda Peet's marvelous turn as Perry's dental assistant. Director Jonathan Lynn helmed a few losers (*Greedy*, 1994; *Sgt. Bilko*, 1995; *Trial and Error*, 1996), but Mitchell Kapner's lively script here rekindles the brisk playfulness that made Lynn's best effort, *My Cousin Vinny* (1992), so much fun to watch. *(Rated "R" for language, adult and sexual situations, nudity, dentistry, and violence.)*[41]

---

41 Note: For the record, due to the editor's vacation schedule, the above three columns were published in *The Brattleboro Reformer* as follows: no column was published July 20; my

August 10:

It is, of course, mere coincidence that two direct-to-video dragon fantasies, ***DRAGONHEART: A NEW BEGINNING*** (1999) and ***KOMODO*** (2000), hit the shelves this week. But as the recent hit *Magnolia* (see review below) asserts, there's no such thing as "mere coincidence" — even in the lowly world of direct-to-video films.

    Dragonheart: A New Beginning immediately betrays the premise of the original *Dragonheart* (1996). It turns out that Draco the dragon *wasn't* the last of his kind, really; his offspring, Drake, is voiced by Robby Benson (1970s teen actor and the voice of Disney's revered Beast in *Beauty and the Beast*), a sorry step down from Sean Connery's rich vocal characterization of Draco; and Chris Masterson (co-star of Fox-TV's *Malcolm in the Middle*) personifies an equivalent plunge from the original's knightly hero played by Dennis Quaid. Scruffy, scrappy Masterson stars as Geoffrey the stable boy, who befriends the innocent young dragon Drake. Geoffrey aches to achieve knighthood despite his lowly peasant stature in a troubled feifdom ruled by an addled king (Ken Shorter), who is the puppet of his evil advisor Osric (Harry Van Gorkum, delivering the film's only effective performance). Enter an enigmatic duo from far-away China, the elder Kwan (Henry O from

---

July 20th column was published on July 27; for the August 3 column, the editor combined my reviews of *The Beach* and *The Ninth Gate*, and ran the review of *The Whole Nine Yards* as a *"Recent & Recommended"* sidebar. I have presented the columns here, however, as they were originally written.

Romeo Must Die) and youthful Lian (Rona Figueroa, who also sings the closing tune *"My Heart Goes With You"*), seeking "the last dragon" (ya, sure, right) in hopes of averting a dire prophecy.

Though the original *Dragonheart* was a flawed fairytale at best, the sequel embraces few of its virtues. Despite the picturesque Slovakian locations and a couple of amusing conceits (dragon flatulence, anyone?), the venture is undone by Doug Lefler's listless direction, the lackluster cast, and Shari Goodhartz's vapid script which buries its few trump cards (including a surprising climactic twist) beneath painfully inane dialogue. Younger viewers may enjoy the movie, and parents can rest easy with the film's "PG" rating (for its timid action sequences), but older direct-to-vid fare like *Dragonworld* (1994) offers more rewarding entertainment.

Keep the little ones away from **Komodo**, though, which earns its "PG-13" rating with splashes of gore, stronger language, and one seat-jumper jolt in its first act. *Komodo* eschews the talkative flying reptiles and cozy distance of *Dragonheart*'s 10th Century medieval setting to establish a contemporary colony of "real" Komodo dragons lurking on an isolated island off the coast of North Carolina. Preteen Patrick Connally (Kevin Zegers, who starred in the *Airbud* series, Bram Stoker's *Shadowbuilder, A Call to Remember*, and as a stigmata-suffering lad in an episode of *The X-Files*) is traumatized when he alone survives a dragon attack on his family. A couple of years later, a therapist (Jill Hennessy) drags now-teenage Patrick and his caseworker (Nina Landis) back to the island in a dubious bid to restore the lad's memory. The dragons are only too eager to oblige. Patrick goes feral as the rest of the cast stupidly separate and dash into the darkness alone to chum the lazy script by Hans Bauer (*Anaconda*) and Craig Mitchell; enter a pair of lethal characters (Billy Burke and Paul Gleeson) under orders of a loathsome corporate executive (Simon Westaway) to kill the interlopers along with the dragon population. It's not much of a movie, though the dragon effects by Tippett Studio (handling the CGI) and John Cox creature workshop (live-action animatronics) are superior.

The peripheral (*Dragonheart*) and direct (*Komodo*) involvement of Phil Tippett Studios links both efforts with their proper cinematic precursors: special effects master Ray Harryhausen's distinctive stop-motion-animated creations of the 1950s, '60s, and '70s. The best of Harryhausen's films — *The Beast from 20,000 Fathoms* (1954), *20 Million Miles to Earth* (1957), *The 7th Voyage of Sinbad* (1958), *Jason and the Argonauts* (1963), etc. — entertained generations of young and young-at-heart film audiences. Harryhausen inspired a generation of special effects visionaries like Phil Tippett, who created stop-motion creatures for the *Star Wars* trilogy, *Dragonslayer* (1981), and *Robocop* (1987) before ushering in a new age of CGI-monsters with his efforts on *Jurassic Park* (1993). Tippett became a key transitional artist in the field, refining his own studio's repertoire with the direct-to-video *Tremors 2: Aftershocks* (1996) en route to the state-of-the-art CGI-monster effects for *Starship Troopers* (1997). During this period, Tippett also worked on the design of Draco the CGI dragon for the first *Dragonheart* (though Industrial Light

& Magic executed the final effects work); hence, his pivotal role in this discussion.[42]

Despite their meager budgets, direct-to-video productions like *Komodo* and *Dragonheart: A New Beginning* offer invaluable room to experiment; the lower resolution of video offers a forgiving vehicle for CGI effects. With their toxic saliva and beaded bullet-deflecting hides, *Komodo*'s titular dragons look alive, but they have limited appeal as monsters (ambulatory appetites with no personality). Sadly, *Komodo* is sub-*Jurassic Park* by design every step of the way, giving Tippett Studios veteran Michael Lantieri precious little to work with on his debut directorial feature. Still, *Komodo* boasts the superior dragons: *Dragonheart*'s sequel sports competent but cartoony digital visual effects by Metrolight Studios, Inc. sans the lively character animation and supple surface textures that made Sean Connery's Draco such an engaging character. Drake is conceptually a far more personable creature than *Komodo*'s impassive eating-machines, but he remains a scaly cipher. As long as Hollywood's finest special effects maestros remain strait-jacketed by unimaginative "commercial" claptrap like *Komodo* and *Dragonheart: A New Beginning* — not to mention *Star Wars: The Phantom Menace* or recent theatrical extravaganzas like *The Hollow Man* — their skills will be wasted.

Long before CGI and the digital effects revolution, stop-motion animator Ray Harryhausen was shrewd enough to co-produce almost all of the films he worked on, exercising far more creative control over every as-

---

[42] My interview with Phil Tippett, originally published in *Animato!* magazine, will appear in the upcoming *Gooseflesh* volumes from Black Coat Press.

pect of their production and completion than most special effects experts had before, or have since. By doing so, Harryhausen fleshed out his own fantasies from the conception stage to the big screen, crafting entertainments and a few classics that bore his distinctive personality. But Tippett, Lantieri, and their peers in the effects field have yet to emulate Harryhausen's example and seize comparable control of their destinies. Of course, considerable consolidation of studio power is concentrated against their ever doing so; still, one hopes a breakthrough artist will emerge, able to creatively select, shape, and control the narrative vehicles for their CGI visions as decisively as Harryhausen shaped his own. However primitive Harryhausen's techniques may seem to today's audiences, there's no denying the enduring heart, soul, and magic of the man's creations — magic that continues to elude the staggering technical accomplishments of the new generations' digital technology. Until the digital-age artists conceive and realize their own visions, they will remain slaves to studios, producers, writers, and directors whose impoverished, impersonal fantasies are hardly worth their — or our — time and attention.

There's real magic to be savored in Paul Thomas Anderson's *MAGNOLIA* (1999), an incredible film that weaves a complex tapestry of dramatic vignettes and characterizations into an organic whole that is more than the sum of its parts. Building on the multi-layered narratives director Robert Altman (*M*A*S*H, McCabe and Mrs. Miller, Nashville*, etc.) pioneered in the 1960s and '70s, Anderson's previous feature *Boogie Nights* (1997) showcased a diverse set of characters to chronicle the rise and fall of a young porn-star (Mark Wahlberg) over two decades; it remains a remarkable film, but *Magnolia* is a far more ambitious venture. Anderson casts an even wider net over a much narrower time frame to track the complex connections between nine people (and their many associates and acquaintances) in a single, fateful 24-hour period in San Fernando Valley, California. A remarkable cast (including Tom Cruise, Jason Robards, Julianne Moore, John C. Reilly, Philip Seymour Hoffman, William H. Macy, and many more) bring these people to vivid life as they interact in unexpected ways, each stumbling toward their respective redemption, damnation, or oblivion.

Clocking in at over 180 minutes, *Magnolia* is a demanding but rewarding masterpiece. It isn't out to please; its unflinching dissection of human foibles and frailties will have many of you squirming — as will the revelatory climax, which establishes *Magnolia* as one of the few truly Fortean films ever made. The writings of Charles Fort (*The Book of the Damned, Lo!, New Lands*, and *Wild Talents*, the latter title the only one which is overtly referenced in the film) documented events which orthodox science refused to acknowledge, much less investigate. In writing these books, Fort evolved a philosophy that asserted that extraordinary events we dismiss as chaos, coincidence, chance, or impossibilities were actually manifestations of mysterious forces at work beyond our comprehension. Fort believed these forces were integral and essential to our existence; the bizarre events he traced in his books provided hard evidence of patterns we were too vain, blind, or inconsequential to discern. The Fortean Society (founded in

1931[43]) has carried on Fort's ground breaking work, keeping his books in print and publishing *The Fortean Times* magazine to extend his efforts and philosophy into the new Millennium. Fort documented many inexplicable events like those which open and conclude *Magnolia* (however outrageous you might find the final act, rest assured such things can and do happen).

There have been other Fortean films — Peter Greenaway's *A Zed and Two Noughts* (1988) comes to mind[44] — but no filmmaker before Anderson has so fully embraced or persuasively argued the validity of Fort's beliefs. That he does so by drawing us so completely into the lives of his characters opens our eyes to fresh perceptions of our own. Anderson reaches a bit too far at times (though Aimee Mann's songs are integral to the film, the moment when the characters begin to sing along with Mann is a major miscalculation, a dramatic breach I found much tougher to swallow than the notorious Fortean climax; still, it's a lovely conceit, deftly executed), but such missteps only emphasize the courage of the endeavor. *Magnolia* is a challenging, audacious, entertaining, ravishing experience, a key work (along with *American Beauty, Being John Malkovich, Fight Club*, and others) in a bracing new era of American cinema. Don't miss it; highest recommendation! *(Rated "R" for strong language and emotional content, adult and sexual situations, violence, alcohol and drug use.)*

---

[43] FYI, Charles Fort refuted and refused to join the Fortean Society.

[44] See *Blur, Vol. 1*, pp. 187-188.

August 17:

THE CIDER HOUSE RULES (1999), like director Lasse Hallstrom's best work (*My Life as a Dog*, 1985 and *What's Eating Gilbert Grape?*, 1993), thrives on the akimbo coming-of-age dramas and peculiar tragicomic rhythms characteristic of novelist John Irving's work. Small surprise, then, that these two storytellers make such a fine match with *The Cider House Rules*, with Hallstrom working from Irving's own Academy-Award winning adaptation of his best-selling novel. The story of orphan Homer Wells (Tobey Maguire) and his rite-of-passage to adulthood after leaving the St. Cloud orphanage to work and live in a New England orchard toward the close of World War 2 is peppered with overtly Dickensian characters and flourishes, but Hallstrom negotiates the potential minefield with telling grace and affection.

As he stakes out his own path in the wide world outside, Homer remains anchored by his ties with his surrogate siblings and "father," Dr. Larch (Michael Caine delivering a warm, winning performance); indeed, the narrative structure is defined and framed by those relationships. Homer reluctantly practices the medical skills he learned at the orphanage as his world view is irrevocably altered by his brush with a very different patriarch — Mr. Rose (Delroy Lindo of *Clockers, Romeo Must Die*, etc.), head of the nomadic migrant pickers who work at the orchard — and Homer's first love, Candy (Charlize Theron of *The Devil's Advocate, Mighty Joe Young, The Astronaut's Wife*, and *Reindeer Games*). Cloying as all this should be, it works, maintaining its balance even as the dark center of Irving's novel (involving abuse, abortion, incest, and profound loss) asserts itself.

Taken at blunt face value, the film is essentially a pro-abortion parable, but its rich cast of characters, tactile sense of time and place, and engaging storyline elevates it beyond mere polemic. Just as Homer's orphanage roots strengthen and define his character throughout, the film itself is immeasurably enriched by the imaginative conviction of its scenes at St. Cloud, which thread back and forth throughout the narrative tapestry.

Though Michael Caine deservedly won the Oscar for his role, Tobey Maguire's performance is the ripe core of the apple here. This young actor has carved out a definitive niche as one of his generation's finest performers in Ang Lee's *The Ice Storm* (1997) and *Ride with the Devil* (1999; new to video and highly recommended), Gary Ross' *Pleasantville* (1998), and others. While all eyes have been glued to Leonardo DiCaprio and his ilk, Maguire has quietly asserted himself with a quiet presence and dignity that marks him as an actor well worth watching. *The Cider House Rules* also boasts local interest, what with John Irving having lived hereabouts until recently, and as it was filmed in and around Dummerston, Brattleboro, Vermont, and the neighborhood (including the instantly recognizable Northfield Drive-In in Massachusetts!). What are you waiting for? Take this one home tonight. *(Rated "PG-13" for adult content, frank medical language and a few harsh words, adult and sexual situations, nudity.)*

Whatever your attitude toward Julia Roberts, don't miss **ERIN BROCKOVICH** (1999). I'm sorry I passed it by when it was in theaters (if you steady readers recall my reviews of *Notting Hill* and *Runaway Bride*, I'd had quite enough of Julia around that time).[45] Thankfully, I had to watch *Erin Brockovich* for this column; it's the best thing the actress has done in years.

Roberts stars as Erin Brockovich, a twice-divorced, impoverished single mother of three who insinuated herself into a job with a California legal firm in the early 1990s and — sans any prior formal education — almost single-handedly pieced together a class-action lawsuit against a major corporation (Pacific Gas & Electric) responsible for the lethal contamination of a small town's water. The story is true, and Roberts, co-stars Albert Finney (as Erin's boss Ed Masry) and Aaron Eckhart (as biker lover George), screenplay writer Susannah Grant, and director Steven Soderbergh find an ideal chemistry for putting across its nuances and essentials. Similar subject matter informed the recent John Travolta vehicle *A Civil Action* (1998), a noble effort undone by its compromised courtroom dramaturgy that sidestepped the human suffering and loss at its core.[46] *Erin Brockovich* is a much better film. It confronts, communicates, and empathizes with the agonies of the victims of PG & E's toxic Chromium 6 dumping practices while maintaining a rigorous focus on Erin's story.

This is a tough juggling act, but the film follows its heroine's lead — breezy, brash, bold, mercurial and direct — without skirting the legal, moral, and scientific complexities of its case and story. Roberts makes the most of a plum role that places her firmly on the side of the angels. Brockovich was and is a moral crusader fired up by righteous indignation against an uncaring world and its most devious agents, and Roberts savors every

---

[45] See *Blur, Vol. 1*, pp. 113, 188-190.

[46] See *Blur, Vol. 1*, pg. 33.

setpiece that pitch Erin against idiots, oppressors, and smug superiors. More importantly, she conveys Erin's loving but strained relations with her kids, lover (who takes care of her children while she's out fighting the good fight), and boss, whom she inadvertently walks on or over in her crusade to bring relief to Hinkley's citizens and bring the culprits to justice.

Erin is the heart of the film, beating steady and true. As outrageous as Roberts' outfits seem throughout, by all reports her portrayal and wardrobe are true to her real-life role model, who has a cameo as a diner waitress and registers strongly in the DVD bonus materials (particularly the "Spotlight on Location" short detailing the making of the film; the DVD also boasts almost thirty minutes worth of deleted scenes!). It's stirring to see and hear Erin herself in these extras; she seems as forthright, aggressive, engaging, and honest as the film paints her to be, a true heroine for the Millennium. If only she were running for the Presidency...

Though the film's narrative mechanism runs like clockwork and could easily have become arch or insufferable, director Soderbergh (*Sex, Lies, and Videotape*, 1989; *King of the Hill*, 1993; *The Limey*, 1999[47]) orchestrates it all with a rakish skill and attention to time, place, and characters that recalls Jonathan Demme's best early work (*Citizen's Band*, 1988; *Melvin and Howard*, 1980; *Who Am I This Time?*, 1982). The ensemble cast is excellent throughout, with Finney and Eckhart at their most beguiling playing off Erin's bullying dynamo. Finney's role is hardly a stretch, coasting on the veteran actor's easy charm, but it's hard to believe the patient, put-upon dreamboat George is played by the same per-

---

[47] See *Blur, Vol. 1*, pp. 241-243.

former who embodied misogyny and misanthropy so palpably in Neil LaBute's scathing *In the Company of Men* (1996). This is shamelessly populist filmmaking of the highest order; Recommended. *(Rated "R" for language, adult and non-explicit sexual situations.)*

Recent & Recommended:

Back in the mid-1980s, a Brit friend of mine once registered his bemusement with the American term "dysfunctional families" — "that's just how all families are," he commented. This lingering memory asserted itself recently as I watched Tim Roth's quietly harrowing feature-film directorial debut **THE WAR ZONE** (1999), an unflinching dissection of the corrosive impact incest has on a London family who uproot and move to a remote seaside residence. While top-drawer American actors like Edward Norton (who made his mark as a performer with confrontational fare like *American History X*) make their directorial debuts with romantic fluff like *Keeping the Faith* (1999), British actors move behind the camera to cut their teeth with stronger fare. Gary Oldman made the jump with *Nil by Mouth* (1996), mining his own working-class background to depict a Cockney family's private hell under the ruthless fist of drunken patriarch Raymond (Ray Winstone); Roth follows suit. Where Oldman adopted the cinematic shotgun tactics of a thug appropriate to his material, Roth cuts to the heart with the precision of a surgeon.

Roth casts Ray Winstone as another monster father whose covert evil and cool denial ravages home and hearth as irrevocably as Raymond's rage totaled his own in *Nil by Mouth*. Winstone eschews the bellowing theatrics of *Nil by Mouth* to create a soft-spoken sexual predator who sustains apparent family harmony with his wife (Tilda Swinton of *Orlando*, 1992, and *The Beach*), newborn daughter, and teenage son Tom (Freddie Comliffe) while slaking his carnal appetite with his teenage daughter Jessie (Lara Belmont). Scarred by a car accident he feels responsible for and troubled by his own awakening sexuality, Tom's accidental glimpse of their incestuous relations sets this spare tragedy in motion. The revelation eats away at Tom as he stumbles toward increasingly devastating confrontations with sister (stirring her own repressed shame, anger, and agony), mother, and — inevitably — the father. Like *Nil by Mouth*, Roth's *The War Zone* charts the echoes of abuse across generational lines. Tom's implacable, haunted gaze defines the film; we, too, cannot look away as the fragile illusions the family sustains are shattered in the wake of the awful truth. The film concludes with one of the most chilling final shots in recent memory.

Highly recommended, but a stern warning: due to the strong dramatic content and a shockingly explicit key sequence, this film is definitely *not* for children or impressionable viewers. Adult survivors of sexual abuse should approach with extreme caution, or skip the film altogether; this is very potent, possibly toxic, fare. *(Rated a very strong "R" for language, adult and sexual situations, nudity, onscreen sexual activity, and violence.)*

August 24:

AROUND THE FIRE (1998) is being promoted as a celebration of the (Grateful) Deadhead and Phish scene, but it is actually a coming-of-age drama that would have passed as a TV "Movie of the Week" in the 1970s —

meaning it's a bummer, man. The language is harsher, the sexuality riper, the drug use and abuse truer to its scene, and the portrait of the 1990s music tribes far more believable and sympathetic than '70s TV fare afforded its respective rock and hippie scenes, but the narrative arc is pure formula and the casting is TV-movie perfect.

The troubled lead Simon is played by Devon Sawa — post-*Casper* (1995), *The Boys' Club* (1996), and *Wild America* (1997), pre-*Idle Hands, SLC Punk* (both 1999)[48], and *Final Destination* (2000) — sporting various-length hair extensions to convey the passing of time in the stormy rites-of-passage. The archetype is a familiar one, a fixture for prior generations of teen actors from Linda Blair to Scott Baio to Leonardo DiCaprio. Sawa isn't an embarrassment, but he doesn't bring much more than his lanky good looks and sunny-to-surly range to the role.

True to the TV formula, the male patriarchal focus dominates: female characters either lend support, fail, or betray the male leads. Plagued by vague memories of his mother's departure and death, and rocky relations with his dad (Bill Smitrovich) and stepmom (Lisa Burgett), Simon strikes up a friendship in boarding school with laid-back Andrew (Eric Mabius of *Welcome to the Dollhouse, Black Circle Boys*, and *The Crow: Salvation*). Andrew introduces Simon to the pleasures of marijuana and the bohemian brotherhood of the tribal concert circuit, where Simon meets lovely Jennifer (Tara Reid of *American Pie, Body Shots*, and *Cruel Intentions*). In short order, Simon and Jennifer are an item and fellow "head" Trace (Colman Domingo) shows Simon the ropes on dealing acid before the lad's anger, despair, and

---

[48] See *Blur, Vol. 1*, pp. 43-44, 70-71.

rootlessness steers him into drug abuse, freak-out, arrest, and incarceration in a rehab clinic. Thanks to tough-love therapist (Charleyne Woodard), healing reconciliations indeed manifest, but not before Simon's downward spiral unreels in the time-honored tradition of *Go Ask Alice* (1973), *Sarah T. - Portrait of a Teenage Alcoholic* (1975), *The Death of Richie* (1977), and other cautionary after-school specials and TV movie teen-angst melodramas.

Sure, the genre is rooted in reality, but like most of its ilk *Around the Fire* is out of tune with the very generation it's about. Local teenagers suffer far rockier roads than Simon, but the film shuns fresh intimacies, extremes, or tragedies that might set *this* troubled teen apart or make his story worth the telling. The "troubled teen" formula trivializes the personal and social issues it pretends to address as the cliches assert themselves: color-tinted flashbacks of the traumatic primal scene which must be decoded; ersatz simulations of being stoned and tripping; coy side-stepping of any meaningful confrontation until the obligatory degradations run their course.

At least producers and co-writers John Comerford and Tommy Rosen avoid the usual scape-goating of the countercultural characters these films categorically indulge. The subculture Simon embraces contains the seeds of destruction and redemption, and the film clearly depicts his undoing due to his own opportunistic decisions, addictive behavior, and self-destructive ire at his father. En route, the film effectively evokes the allure and carnival comforts of "the tribe," capturing the Deadhead/Phish scene's extension (and reduction) of 1960s' alternative lifestyles to sampler "weekend retreats" for contemporary middle-class youths seeking their own sense of community and family. The concert scene provides a taste of freedom and meaningful alternatives, commercial enough to sustain its nomadic carnival festivities, but commitment to any substantial political, communal, or personal ideals or change remains out of reach. The "tribe" does, however, provide a core around which many young adults build their own relationships and circles of contact, as Simon does here. Genres evolve incrementally, and this is *Around the Fire*'s sole progressive achievement.

Around the Fire isn't perceptive or aggressive enough to explore its characters or trappings beyond the formulaic parameters. Nor does its budget allow for any real interaction with the music scene it dances around: the soundtrack features tunes by Phish, Grateful Dead, Bob Marley, Dire Straits, etc., but not a single band is shown onscreen. *Around the Fire* has its merits, notable among them a tidy recluse named "Doc" (Stephen Tobolowsky) who cooks up his own distinctive brand of LSD and determines the worthiness of potential dealers based on their knowledge of Dead arcana, and the most amusing onscreen cast credit of the month ("Vegan Gooball Man: Manny the Hippie"). Bring on the Gooball, Manny. *(Rated "R" for language, drug abuse, nudity, adult and sexual situations.)*

The promotional tagline for **SUPERNOVA** (2000) reads, "In the farthest reaches of space, something has gone terribly wrong." The truth is, in the dark corners of Hollywood something went terribly wrong; or, to paraphrase the ballyhoo for *Alien* (1979), the wellspring for this ongoing science fiction breed, "In space, no one can hear you cutting." *Supernova* is the latest botched big-budget studio science fiction feature, joining *Event Horizon,*

Sphere, and others. The real pisser is that eleventh-hour studio tampering sabotaged *Supernova*. Thankfully, the DVD of *Supernova* provides some insight into the butchery by preserving the vital organs that were so thoughtlessly removed, proving that *Supernova* was a contender.

Though the cast is terrific (including Angela Bassett, James Spader, Lou Diamond Phillips, and more), the story elements are familiar, to say the least. While on a 120-day duty, medical rescue vessel Nightingale 229 responds to a mysterious distress call (*à la Queen of Blood, Planet of the Vampires, Alien*, etc.). The crew brings aboard a mysterious alien artifact (*à la Atomic Submarine, 2001: A Space Odyssey, Sphere*, etc.) and a sole human survivor who appears normal but is undergoing a biological transformation due to an unknown and probably alien catalytic agent (*à la The Quatermass Experiment, Night of the Blood Beast, Alien, Xtro*, etc.), thus endangering all on board (*à la It! The Terror From Beyond Space, Alien, Creature, ad infinitum*). After the revelation of the potential threat to the known universe, including home planet Earth (*à la Alien, The Thing*, etc.), the dwindling crew must eliminate the alien intruder and artifact before the suicidal self-destruct of the ship runs its course (*à la Alien, Aliens*, etc.).

I've cited the obvious cinematic sources in this cursory synopsis, but bear in mind these elements were old hat in literary science fiction decades ago, codified by A.E. Van Vogt's first published short story *"Black Destroyer"* (1939), the definitive source for the entire "murderous alien menace on the ship" subgenre. *Supernova*'s screenplay (credited to David Campbell Wilson) was definitely hip to its sources, incorporating overt references to "the Van Vogt colony" and the self-referential

"Titan 37 mining facility" (evoking William Malone's *Creature* aka *Titan Find*, 1985, a cheap *Alien* pastiche that was Malone's first major film; Malone retains a story credit here, most likely drafted before his recent writer-director stint on the *House on Haunted Hill* remake). But in its current video form — which supplants the January 2000 theatrical "PG-13" rating with a spicier "R" rating — *Supernova* is a muddled mess, sagging beneath the long, dark shadow of its livelier and more coherent precursors.

Alien informs the film in more ways than one, as credited director "Thomas Lee" is a pseudonym affixed after final edit was taken away from on-set director Walter Hill (*The Warriors*, 1979; *48 Hours*, 1982; *Streets of Fire*, 1984; *Trespass*, 1992; etc.), who co-produced and co-scripted the original *Alien*. Hill stepped in during preproduction to replace Australian director Geoffrey Wright (*Romper Stomper*, 1992); when parent studio MGM-UA wrested editing control from Hill, Jack Sholder (*The Hidden*) and none other than Francis Ford Coppola (*The Godfather, Apocalypse Now*, etc.) recut the film. Curiously enough, this kind of revisionary editing work informed Coppola's efforts in the very early 1960s for producer Roger Corman, converting Russian science fiction features Corman purchased US rights to (primarily for their special effects footage) into drive-in fodder like *Battle Beyond the Sun* (1962); ah, how the mighty have come full circle.

Little wonder, then, that Hill wanted his name off the final product; in its present form, *Supernova* is a skeletal remnant of the film Hill completed, and a sterling example of the dangers of filmmaking-by-committee.

Thankfully, the DVD offers a generous selection of "deleted scenes." As with MGM-UA's DVD of David Nutter's *Disturbing Behavior* (1998, a fine film which also suffered from studio tampering), comparison of the deleted sequences with the final studio cut offers a marvelous crash-course on how comparatively little cumulative running time can make or break a motion picture. The cuts seriously cripple the film: gone, for instance, are the succinct characterizations of pilot A.J. Marley (Robert Forster of *Jackie Brown*, who is less than a cipher in the final edit) and co-pilot Nick Vanzant (James Spader), who becomes the nominal hero after Marley suffers his dire fate. Gone, too, is the lovely prologue which perfectly framed the movement of the original (cut) downbeat ending — which, by the way, featured the titular "supernova," lending coherence and a real conclusion to the film. The loss of Titan 37's male computer "George" and a crew member's gory demise are inconsequential, but the fate of the monstrous Karl Larson (Peter Facinelli of *Can't Hardly Wait*) in the original climax was an essential element. Most devastating of all was the loss of an absolutely crucial sequence in the bowels of the Titan complex as Vanzant discovers Karl's son Troy (Knox Grantham White, voiced by Kerrigan Mahan; both credits inexplicably appear on the final studio version), who has been transformed into a grotesque fetal adult mutation by prolonged exposure to the overtly phallic, translucent alien artifact.

Supernova was never a great film by any stretch of the imagination, but it clearly was a much better film than it is now. I can only recommend the DVD release; viewing the deleted scenes after the feature, one can flesh out the missing narrative elements and envision the film that once was. The video version of *Supernova* is yet another testimony to Hollywood studio stupidity, cowardice, and waste... and we already have plenty of those. *(Rated "R" for strong language, gore, violence, nudity, adult and sexual situations.)*

Recent & Recommended:

GHOST DOG: THE WAY OF THE SAMURAI (2000): The latest film from fiercely-independent American director Jim Jarmusch is delightfully true to the deadbeat rhythms, cool, wit, and vigor of his best work (*Stranger Than Paradise*, 1984; *Down By Law*, 1986; *Mystery Train*, 1989; *Night on Earth*, 1991; and *Dead Man*, 1995). Jarmusch goes with the flow of his chosen cross currents, melding Eastern philosophy and archetypes, urban hip hop culture, dysfunctional gangster stereotypes, and classical Western setpieces with mesmerizing insouciance.

In an unnamed New Jersey city a single beat ahead of (or apart from) today, an impoverished clutch of Italian mobsters take out contracts on one another and loner hitman Ghost Dog (Forest Whitaker of *Good Morning Vietnam, Bird, The Crying Game*, etc.) lives amid his beloved pigeons on a rooftop, religiously adhering to the code of the samurai while serving his master, Louie (John Tormey). Conflicts arise when Ghost Dog is forced to lash out at Louie's circle of wiseguys when they put out a contract on both assassin and master, compromising Ghost Dog's devotion to the path and his master as complications inevitably arise. But this is hardly a cops-and-crooks action movie; it's sheer poetry.

Jarmusch punctuates and frames the narrative with quotations from the samurai text *Hagakure*, detailing the path of the warrior as a spiritual calling. Whitaker beautifully embodies his character's devotions — gentle, focused, methodical, and lethal. Jarmusch gleefully plays Ghost Dog off his few friendships (Isaach de Bankole as a French-speaking ice-cream man and Camille Winbush as streetwise little girl Pauline) and the quiet lunacy of the morally and financially bankrupt mobsters (Cliff Gorman, Henry Silva, Victor Argo, Gene Ruffini) and the mysterious Louise (Tricia Vessey), perpetually watching bad cartoons surrounded by her father's goons. The film sustains its own uncanny vision and pace, to the beat of a great original score by RZA (formerly of Wu Tang Clan), who makes a cameo. *Ghost Dog* is a marvelous film; Highly recommended! *(Rated "R" for language, gunplay, violence, and adult situations.)*

August 31:

Football fans have much to rejoice over this weekend, with Oliver Stone's *ANY GIVEN SUNDAY* (2000) hitting video stores across the country tomorrow morning (enjoying a rare Friday video street date instead of the usual Tuesday). Stone brings all his visceral cinematic skills to bear, downplaying off-field soap opera for as much on-the-field football play as the 157-minute running time allows (over an hour of the film is in-your-face football action). Though there's no conspiracy theories or serial killers at work, Stone's dissection of a sport torn asunder by big business, sponsor city politics, family proprietors, player egos, and corporate media prompted the NFL to refuse to cooperate with the production.

We meet the key players in the opening moments: Miami Sharks' coach Tony D'Amato (Al Pacino) is under the gun to deliver wins during one of his team's tougher seasons, with star quarterback (Dennis Quaid) suffering an incapacitating injury and hotshot replacement Willie Beaman (Jamie Foxx, far from his usual comedic roles) suffering a swelled head and insufferable ego. Add to the pressure cooker a general manager (Cameron Diaz) who, as one official (Charlton Heston in a cameo) notes, would "eat her young" to get her way; a corrupt team doctor (James Woods) willing to overlook potentially-fatal conditions as he sees fit; and team mates (including LL Cool J) who've had their fill of Beaman and are eager to throw him to the lions. Tension builds as Stone strains to capture every nuance with his patented kinetic style, though he's clearly in a more playful mode here, casting himself as a sports announcer. The games themselves are rendered with the twitchy clarity of *Saving Private Ryan*'s Normandy invasion, and Pacino holds it all together with anchor support from vet football star and action actor Jim Brown as his assistant coach.

Any Given Sunday builds to the inevitable to-the-wire playoff game ("three yards to go, four seconds, one play") between the Sharks and the Dallas Knights. The arcane "blazing eye" logo of the Knights is one of Stone's most flamboyant flourishes, foreshadowing the game's most gut-wrenching turn, a fleeting dose of the old Stone ultra-violence that's risible in the context of this film. Stone otherwise plays it by the rules — the new rules of high-stakes media football, that is — lacing the field hijinks with asides directed at television's aggressive corruption of the sport. Could it be Stone has become a team player? Well, not quite: don't be too quick to fumble for the remote as the final credits appear, because *Any Given Sunday* has one more zinger up its sleeve. Though *Any Given Sunday* is ultimately much ado about nothing, Stone, Pacino, and the ensemble cast give it all they've got, making this a lively evening or Sunday afternoon entertainment. *(Rated "R" for strong language, casual alcohol and drug abuse, nudity, adult and sexual situations, and violence.)*

I DREAM OF AFRICA (2000) is a high-pedigree production, directed by Hugh Hudson (*Chariots of Fire, Greystoke: The Legend of Tarzan*, etc.) and scored by maestro of the epic film Maurice Jarre (*Lawrence of Arabia, Doctor Zhivago*, etc.). It boasts lovely cinematography (by Bernard Lutic) and impeccable credentials, but remains an oddly listless affair. While living *la dolce vita* in Italy, privileged divorcée Kuki Gallman (Kim Basinger) and her new husband Paolo (Vincent Perez) survive a traumatic auto accident that shatters their lives and sends them packing for a remote corner of Kenya, Africa. They trade the European comforts of the rich for the dusty comforts of, well, wealthy white African colonials living on their 100,000 acre ranch, and thereby hangs the tale. Paolo embraces the live-for-the-moment excitement of traveling the continent with fellow white transplants, leaving Kuki to fend for herself to raise their son Emanuela (played as a youth by Liam Aiken) amid the sun-baked savanna.

Based on author and conservationist Kuki Gallman's autobiographical novel, *I Dream of Africa* passes less like a dream than a fragmented memory of a dream: vague, unfocused, anecdotal, and distant. Kim Basinger's glacial performance defines the odd vacuum of the film, though Kuki's life story should provide plenty of raw material for a plum role as the family's crusade against local poachers ultimately exacts a terrible toll (as does Emanuela's affection for reptiles). What little spark the film musters derives from Perez's performance as Paolo and Garrett Strommen's as seventeen-year-old Emanuela (bearing a striking resemblance to Perez); both of them are confident, reckless, self-absorbed, and utterly likable, emphasizing Basinger's poor-little-rich-girl aloofness.

Lacking the emotional core of, say, *Out of Africa* (1985), the visionary allure of Nicolas Roeg's *Walkabout* (1971), or even the lively funk of an old *Tarzan* movie, *I Dream of Africa* lurches from setpiece to setpiece without leaving much of an impression. The final line of Kuki's narration refers to "the job to be done" in Africa: "Now, it is my privilege to look after Africa herself." We are meant to associate this with Gallman's conservationist efforts, but Basinger's arrogant delivery rings false. Her maternal tone defines the same imperialist colonial agenda that made the African adventure genre such an anachronism by the mid-1960s. *(Rated "PG-13" for partial nudity, strong language, and adult situations.)*

***PRINCESS MONONOKE (MONONOKE HIME**, 1998)* is my video pick of the week. This marvelous anime epic is one of the major video releases of the year, a feature-length animated fantasy from Japan's premiere animator and fantasist, Hayao Miyazaki (*My Neighbor Totoro, Kiki's Delivery Service* and *Warriors of the Wind* [49]). Though the English-dubbed version (scripted, in part, by novelist and Sandman comic creator Neil Gaiman) loses some of the richness of the original in the

---

[49] This was the 1985 US release title of Miyazaki's *Nausicaa of the Valley of the Wind* (1984), in cut and dubbed form, shorn of 32 minutes.

translation and sports a couple of laughable lines of dialogue, *Princess Mononoke* is an energetic, engaging, breath-taking creation.

During Japan's rugged Muromanci medieval era (15th to 16th century), a remote mountain village is attacked by a maddened creature that is killed only after it infects the young warrior Ashitaki (voiced by Billy Crudup) with a mysterious malady. Banished from his village, Ashitaki follows the invading beast's trail back to the source of the infestation, where a fortified clan of ironworkers under the rule of the cunning matriarch Lady Eboshi (Minnie Driver) are denuding the forests and at war with powerful animal tribes and spirits. Spearheading the forest creatures' defenses against the ravages of Eboshi and her clan is the feral Princess Mononoke (Claire Danes), raised by an albino she-wolf (Gillian Anderson) who is goddess to her species. Ashitaki forges an uneasy alliance with Mononoke, though his efforts are stymied by the secret agenda of an opportunistic monk (Billy Bob Thornton), the escalating violence between the forces of man and nature, and the mystical primal being which lives in the deepest regions of the forest.

This dense, powerful saga is a genuine epic in every sense of the word, tapping potent mythic wellsprings to explore fundamental issues of man and nature, technology and ecology, darkness and light. Viewers expecting a sort of simplistic Disney narrative are in for a real surprise: like all of Miyazaki's work, *Princess Mononoke* constructs and probes its invented universe with the moral rigor and complexity live-action Japanese filmmakers like Akira Kurosawa bring to their best work. There are no easy dualistic definitions of good and evil: each side of the struggle has their own goals, beliefs, and hard-earned prejudices, and the morality play is punctuated by surprising shifts in allegiance as Miyazaki's characters struggle to understand and/or control the awesome forces at work. Thus, *Mononoke* rewards repeated viewing as few other recent animated films do.

Furthermore, though I heartily recommend *Mononoke* to all but the youngest and most impressionable viewers, this is an often violent masterpiece (it does not wallow in mayhem: the bloodshed, when it comes, is brutal and direct). The moral complications and complexities of its plot may bewilder younger children, but then again, the moral universe of the classic fairy tales never was as cut and dried as the Disney versions were. Be aware, too, that this is a film of rare, dazzling beauty, with a profound sense of, and connection to, life: among Miyazaki's most memorable conceits are the spectral, baby-like forest spirits, who shake their heads like rattles and populate the trees like fireflies. This is a magnificent film.

Miramax/Disney have done a shameful job mismarketing *Mononoke* in its truncated theatrical, delayed video, and long-delayed DVD releases; it could hardly have been worse if they had set out to deliberately bury the film. After rave festival reviews from the major critics (including *The New York Times, Time* magazine, Roger Ebert, and others), the film enjoyed a strangely abbreviated theatrical release, shifting from playing for months in select urban art houses to scarce third-run and college venues, without any open theatrical rollout between the two extremes (even though the almost simultaneous blockbuster theatrical success of Warners' US release of the first *Pokemon* feature instantly opened venues to a potential anime goldmine). The subsequent video release was delayed no less than *four times*, and the DVD was further delayed (from August 2000 to late December 2000) to accomodate the addition of a Japanese audio track demanded by outraged anime fans on a variety of online discussion boards (note the track is not cited on the actual DVD box art, indicating that the printing had already been completed prior to the reconsidered addition of the Japanese track, noted only by a sticker on the shrinkwrap). There are no other significant extras, typical of Disney/Miramax genre releases, another missed opportunity given the wealth of material that was available.

Could it be that Disney is passively burying the entire Miyazaki oeuvre whose exclusive international rights (outside of Japan) they now own? Many Japanese anime industry professionals and fans believe so. As more time passes, it's hard not to believe such is the case. There's been no orchestrated attempt to mount any public awareness of this remarkable body of work the corporation is keeping under lock and key. *Kiki's Delivery Service* was released without any significant notice or marketing support, and *Mononoke*'s release has been botched from Day One. The repeated delays of *Mononoke*'s street dates robbed retailers of any confidence or interest in the title, which was released on video at rental rather than sell-through prices.[50] Furthermore,

---

[50] In the video market, new titles were usually released at rental pricing – between $49.95 and as much as $120 per copy – rather than sell-through pricing (at this time, $14.95-29.95 were standard retail prices for sell-thru titles). Only later would rental-priced titles be re-released at sell-through prices. Customers were regularly confused by this staggering difference in pricing, assuming as they did that *all* new videos were sell-through priced. For the most part, with the phasing out of

the scant studio industry promo never linked the title with Miyazaki's other works (including *Kiki*, which one would think Disney has a stake in promoting in conjunction with *Mononoke*), the Disney animated classics, or indeed any anime (in fact, the two titles studio promotions linked with Mononoke for retailers were — I kid you not — *eXistenZ* and *Velvet Goldmine*!). *Mononoke*'s theatrical poster offered a surprisingly grim graphic design, dominated by a brown circular stone carved with a relief likeness of the Princess, hovering over a smoky, ominous image of Lady Eboshi's Irontown (reportedly, Miyazaki's interests had final approval over this graphic, so it is hard to fault Miramax completely). *Mononoke*'s final slipsleeve and DVD box art offers drab, utterly pedestrian packaging which makes the film look like a *Star Wars* rip-off, with an androgynous Ashitaki crossing swords (rendered like lightsabers) with an unseen opponent. Sans any hint of the powerful, primal imagery Miyazaki creates, or the most marketable iconic aspects of the feature — Mononoke astride the outsized Albino wolf, or the ravishing forest interior oasis where the primal forest spirit dwells — the packaging grossly misrepresents one of the best films of this or any other year.

As for the rest of Miyazaki's incredible work... silence. Arguments from the Disney quarter that the violent nature of *Princess Mononoke* accounts for their tentative attention to the title simply don't hold water in regards to the rest of Miyazaki's features. These rank among the greatest adventure and fantasy films ever made, period, and certainly among the greatest animated

---

vhs and retail pricing of DVD, this pricing structure has been dramatically revamped since 2002.

features in history. It's as if Disney fears their own animated features might suffer by comparison (well, they do). Despite the previews on Disney's 1999 video release of Miyazaki's marvelous *Kiki's Delivery Service* announcing the then "upcoming" release of *Laputa* on video, it has yet to surface, and there's been no announcements for the other Miyazaki features Disney/Miramax bought as a package deal. Fox's clamshell video release of *My Neighbor Totoro* is still available from most outlets and distributors.[51] When I inquired about the fate of *Laputa* months ago in my capacity as a video store manager and member of the New England Buying Group, the Disney rep said there were no plans for *Laputa*, but *Castle in the Sky* was being discussed as a possible 2001 release... not knowing they are *one and the same film*! Disney doesn't even know what they have, and seem uninterested in notifying their personnel of its true nature. One hopes that Disney and Miramax will soon see the error of their ways and rectify the situation.

Sad as this state of affairs remains, in December 2000 Disney finally released *Princess Mononoke* on DVD ($32.98) in an opulent 1.85:1 anamorphic widescreen transfer, with a production featurette and three optional soundtracks: 5.1 Japanese, 5.1 English, and 2.0 French. In either format, this is a film we can savor for years to come.

Don't pass up *Princess Mononoke* because it's animated, or be misled by Miramax's sorry packaging.

---

[51] As was Fox's no-frills, fullscreen DVD release, too, at the time this review was originally written and published.

Highly Recommended! *(Rated "PG-13" for violence and sometimes horrific imagery.)*[52]

---

[52] This is the revised, expanded version of the *Princess Mononoke* review, hence its reference to the DVD release, which was in fact delayed until December of 2000 and unavailable for review in the August *Video Views* column as it originally was published. This complete review was published in *Video Watchdog* #72, June 2001, pp. 17-19. The major revisions to the *VW* review begin with the paragraph that opens, "Miramax/Disney have done a shameful job mismarketing Mononoke...," supplanting what was a single paragraph in the *Reformer* review. The final paragraph of the August 30 *Video Views* column originally read:

"Miramax/Disney have done a shameful job mismarketing Mononoke *in both its truncated theatrical, delayed video, and long-delayed DVD releases; it could hardly have been worse if they had set out to deliberately bury the film. After a truncated theatrical release (the film went from playing for months in a Boston theater to a single Vermont showing in Bellows Falls!), the video release has been delayed no less than five times, and the DVD will not be available until December of this year or January of 2001. Don't pass up* Princess Mononoke *because it's animated, or be misled by Miramax's utterly pedestrian packaging (which makes the film look like a* Star Wars *rip-off) — you'd be missing one of the best films of this or any other year. Recommended!"*

Also note that Disney finally 'saw the light' after their initially tentative festival and select urban theatrical release of Miyazaki's *Spirited Away* (2003) yielded raves, solid boxoffice, and netted an Academy Award for Best Animated Feature. With a push from Pixar's John Lassiter, Disney subsequently gave *Spirited Away* a proper theatrical release and used it to spearhead a proper vhs/DVD release of three Miyazaki features. At the time of this book's publication, Disney has released almost *all* of Miyazaki's and Studio Ghibli's features on video and DVD in deluxe editions with handsome packag-

Recent & Recommended:

RIDE WITH THE DEVIL (1999): Director Ang Lee (*The Wedding Banquet, Eat Drink Man Woman, Sense and Sensibility, The Ice Storm*) captures the agonies and rites-of-passage of America's last generation to deal with war on their native soil. In the final spasms of the War Between the States, orphaned Missouri farm boys Jake (Tobey McGuire) and Jack (Skeet Ulrich) take up arms to avenge their slain families, joining the guerrilla rebel Roughnecks in their extended campaigns against the Union Jayhawks and any who were sympathetic to the Union. Joined in their bloody struggle by a freed slave (Jeffrey Wright) and swayed by their affections for a Confederate widow (Jewel), Jake and Jack mature amid the decreasing fortunes of their vigilante cause and escalating manhunt against the Roughnecks.

The first act is jarringly violent, but the vivid bloodshed is necessary to Lee's narrative, as the Roughnecks grow numb to the violence, inciting their comrades (including Jonathan Rhys Myers) to embrace even more extreme measures that inevitably consume them. Critics gave *Ride With the Devil* a cold reception, and the film's arc from bracing mayhem to a measured, contemplative pace as Jake regains his moral equilibrium to settle down will put off casual fans of action films, revenge tales, or traditional westerns. But I think this is an extraordinary

---

ing, excellent extras, and aggressive promotion. For more on Disney's handling of *Mononoke*, see my chapter on the film in *Prince of Stories: The Many Worlds of Neil Gaiman* by Hank Wagner, Christopher Golden and yours truly (St. Martin's Press, 2008), pp. 421-426.

gem. The time and place is vividly rendered, and McGuire's slow awakening to fresh possibilities is profoundly moving; we share his need to find a way out of the war's vortex. Lee's Asian-American meditation on war-torn youths' attempts to find their way in a ravaged homeland resonates with its own integrity, adding another worthy film to his canon. *(Rated "R" for sometimes extreme violence and gore, adult and sexual situations, nudity, and strong language.)*

September 7-14:

MEDIA MEDEAS: PSYCHOS, TYRANTS & DREAMERS [53]

Please, don't look away. Stay with me, I beg you. There's something important to be considered here, something more than just this week's new video releases, though they are the catalyst for this discussion.

Back in 1993, I caught Jennifer Lynch's first and (to date) only feature film, *Boxing Helena*, at a local Massachusetts theater. The film was preceded by an inordinate amount of negative publicity surrounding the film's controversial narrative (a male surgeon's obsession with an unattainable woman prompts him to surgically remove her limbs and imprison her in his home)

---

[53] This was originally published as a two part article, *"Psychos, Tyrants, and Dreamers."* I have slightly revised the published version to consolidate it into single essay. Only the transitional passages have been deleted; this is the definitive version. Abridged versions of this essay's comments on *Titus* and *American Psycho* were published as self-standing reviews in *VMag* #34, October 2000, pp. 38-39.

and a costly court verdict against Kim Basinger for her eleventh-hour abandonment of the project to the tune of $9 million in damages. Given the ballyhoo, I wasn't surprised at the aggressive feminist protesters in the theater lobby who noisily tried to keep viewers like myself from entering the theater, nor was I surprised when a brief conversation with two of the protesters revealed that *none* of them had actually seen the film.

What did surprise me was their vehement attack, sight unseen, upon a film made by a woman: just the buzz over its violence-against-women content was enough to poison the film. Never mind the enormous difficulties writer-director Jennifer Lynch (daughter of director David Lynch) had overcome to bring her brainchild to the screen; never mind the film's tasteful handling of its bizarre, fairy-tale like parable; never mind the fact that the violence was essentially offscreen; never mind its dissection of male sexuality in which the victimizer is undone by the very woman he vainly tries to control, imprison, and objectify. Never mind that it was, blatantly, a feminist work, railing against misogyny and patriarchal, possessive presumptions. *Boxing Helena* wasn't a great film, but it was a compelling and haunting effort, an adventurous and challenging first film. Far more haunting, though, was the spectacle of female protesters aggressively attempting to silence a female filmmaker by driving her meager audience away (they — along with studio indifference, critical putdown, and popular opposition to the film — succeeded: Jennifer Lynch has yet to make another film).

Which brings us to the subjects at hand, two current new releases by contemporary, cutting-edge female filmmakers: Mary Harron's inspired adaptation of Bret Easton

Ellis' reviled 1991 novel *AMERICAN PSYCHO* (2000) and Broadway theatrical director Julie Taymor's *TITUS* (2000), a splashy adaptation of William Shakespeare's despised *The Most Lamentable Roman Tragedy of Titus Andronicus* (1592-94). "Splashy" is indeed the operative word here, as both films are awash in blood and gore essential to their source material.

We are told (and assume) female audiences are repulsed by such mayhem. Casual observation would seem to confirm this assumption: I see it first hand every week in the video store, though there are notable exceptions to the rule (lots of women love vampire movies, you know).

This past weekend, I was among a group of people at a Labor Day party enjoying a discussion between two knowledgeable, earnest, articulate women about recent movies they'd seen (*Sunshine* and *Life is Beautiful* prominent among them). This prompted someone to ask what videos were out this week; when the title *American Psycho* was uttered, the conversation stopped cold. The message was clear: no one was interested in discussing *that* movie. The keyword "psycho" — an exposed cultural nerve since novelist Robert Bloch and director Alfred Hitchcock elevated it to the pantheon of horror in 1960 with the original *Psycho* — was perhaps enough, though I suspect the memory of the public outrage provoked by the explicit misogyny and harrowing sexual carnage of Ellis' novel was a factor, too (a quick refresher: Ellis' original publisher dropped the book just prior to publication in a storm of heated criticism; its subsequent debut under another imprint was greeted with scathing reviews). It was as if there was nothing to discuss, and any attempt to pursue discussion would have been an affront.

But there's a great deal to discuss here. The fact is that some of our key female artists are drawn to explicitly violent fare, despite the ongoing feminist struggle against pornography and imagery of violence directed against women. In occasional harmony with the feminist outrage is the ongoing political and cultural damnation of "sex and violence in the media" as if it were a localized contagion. But the debate too often relies upon simplistic, knee-jerk rhetoric; the intrusion of overtly violent novels, songs, and films by women only complicates the issues in ways too uncomfortable to contemplate. If the assumption that female audiences are repulsed by the fusion of "sex and violence" has any validity, why is it that so many female and feminist poets, musicians, artists, authors, and filmmakers continue to embrace such volatile material?

While it's easy to dismiss genre fare from women directors like Mary Lambert (director of *Pet Semetary and Pet Semetary 2*), Katt Shea (*Poison Ivy; The Rage: Carrie 2* [54]), and Kathryn Bigelow (*Near Dark, Blue Steel, Strange Days*), it's harder to so blithely sweep *Titus* or *American Psycho* under the rug. The artistic credentials of their creators (male and female) are too refined; the thrall of the films themselves too uncanny to shake. Indeed, the violence (often overtly sexual in nature, and indeed directed against female as well as male characters) is intrinsic to their dramatic dissections of issues of great concern to feminism: the oppressive, repressive, and destructive urges of patriarchal domination; the ravages of misogyny; the dynamic of rape and sexual subjugation. In short, how is any artist, female or

---

[54] See *Blur, Vol. 1*, pp. 69-70.

male, to address volatile issues related to sex and violence without depicting sex and violence?

Like Jennifer Lynch before her, Mary Harron (who directed and co-scripted the remarkable *I Shot Andy Warhol*, 1996) struggled against enormous studio opposition and interference to mount and complete *American Psycho* according to her own vision. Fascinated by the novel's ruthless portrait of the misanthropic Reagan Era elite, she passionately wanted to make this film. Fresh from the Broadway success of her triumphant stage production of Disney's *The Lion King*, Julie Taymor handpicked *Titus Andronicus* for her film debut. Taymor embraces the Bard's most reviled play to address such issues with bold imagery of male power, domination, and futile circles of vengeance. Though Shakespeare scholars have tried to excise *Titus* from the Bard's canon (arguing the validity of his authorship) with no less a critic than T.S. Eliot dismissing it as "one of the stupidest and most uninspired plays ever written," Taymor saw fresh potential in this least-filmed of all Shakespeare plays (the sole previous film version was telecast in February 1985 by the BBC).

Paradoxically, the excesses which attracted Harron and Taymor to these self-consuming patriarchs and misogynists are the very elements that will keep many potential viewers at bay (just as their verbal sophistication, sharp wit, and unnerving intelligence will put off bloodthirsty action or horror fans lured by the promise of cheap thrills). There's nothing subtle about either Shakespeare's or Ellis' setpieces, and neither Harron or Taymor spare audience sensibilities. Unlike Jennifer Lynch's *Boxing Helena* — an overtly dreamlike experience that skirted any onscreen bloodshed that might disrupt its fairy-tale atmosphere — both *American Psycho* and *Titus* are lovingly mounted catalogues of emotional and psychological cruelty punctuated by jarringly physical bouts of violence (rape, torture, impalements, dismemberment, cannibalism, and more). Though neither film can be accused of exploitation, they are as vividly horrific as Tobe Hooper's *The Texas Chainsaw Massacre* (1974) or Jonathan Demme's *Silence of the Lambs* (1991; two films which are more alike than many would care to admit).

Titus opens with an anachronistic procession of Roman centurians and 20th-Century tanks, a fusion that would seem more imaginative or daring had we not already been exposed to so many Shakespeare adaptations set in the contemporary world (Ian McKellen as *Richard III* in 1930s London; the Leonardo DiCaprio/Clair Danes *Romeo + Juliet*; Ethan Hawke as a modern Manhattan *Hamlet*). Nevertheless, the display of raw male power is appropriate: the grind of the treads and thrust of overtly phallic tank turrets convey more than the march of spear-toting soldiers could. Taymor proceeds with her fusion of old and new via the ravishing set and costume design, concocting a Felliniesque netherworld that never loses its focus on the commanding performances that anchor the film.

Anthony Hopkins is the Roman General Titus, who returns triumphant from his campaigns with the captured Goth Queen Tamora (Jessica Lange) and her three sons in chains. Despite her pleas for mercy, Titus sacrifices one of her sons to appease the gods and his army's thirst for Goth blood; his first mistake, as Tamora thereafter schemes to avenge the deed. Titus also turns down the Senate's petition for him to rule Rome, selflessly crowning the decadent Saturninus (the ratlike Alan

Cumming) Emperor to appease the candidate's outspoken advocates; his second mistake, as Saturninus joins forces with Tamora, her sons, and the scheming Moor Aaron (Harry J. Lennix, delivering a powerhouse performance) to make Titus' life a living hell. Titus' daughter Lavania (Laura Fraser) suffers at the hands of Tamora's sons: the unveiling of the atrocities committed against Lavania — her tongue cut out, her severed hands replaced with twigs spread like cruel, broken mockeries of fingers — is among the film's most devastating images, embodying and externalizing the rape victim's inner emotional and psychological wounds. This provokes Titus to mount his own reign of terror against their tormenters until (to quote the climax of Romeo and Juliet) "all are punished."

Powerful as *Titus* undeniably is thanks to Taymor's energetic direction, the eye-drugging visuals, and the marvelous performances dominated by Hopkins and Lennix, the mayhem is at times risible. Horrible as Lavania's fate may be, her plight becomes increasingly absurd in the context of *Titus'* climactic excesses, and Taymor shamelessly plays it for all it's worth. It's almost impossible not to chuckle when Titus bids his handless, tongueless daughter to take his own severed hand in her teeth like a dog as he cradles his murdered sons' jugged heads: this tableau is simply *too much*, the flamboyance of the staging inviting cruel laughter.

The horrors in **American Psycho** often invite laughter, too, as a victim (Jared Leto) mocks the newspaper pages spread on the sterile apartment floor (to sop up his own blood) while titular psycho Patrick Bateman (Christian Bale) blithely dons a raincoat and offers his pretentious critique of Huey Lewis and the News' *"Hip to Be*

Square" before burying an axe in the sap's skull. What-ever laughs *Titus* elicits are a byproduct of the Bard's shameless pre-Grand Guignol excess and director Julie Taymor's campy flourishes; in *American Psycho*, the savage humor is essential to the film's relentless agenda.

Bateman spouts progressive humanist rhetoric like a Presidential candidate on an election-year convention floor mere moments after shouting to an uncaring woman bartender, "I want to stab you to death, then play with your blood." He rhapsodizes over banal tunes by Robert Palmer, Whitney Houston, and Phil Collins, then quotes notorious Wisconsin cannibal-killer Ed Gein to his friends. Whenever uncomfortable, Bateman wields his exit line, "I've got to return some videos." Among the film's canniest moments are the showdowns between its perfectly coiffed suit-and-tie Wall Street merger-and-acquisitions professionals, challenging each other with their business cards like gunfighters in a Sergio Leone spaghetti western. As each card is presented, the sound-track hisses like a provoked lizard, and the veins start to bulge. The alpha-male's trump card not only wins, it provokes another bloodbath.

Such black comedy was essential to *American Psycho*'s precursors, from Charlie Chaplin's caustic *Monsieur Verdoux* (1947, echoing countless Bluebeard kill-ers while foreshadowing Bateman's lady-killer appeal and appetite) to stylish obscurities like Mario Bava's *A Hatchet for the Honeymoon* (1969, from which *American Psycho* lifts its mad protagonist's opening mono-logue). Like Chaplin's Parisian bank cashier profiteering from the dispatch of wealthy widows and *Hatchet*'s dis-turbed bridal-apparel designer (Stephen Forsyth) com-pelled to butcher his models, Patrick Bateman (the name an overt reference to Psycho's Norman Bates) is a "babe magnet," effortlessly luring potential victims into his coils. Bateman is also a cold, beautiful, steel-eyed monster whose impossibly handsome features hide one of the screen's most dangerously alluring sociopaths. In the opening moments, Bateman peels a facial cosmetics mask off like a snake's skin as he announces his utter lack of human empathy or identity: "I simply am not there."

In short order, we come to understand that in his own mind, all that sets Bateman apart from the Wall Street wolves he runs with is his capacity to act upon his basest impulses. For instance, when Bateman kills the peers who trumps his own business card; it is one of the few contextually 'motivated' killings, heeding the territorial imperative to maintain his rank in the wolf pack by eliminating a competing alpha-wolf. Though Harron necessarily downplays the graphic extremes of Ellis' novel (which would have never been permitted to reach the screen if filmed verbatim from the text), the progression of Bateman's crimes is clear. Most of his victims (and potential victims) are women, pale, wan, and unable to stand up to Bateman's feeding frenzies. These escalate from an offscreen encounter that leaves Bateman shrieking the morning after at the Chinese laundry proprietors who refuse to clean his bloodied bedclothes, to two successive evening sessions with a wary streetwalker (Cara Seymour) and selected female companions that culminate in the film's most excruciatingly horrific sequence. (Though the unrated version may suggest bloodshed closer to the novel, the only difference between the 'R'-rated and unrated versions is about 40 non-explicit seconds of sexual activity during the first encounter in Bateman's apartment.)

Among the novel's cruel jests to which the film clings and expands upon is the inability of Bateman and his cronies to tell each other apart: in the first scene, none of them can identify a business associate sitting across from them in a posh Manhattan restaurant. Bateman and his associates share the same obsessive narcissism and interchangeable uniforms of affluence: the suits, glasses, and haircuts. They revel in the same casual misogyny, racism, anti-semitism, homophobia, misanthropy, and hedonistic appetite for impersonal sex and readily available drugs, wallow in the excesses of privilege and wealth. This homogeneous confusion is the key to Bateman's ability to hide his secret life — and his undoing. It's also central to Mary Harron's adaptation (co-scripted with Guinevere Turner). Sans his rage and the murders, Bateman feels no distinction from those of whom he is so openly contemptuous and covetous. This is the black heart of the film, essential to unraveling its disorienting final act.

Just as Harron's marvelous first feature *I Shot Andy Warhol* detailed the depleted male culture that spurned and enraged outsider Valerie Solanas (Lili Taylor), *American Psycho* lovingly constructs Bateman's environment. Though no glib explanation is offered for his violent behavior, the suffocating vacuum he swims within provides a fertile context for his carnal crimes. Harron neither condones nor excuses Bateman's atrocities; she contextualizes them, just as she did Solanas' madness in *I Shot Andy Warhol*. Indeed, Solanas' desperation, vicious anti-male rhetoric, and explosive expression of that rage (her attempted assassination of Warhol) is perfectly mirrored by Bateman's affluence, misogynist compulsions, and homicidal expression of his rage; the films are perfect companion pieces. Solanas and Bateman are polar opposites adrift in their respective "scenes" in materialistic 1980s Manhattan, equally covetous of what they cannot have or take, equally lost and self-loathing, and ultimately as lethal. In place of Warhol's junkie daze and parasitic entourage, Harron ruthlessly exposes the seething corruption of *American Psycho*'s chameleon yuppies and the frail females in their orbit. She devotes considerable screen time to the women spared Bateman's frenzies: his fiancee (Reese Witherspoon) is a vacuous society climber, his mistress (Samantha Mathis) a dazed pharmaceutical junkie engaged to a gay man, his secretary (Cloe Sevigny) a naive waif blind and deaf to the true nature of her employers. They are as birdlike as the males are reptilian.

I am not arguing that the graphic extremes *Titus* and *American Psycho* revel in are essential to any or all intelligent narrative dissections of patriarchal values and their destructive potential. Quite the opposite can be true, as evidenced by another new video release, **THE LATHE OF HEAVEN** (1980). Essentially pacifistic in nature, **Lathe of Heaven** eschews any overt physical violence: the violence committed here is once again one of male hubris leveled against our identities, our freedom to choose and determine our shared future -- perpetrated by a ruthless patriarch assuming he has the right (once the power is within his reach) to shape our destinies according to his master plan. Yes, *The Lathe of Heaven* was directed by two men — David Loxton and Fred Barzyk — but this insightful science fiction parable was lovingly adapted (by Diane English and Roger E. Swaybill) from Ursula Le Guin's 1971 novel. Thus, *Lathe of Heaven*, too, raises a distinctively female voice; Le Guin remains one of our most remarkable women novelists, making her mark with deservedly award-winning masterpieces like the challenging gender-bender parable *The Left Hand of Darkness* (1969), the utopian *The Dispossessed* (1974), the marvelous *Earthsea* books (1968-90), and many others. Her voice rings loud and clear in the film adaptation of *The Lathe of Heaven*, which remains remarkably true to its source text.

Le Guin's story posits a bleak, polluted future in which a dreamer named George Orr (Bruce Davison) is capable of altering our shared universe through his dreams: upon awakening, Orr finds the world has been irrevocably altered, with he alone cognizant of the transformation while harboring a memory of the reality that once existed. Desperate for help, Orr submits to the care of psychiatrist Dr. William Haber (Kevin Conway), who comes to consider Orr's uncanny ability a tool — Haber's tool for reshaping the shared future of the planet. After a single dream reestablishes Haber with his own research facility and considerable base of power, Haber tackles greater concerns with obsessive fervor: pollution, disease, racism, hunger are "solved" through Haber's manipulation of Orr's dreams — but always at an unexpected price that courts greater global disaster. As Haber's patriarchal, paternalistic determination to play God has increasingly devastating results, Orr rebels until the final confrontation between dreamer and dream-shaper takes its toll.

Le Guin's tale is a potent one, and *Lathe of Heaven* remains a powerful and imaginative science fiction film despite the relative paucity of its means. Originally produced by PBS parent station WNET-13 of New York for less than $800,000 and broadcast in January 1980, *Lathe of Heaven* became a "lost film" after its final PBS showing in 1983; the rights to the Beatles song *"All You*

Need is Love" (essential to Orr's awakening process in the latter part of the narrative) apparently kept the film in the vaults until just recently. Thankfully, the recent June 3, 2000 rebroadcast and last week's video release of *Lathe of Heaven* rescue this modest but memorable gem from oblivion (despite PBS' publicity, note that *Lathe of Heaven* was *not* PBS' first made-for-TV movie: that honor belongs to a truly "lost film," a prior slice of science fiction heaven entitled *Between Time and Timbuktu; or, Prometheus-5*, broadcast March 13, 1972, an adaptation of Kurt Vonnegut's works also produced by Loxton and Barzyk for WNET-13). While one is tempted to summarize the film as "be careful what you dream or wish for" (as in W.W. Jacobs' venerable short story *"The Monkey's Paw"*), such simplistic morals fail to embrace the lucid dissection of power and its abuses central to the film and Le Guin's novel. The key lies in its title, derived from a Taoist quote from Chuang Tse: "Those who heaven helps, we call the sons of heaven... They do not reason by using reason. To let understanding stop at what cannot be understood is a high attainment. Those who cannot do it will be destroyed on the lathe of heaven." These words are spoken in the film (during Orr's dream encounter with one of the turtle-like alien visitors), and bear careful scrutiny.

Thus, *The Lathe of Heaven* is as much about the clash of Eastern and Western philosophies as it is about creation vs. destruction, the futile imposition of conscious will upon the wellspring of the unconsciousness, or patriarchal attempts to control cultural realities. We would do well, as a people, to heed such lessons. In one of her illuminating, impeccably reasoned discussions in *The Language of the Night: Essays on Fantasy and Science Fiction* (1979), Le Guin persuasively argued that self-censorship was the most destructive form of censorship; that which we do not create due to fear of external censorship, censure, or lack of a lucrative marketplace may be of vital importance. In an era when fear of school violence prompts swift silencing of students who may express their feelings through writing, music, or speech deemed suspect, we must weigh at what price such control is exercised. Likewise, in an era defined by "politically correct" repression of free expression and unreasoned, knee-jerk rhetoric against ill-defined "sex and violence" in our media, we should be careful not to toss the baby out with the bath water.

The Lathe of Heaven is a relatively non-threatening and easily defended work; it has, thankfully, survived the market forces that kept it buried and might have consigned it to oblivion. Far more volatile fare like *Titus* and *American Psycho* are easier to attack or dismiss and harder to defend; they are also, given the perverse irony of our culture, far more marketable commodities because of their violence, and thus appealing to wider audiences in a way pacifist science fiction like *The Lathe of Heaven* never will be. *Titus* and *American Psycho* are flawed films, but they are also undeniably bracing, potent works, among the year's most daring achievements. Their dramatic power is inherently linked to the fresh female perspectives their directors bring to their chosen male subjects and source materials: indeed, given the harsh (and justifiable) charges of misogyny leveled at the source novel, it is doubtful *American Psycho* could have been filmed at all had a female director not been at the helm. Viewed on their own terms *and* within the context of the broader cultural debates concerning gender issues as well as "sex and violence" in the media, they showcase vital voices and visions which deserve careful scrutiny... and which must *not* be silenced, how-ever disturbing they may prove to be.

*(*Titus *is rated "R" for extreme violence, gore, partial nudity, adult and sexual content;* American Psycho *is available in "R" and "Unrated" versions for extreme violence, gore, nudity, harsh language, casual alcohol and drug abuse, adult and sexual content.* The Lathe of Heaven, *having been produced for television, is unrated by the MPAA, but it is suitable for all ages — younger viewers may have difficulty following the adult storyline, and some parents may object to the fleeting nudity.)*

September 21:

Word-of-mouth on **MISSION TO MARS** (2000) was so bad that I skipped the spring theatrical release of this wanna-be epic, the latest from director Brian De Palma (*Carrie, Dressed to Kill, Scarface, The Untouchables, Casualties of War*, etc.). I should have known better. Word of mouth on the video release lets me know that I'm definitely in the minority here, but silly me, I quite like the film. Its script is overly derivative, yes, opening with *Apollo 13* swipes and closing with — well, you'll see. But I found the film itself nevertheless engaging and often quite beautiful, an uncharacteristically sweet en-tertainment from the usually caustic De Palma. I reckon I was just in the right frame of mind for it, and let the ten-year-old in me go for the ride; I was a child of late 1950s and early 1960s science fiction and real-life space travel, and *Mission to Mars* plugged right into those longings.

Twenty years from now, a NASA rescue mission (manned by Gary Sinise, Tim Robbins, Connie Nielsen, and Jerry O'Connell) rockets to Mars to recover the stranded sole survivor (Don Cheadle) of a previous expedition, decimated by contact with a mysterious alien artifact. Sound familiar? Well, it is, with setpieces and narrative concepts lifted from *Quatermass and the Pit* (1967, US title: *Five Million Years to Earth*), *2001: A Space Odyssey* (1968), *Close Encounters of the Third Kind* (1977), *The Abyss* (1989), *Contact* (1998), and others. That was a problem for many critics and viewers, who also found the vintage 1950s dialogue unpalatable.

But *Mission to Mars* is also a pleasant, eye-popping science fiction diversion, an old-fashioned anachronism equally evocative of the 1950s "gee whiz" gadgetry and interstellar exoticism of artist Chesley Bonestell, producer George Pal's pioneer space operas (*Destination Moon*, 1950; *When Worlds Collide*, 1951; *The Conquest of Space*, 1955), and gems like *Robinson Crusoe on Mars* (1964). Most importantly, the film rekindles the sense of wonder fueling those chestnuts, which is what makes the film such a pleasure to watch. Reflecting the humanist science fiction of Pal and Gene Roddenberry (*Star Trek*), *Mission* likewise champions interpersonal relations, commitment, loyalty, and ingenuity; it's also suitable for all ages, a relative rarity in the hyper-violent post-*Alien* and *Terminator* cinematic science fiction universe.

Director De Palma orchestrates the melange of hardware and borrowed narrative debris quite nicely, opening with his trademark sustained single take to establish character relationships and maintaining smooth, graceful visuals and storytelling throughout. As in De Palma's *Mission: Impossible* (1996, which I loathed), the extended suspense sequence at the film's midway point is its strongest asset, beginning with the startling impact of a pin-point meteor strike and concluding with a harrowing act of self-sacrifice.

The DVD is particularly recommended as an ideal showcase for the film's visual and aural feast, enhanced by interactive DVD-Rom features, the documentary *Visions of Mars*, and additional extras offering behind-the-scenes insights, production and CGI-effects secrets, and more. *Mission to Mars* is nothing exceptional (the low-budget *Lathe of Heaven* is a far superior and decidedly more original science fiction feature) but I enjoyed it. Keep high expectations in check and take the film on its own terms and I suspect you will, too. *(Mission to Mars is rated "PG" for a few moments of violence, all involving flying space or Martian debris; there is no interpersonal violence on view.)*

Recent & Recommended:

THE 1,000 EYES OF DR. MABUSE (*DIE 1000 AUGEN DES DR. MABUSE*, 1960) is "Restored and Recommended," a vintage slice of Cold War paranoia that was almost a "lost film" before this crisp Kino restoration rescued it from oblivion. *The 1,000 Eyes of Dr. Mabuse* was the final film from renowned German director Fritz Lang (*Metropolis*, 1925; *"M"*, 1930; *Fury*, 1936; *You Only Live Once*, 1937; *The Big Heat*, 1953; *While the City Sleeps*, 1956; etc.), who was at the time at the end of his rope. By the late 1950s, Lang was reviled in his unforgiving homeland for fleeing the Third Reich's rise to power to lend his talents to Hollywood, and despised in Hollywood for his ongoing feuds with producers. Unable to secure financing for any of his own projects, Lang reluctantly accepted the invitation to return to Germany and resurrect the once-popular super-criminal Dr. Mabuse.

Emerging from the distinctive European pantheon of master criminals like Moriarty, Fantomas, and Judex, the original Dr. Mabuse was an almost super-human villain, capable of controlling the will of his minions and victims with preternatural hypnotic and psychic abilities while blurring his identity amid a disorienting array of assumed personas (an archetype that still holds our fascination, as embodied by Magneto in the contemporary X-Men comics and summer hit film). Lang charted Mabuse's crimes in a dazzling arc of masterpieces beginning with the silent, two-part *Dr. Mabuse the Gambler* (1922) and culminating in Mabuse's demise in an asylum in *The Testament of Dr. Mabuse* (1933). Indeed, the latter's anticipation and pointed attack on the emerging Fascist regime prompted Lang's flight from Germany.

Hitler's shadow also darkens *The 1,000 Eyes of Dr. Mabuse*, set in Berlin's fictional Luxor Hotel that once provided wartime Nazi intelligence with room-by-room access to its guests' secrets via secret microphones and audio surveillance. Here, a contemporary Mabuse acolyte adopts the deceased doctor's evil ways, customizing the Luxor with cutting-edge television surveillance systems to monitor every corner of the vast hotel, masterminding an international web of terrorism via murder, blackmail, and espionage.

The film opens with a jarring assassination of a TV reporter in downtown Berlin traffic, setting the stage for an unwary American financial tycoon (Peter Van Eyck, bringing little more than cool authority to his key role) to be drawn into the faux-Mabuse's web when he rescues a suicidal woman (Dawn Addams). Hot on his heels is the

206

persistent Inspector Krab (Gert Frobe), whose suspicions about the strange happenings at the Luxor soon make him a target as well. There's also a blind psychic, a cold-blooded hitman, a boisterous insurance salesman who is not what he seems, and much, much more... and then, of course, there is the mysterious mastermind who claims to be Mabuse.

What is most striking about *The 1,000 Eyes of Dr. Mabuse* when seen today is its utterly contemporary pacing and its pivotal transitional role in international cinema. With his final film, Lang established the template for the entire 1960s spy genre (particularly the James Bond series and spinoffs like television's *The Man from U.N.C.L.E.*) and anticipated the all-too-real role high-tech terrorism would play in the world arena. Gert Frobe went on to star as one of Bond's most dangerous foes, *Goldfinger* (1964), ample evidence of the Bond franchise's familiarity with Lang's swan song. Here are all the cinematic shorthand devices subsequent Bond films, pastiches, and parodies (from *Get Smart* to *Inspector Gadget*) quickly reduced to clichés — the off-screen villain glimpsed only as a hand twisting knobs beneath ominous surveillance screens or a deformed limb marking his identity; the villains's voyeuristic and almost omniscient ability to see and hear everything; secret panels and doors hiding covert high-tech basement operations; lethal gadgets like the steel needle gun wielded by Mabuse's slab-faced assassin (Howard Vernon, who soon made history as the titular villain of Jess Franco's *The Awful Dr. Orloff*, 1962). Thus, Lang adopted and reinvigorated venerable elements of the serials to fit the darker Cold War ethos. In 1960, these were fresh devices, sparking Mabuse's boxoffice success throughout Europe (though not, alas, in the US). Don't laugh when you see them here — this was the wellspring from which it all flowed, marking Lang as a visionary filmmaker still capable of transforming cinema with his final low-budget effort.

Kino's restoration effort is worthy of celebration, presenting for the first time the film's original German-language version subtitled in English. This is necessary viewing for any true film-lover, and those Bond fans adventurous enough to check out 007's real roots might be surprised how entertaining this lively potboiler remains today. Recommended! *(Produced long before the MPAA Ratings system was initiated, this film is unrated; though it features one moment of vintage 1960s eroticism which seems tame today, this film is suitable for all ages.)*

September 28:

If anyone can make alcohol and drug addiction and cold-turkey rehab look good, Sandra Bullock can. The problem is, addiction and rehab *shouldn't* look good... and that, in a nutshell, is the problem with *28 DAYS* (2000).

Gwen (Bullock) hits her drunken dead-end when she and boyfriend Jasper (Dominic West) trash the wedding of her sister Lilly (Elizabeth Perkins), culminating in Gwen's theft and destruction of the marriage limo. Off she goes to rehab, and the film chronicles the clumsy ordeal and tedium of the titular 28 days in the clinic. But it insistently downplays the drama of the situation in order to accommodate the entertainment requirements of a Hollywood star "vehicle."

Gwen's counselor is played by Steve Buscemi, who is himself "a drug addict, alcoholic, compulsive gambler-slash-liar" (having presumably checked himself into rehab after trashing the wedding in Adam Sandler's *The Wedding Singer*). Buscemi is fine in the role, but he's incapable of elevating the material with so little screen-time amid such false high spirits. Gwen's fellow rehab peers (Diane Ladd, Marianne Jean-Baptiste, Reni Santoni, etc.) are stereotypes; her roommate Andrea (Azura Skye) is preordained for tragedy; and eccentrics like Gerhardt (Alan Tudyk) are caricatures played for laughs, providing comic relief whenever the substance of the film threatens to get in the way of a good time.

Time and time again, Susannah Grant's script and Betty Thomas' direction flinch from its edge: Gwen's wake-up arrives when she takes a dangerous plunge during her escape attempt, but she's rescued by the arrival of baseball-star-hunk-in-recovery Eddie Boone (Viggo Mortensen). Gwen's memories of her childhood with alcoholic mom unreel with TV-movie timing, but are never jarring or intrusive. Her plight is increasingly played for cozy inspiration and sitcom situations, laughs, and bathos which trivializes the subject. However dated or pat its ending may seem today, *The Lost Weekend* (1945) portrayed much of what *28 Days* pretends to, and did so with far more honesty and power; there isn't a second in *28 Days* that approaches the impact of Ray Milland's performance, much less his genuinely terrifying delirium nightmare (the hole in the wall, the mouse, the bat, the terrible stream of blood).

In its shallow determination to preach while keeping Bullock's charm at center stage, *28 Days* betrays its aspirations. Some may consider this entertaining, but others (like myself) find it insulting. The recent *Jesus' Son* (2000) offers a far more vivid, honest, chaotic, and challenging portrait of addiction and redemption — but then again, it isn't as safe, cozy, or "funny" as the populist *28 Days*. Which is, my friends, exactly the point. *(Rated "PG-13" for depictions of alcohol and drug abuse, strong language, nudity, adult and sexual situations, and some violence.)*

FINAL DESTINATION (2000) proffers a fresh spin on a venerable horror archetype, whipping up a lively rollercoaster ride for willing viewers. While boarding an international flight on a class trip to Paris, Alex (Devon Sawa of *Idle Hands* and *Around the Fire*, giving his best performance to date) has a terrifying premonition of disaster and flips out. In the ensuing melee, he and six others are forced to leave the plane, which departs without them. While arguing in the lobby, they watch in horror as the aircraft explodes moments after liftoff. But Death will not be cheated — one by one, Alex's surviving classmates and French teacher succumb to the Reaper's fatal touch. Increasingly alienated and distressed by his frightening premonitions, Alex struggles to cheat Death anew by determining the pattern of events leading to each grisly demise. Can he save their lives again, or are they merely postponing the inevitable?

Like the recent *Disturbing Behavior* (1998), *Final Destination* boasts behind-the-camera credentials from *The X-Files* and lives up to their promise. The producer/co-writer/director team of James Wong and Glen Morgan were responsible for some of *The X-Files* finest episodes (including *"Home,"* my personal favorite of the series' horror one-shot stories), and they squeeze some real chills, jolts, and surprisingly strong characterizations from a plot that could have been just another teen body-count fest. As in *"Home,"* Wong and Morgan spike the concoction with some satiric barbs: in *"Home,"* a beloved Johnny Mathis standard foreshadowed the gruesome mayhem, just as John Denver's feel-good tunes cue the horrific setpieces here. *Final Destination* is great fun, but it falls short of being a great horror film — it's too mechanical a thrill-ride to really explore its theme, skirting depth to rush to the next shock (most of which work marvelously on first viewing, though one extended horror sequence stretches its atrocities to laughably Rube Goldberg-like extremes). Nevertheless, this is the best mainstream horror outing the video season has offered thus far, and well worth an evening rental. *(Rated "R" for violence, gore, strong language, and mature themes. This is NOT suitable for younger viewers.)*

September 28: [55]

As tag-team wrestling matches prove time and time again, one finds friends in the oddest corners of the ring. As head writer and supervising producer of *Saturday Night Live* and co-screenwriter of Eddie Murphy star vehicles *Coming to America, Boomerang*, and both *Nutty Professor* movies, Barry Blaustein seems an unlikely candidate for making the ultimate wrestling exposé feature, but there ya go: Barry's the man. While keeping his seat on the Eddie Murphy career express train, Blaustein spent five years bringing **BEYOND THE MAT** (1999) to the big (and now not-so-big) screen — two years preparing, and three years filming, yielding over 50 hours of footage.

---

[55] This review was published, in truncated form, as part of the September 28 *Reformer Video Views* column. But it was published in this, its complete form, in the January, 2001 issue of *Rampage* magazine, under the pseudoname "Sweaty Steve the Bee."

Out of all that, Blaustein has sculpted a lively, insightful 108-minute (unrated version, natch) behind-the-scenes portrait of our favorite spectacle sport, and a sometimes scathing peek behind the curtain of the billion-dollar WWF empire currently ruled by Vince McMahon. En route, Blaustein also captured (and played a key role in) a crucial shift in madman Mick Foley's fifteen-year wrestling career, all which makes *Beyond the Mat* a must-see video and DVD event for fans of the sport.

Blaustein wears his love for wrestling on his sleeve. He's in awe of the stars and loves the flamboyant theatrics — the ballyhoo, the costumes, the music, the spectacle — of the matches. The film opens with his childhood memories of watching TV matches and his first live match, and the revelation that the wrestlers had lives outside of the ring. "This guy has a family," Blaustein realized, wondering "what kind of father does *this* for a living? Who are these guys?" (A sardonic clip from Woody Allen's *Hannah and Her Sisters*, 1996, finds Max Von Sydow concluding this opener with the quip, "Can you imagine the level of a mind that watches wrestling?" Well, yes we can, Max.) Blaustein's genuine affection for the wrestlers carries the day, as does his curiosity about what makes one of today's top American entertainment and licensing businesses tick. *Beyond the Mat* delivers the goods in spades.

"We're in the business of creating monsters," Vince McMahon tells us early on, and Blaustein offers tantalizing glimpses of the process: football superstar Darrin Drozdov's job interview demonstrating the projectile-vomiting skills that earned him the moniker "Puke"; the key debut pay-per-view *Extreme Championship Wrestling* match, with a glimpse of ECW founder and executive producer Paul Heyman's modest NY suburb operation; a trial pro opening match for California's All-Pro Wrestling Camp's amateurs Mike Modest and Tony Jones. The flip side of the success stories we all know are quickly proffered: interviews with disgruntled WWF vets like Justin Incredible, Al Snow, Afa the Wild Samoan, and the eccentric Coco B. Ware offer a sobering view of the business of the mat, and the canny observation "There's no money in wrestling on the independent level" echoes through much of the rest of the film. Small wonder the powers that be — the WWF, the WCW — guard their assets with such ferocity, and aspiring up-and-coming tribes like Heyman and his ECW up the ante so brutally to compete, offering venues for young turks and old-timers alike.

Texan wrestling vet Terry Funk shows us the ropes, still cooking well into his fifties and in the autumn years of over three decades in the ring. Beloved by fans, fellow professionals, and director Blaustein, Funk's association with the project opened doors; we should all be thankful. Through Terry, our eyes are opened to the realities behind the sport: his deep love for the profession; the living it has provided for this pious, loving man and his family; and their profound concern for his deteriorating health after years of escalating physical abuse.

The DVD offers even more Funk, via a full-length commentary track in which Blaustein interviews Funk. It's well worth an additional viewing of the film as Funk discusses his own formative years as a viewer and participant; Vince McMahon's and the WWF's business practices; the wrestlers' obligations to the owners, promoters, and TV sponsors, and the creation of "storylines" for the matches; his role in, and the necessity of, ECW's mayhem ("initiator of the really, truly high-risk maneuvers... because ECW had to be different... we had to go beyond"); and harrowing observations about being stabbed by a fan in Corpus Christi, the death of Owen Hart, and its impact on Owen's brother Brett. At one point, Terry associates the unthinking exposure of his own children to the brutality of his profession with emotional child abuse; clearly, *Beyond the Mat* prompted Funk to reassess his own relations with his family, retiring (again) from the ring in June 1999. In the film itself, a doctor's matter-of-fact assessment of Funk's knee damage and the faces of his wife and (now adult) daughters as they watch Terry dishing out and suffering punishing ECW extremes only set the stage for *Beyond the Mat*'s revelations about Funk's beloved friend and frequent ringside adversary Mick Foley.

En route, Blaustein's offers a painful portrait of Jake "The Snake" Roberts, offering frank discussion and glimpses of the man's "demons." Sired by the rape of his 13-year-old mother by his pro wrestler father Grizzly Smith (who says to the camera "He was born out of love and I still love him"), scarred by family traumas (the kidnapping and murder of his sister, the accidental electrocution of his stepfather), his marriage totaled by his sex-life on the road, Roberts embodies the toll the profession can take on those who participate. Caught in the vortex of drug and crack addiction amid his career slide, Roberts' painful reunion with his adult daughter is heartbreaking. "Sometimes I realize the person that I hate most in this life is the person I'm looking at in the mirror," Jake somberly explains; still, Blaustein captures Jake's electric presence in the ring, and the respect his peers still hold for him.

Foley — aka Mankind, Cactus Jack, and Dude Love — becomes the clear focus of the film's latter half, culminating in the events surrounding the notorious WWF Anaheim, California Royal Rumble "I Quit" match between Mankind and The Rock. The film dramatically establishes Foley's infamous taste for punishment with a few teasing clips from Funk and Foley's bloody barbwire match in Japan (now available on video in its entirety: see *Gladiators of the New Frontier: TMW King of the Death Match* on video and DVD from Ground Zero Entertainment in censored and uncensored editions, streeting on October 3). "I can absorb more than most people," Foley candidly explains, "and that makes me more marketable" — the secret to his longevity and popularity. He also aspires to "be referred to as the world's most polite wrestler," and it's Foley's genuine good heart, devotion to family and friends, and belief in the shared good will of others (even amid the brutality of the ring) that is his undoing, as the climax of *Beyond the Mat* demonstrates.

Foley brainstormed the match, attracted by the drama his loss would rouse and eager to help his friend The Rock in his climb to the top — but was clearly unprepared for the savagery of the event itself, in which The Rock handcuffed Foley before bashing his skull with a metal chair almost a dozen times. Worse yet, Foley had arranged for his wife Collette and their two young children Dewey and Noel to attend; Blaustein's cameras capture the trauma of the event, which prompted them to flee the stadium before it was over (the complete "I Quit" match can be seen on *WWF Royal Rumble: No Chance in Hell*, 1999); it was a horrifying match then, and after watching *Beyond the Mat*, it's even more horrific.

Its impact on Foley is revealed in a scene that recalls the sobering sequence in the rock documentary

Gimme Shelter (1970) as a different Mick (Jagger) and the Stones watch the footage of the murder of a fan during their notorious 1969 Altamont, California concert. Foley is stunned by the impact of the match on his family: "I don't feel like such a good dad any more," he mutters. Both Terry Funk and director Blaustein's separate commentary tracks note the devastating impact the match had on Foley, citing in particular his horror at his children witnessing the carnage, and his disappointment and anger with the Rock, who didn't even bother to check on Foley after the event. [56] In addition, the *Beyond the Mat* DVD offers two extras with Foley's commentary, "On My Life in Wrestling" (almost 9 minutes in length; during the clips from his barb-wire Japanese match with Funk, Foley says, "I'm not a masochist — well, I just landed on a bomb") and a remarkable assessment of "The Royal Rumble" sequence (clocking in at 20 minutes, 27 seconds). Foley details the game plan between he and the Rock ("five chair shots — and things kind of got carried away... This was my dream, this was my big genius plan") and its irrevocable impact ("I watched this, and then my whole life fell apart"). Foley is polite to a fault about Rock's disregard for the pain he inflicted, but he candidly notes there seems "no real concern in his eyes" and ultimately comes across like a spurned lover: "I'd probably given my body to somebody who didn't deserve or appreciate it." Shortly after seeing the footage of his family watching the match, Foley retired from wrestling.

Beyond the Mat embodies the confrontational 'tough love' of a die-hard wrestling fan taking an expan-

---

[56] Personal note: to this day, because of this, I find it hard to watch *any* film featuring Dwayne Johnson *aka* The Rock.

sive, unblinkered look at the object(s) of his affection, encompassing the heights and aspirations alongside the depths and depravations — the human toll — associated with the sport. Its case histories and harsh lessons apply to all entertainment endeavors based on human exploitation, all the more dramatic for the self-evident (and usually self-inflicted) scars in full view. Those with weak stomachs should steer clear — but this is essential viewing for wrestling fans. I also recommend it to those who could care less about the sport. This is potent filmmaking that stands among the best documentaries of the year. *(Available in both "R" and a slightly longer "Unrated" edition, featuring grueling interpersonal violence, gore, drug abuse, and strong language.)*

October 5:

There's some dumb fun to be had in **THE SKULLS** (2000) — *if* you can swallow the supposed "secrecy" of a covert Ivy League campus men's club that slaps an outsized chrome skull logo on the roof of its supposedly "secret" gothic headquarters like a comicbook society of super villains. Each of the Skulls also carry an outsized "secret" key to their subterranean cult chambers and tote around a "secret" rule book emblazoned with the same gold-foil skull logo and (get this) the *name* of the book's proprietor stamped on to its leather-bound cover. Oh, ya, and even though we're to believe the adult contingent of the Skulls hold elite positions among the country's top-drawer political, medical, and legal professions, the damned fools botch a simple murder-disguised-as-suicide scene central to the film's by-the-numbers narrative. The inevitable car-chase-through-public-roads further ensures the (ahem) "secrecy" of their coven's increasingly homicidal activities. What absolute hogwash. If this is the kind of boy's club shenanigans that reportedly elevates the privileged youth of our nation to Presidential elections, we're in deeper trouble than we know.[57]

Rest assured that *The Skulls* hardly sustains any political agenda, struggling as it does to rub frayed narrative sticks together long enough to spark a reasonable plot. The cosmetically attractive cast is initially engaging, led by likable Joshua Jackson (*Dawson's Creek*) as townie-elevated-to-Skull-status hero Luke McNamara (the name redolent with Vietnam-era echoes), busy Hollywood jock-of-choice Paul Walker (*Varsity Blues, Pleasantville, She's All That*, etc.) as silver-spoon-preppie Caleb Mandrake. Leslie Bibb is Luke's sort-of girlfriend Chloe, serving to remind us that all the all-male antics are, after all, hetero in nature (see final review, below). Luke's pragmatic worries about shouldering the cost of law school without subjugating his ideals to a life-time of debt are utterly believable, as is the desire to "belong" and the seductive Faustian pull of membership in the Skulls (which pays all of its members' tuitions while providing a well-heeled expense fund and a kick-ass set of wheels).

Despite the ominous uber-frat horrors implied, the hazing is a tame affair (especially compared to the real-life, sometimes lethal hazing excesses that plague far less affluent real-life campuses), even after we meet the Skull patriarchy, led by Caleb's corrupt judge father (Craig T. Nelson) and the judge's corrupt senator adversary (William Peterson). Their paternal power struggle

---

[57] As the November 2000 election and subsequent eight years were about to prove, truer words I've never written.

soon draws blood and plays Luke and Caleb for pawns when Luke's journalist roommate (Hill Harper) is found dangling from a rope under suspicious circumstances. Unfortunately, the tangled web of deceit and betrayal trips over its own complications as friction builds under the pressure of the police investigation (led by Steve Harris of TV's *The Practice*) and splitting seams of the Skulls' clumsy cover-up.

Long before the film arrives at its laughable duel-at-ten-paces finale, the cardboard theatrics, thrills, and threadbare characterizations have taken their toll. Director Rob Cohen launched his career with *A Small Circle of Friends* (1980) and scored with *Dragon: The Bruce Lee Story* (1993) before lapsing into high-ticket disappointments like *Daylight* and *Dragonheart* (both 1996). He's turning into another Peter Hyams, who's been crafting slick but empty-headed potboilers for over 25 years now (from *Capricorn One*, 1978, to gory drek like *The Relic* and *End of Days* in the 1990s). In fact, *The Skulls* recalls one of Hyams' livelier confections, the Michael Douglas vehicle *The Star Chamber* (1983), which also sacrificed an initially compelling premise to increasingly insipid mayhem. *The Skulls* is an utterly numb-skulled flick, but it's pulp pacing and shameless stupidity will undoubtably find a receptive audience. *(Rated "PG-13" for violence, strong language, and a fleeting sex scene between Jackson and Bibb.)* Please note: Universal is *not* releasing *The Skulls* on DVD until later this month.

U-571 (2000): In the wake of *Star Wars'* stylish reinvention, subsequent Vietnam-era revisionism, and post-Gulf War delusions, old-fashioned war movies are back in style. Given that, *U-571* is an unpretentious, efficient entry in the genre, eschewing the harrowing claustro-phobic intensity of *Das Boot* (1981) and post-Cold War heat of *Crimson Tide* (1995) to effectively capture the do-or-die melodramatics of classics like *The Enemy Below* (1957) and *Run Silent, Run Deep* (1958). Though only time will tell if *U-571* measures up to their stature, it fulfills its aspirations quite nicely, mounting suspense amid the expected against-all-odds spectacle of men and machines pushed beyond their limits. Troubling as I find the cultural shift toward films glorifying war — a shift hypocritically embraced by the same opportunistic po-litical yahoos currently scoring easy election-year brownie-points by lambasting Hollywood and the mar-keting of "R"-rated fare — it's hard to take as straight-forward an effort as *U-571* on anything but its own terms.

Forget a prior generation's cultural backlash against the military and war: far from the edge of anti-war radi-calism and troubling political questions, *U-571* harbors the post-*Saving Private Ryan* comforts of simply-defined military missions, goals, and ideals. We accept, at face value, the necessity of the rushed U.S. Navy effort to dispatch an American submarine in a race to reach a crippled German U-Boat before the Axis relief vessel arrives on the scene. The German sub carries one of the Third Reich's 'Enigma' de-coder units, which the Allies are eager to secure to break the coded Nazi messages that have kept the Atlantic theater of war firmly in their grip. We also accept the dilemma of Tyler (Matthew McConaughey), denied command of his own vessel until he proves his ability to measure up to the demands of the position. Rest assured that the twists and turns of the mission will test and temper the man.

Under the tutelage of his immediate superior (Bill Paxton, lending sufficient authority to the role) and unswerving devotion of his Chief (Harvey Keitel, who solidly anchors the entire film), Tyler proves his mettle despite the crews' doubts, the insubordination of his most outspoken critics (Erik Palladino, whose sailor would be summarily court-martialled in real life), enemy sabotage, and the necessity of completing their mission in the confines of the crippled German sub. Along with McConaughey, the rest of the young cast (including Jon Bon Jovi, David Keith, and Jack Noseworthy) nicely fill their roles as director/co-scripter Jonathan Mostow helms with admirable professionalism. Mostow lacks the steely intensity of real-WW2 veteran directors like Sam Fuller, but maintains enough of an edge to rivet our attention.

Despite its promotional claims to being "a true story," *U-571* is complete fiction, distilling elements from three actual Allied efforts (two key British missions from May 1941 and October 1942, and a single U.S. mission during June of 1944) into a tightly-crafted dramatization of the ongoing effort to usurp Germany's successful U-Boat control of the Atlantic throughout much of the war. All in all, *U-571* is a solid war drama, and well worth a look. *(Rated "PG-13" for war violence and situations.)* Please note: Universal, in its infinite wisdom, is *not* releasing *U-571* on DVD until later this month.

If you've got a "Take Back Vermont" sign [58] on your front lawn, you'd best steer clear of the deceptively

---

[58] The mention of "Take Back Vermont" signs refers to the 2000 election year's most aggressive campaign slogan, mani-

packaged comedy ***BUT I'M A CHEERLEADER***
(1999). The slow-mo closeups of cheerleader splits
flashing under the credits implies yet another high-
school tale of love lost and found, but the title tune (an
English version of the 1964 French single *"Chick Hab-
its"*) quickly establishes the true perspective of Jamie
Babbit's offbeat movie. As put-upon heroine Megan
(Natasha Lyonne of *Slums of Beverly Hills, Freeway 2*,
etc.) squirms through the sloppy kisses dished out by her
jock boyfriend (Brandt Wille), she's flashing on her fellow cheerleaders' anatomy, lending some validity to her
friends and parents worry over Megan's budding sexual
desires.

In short order, Megan is bundled off to a punitive
rehabilitation camp in the country named True Direc-
tions. Under the stern maternal direction of founder
Mary J. Brown (Cathy Moriarty, sinking her teeth into
her best role in years), Megan's lesbian leanings are only
fanned by the camp's repressive five-step "corrective
gender reorientation" program and her growing attraction to her roommate Graham (Clea DuVall of *The Fac-
ulty* and *Girl, Interrupted*). "Denial is a normal part of
the healing process," Brown assures the gay young
women and men whose conversion to heterosexuality is
her mission, though her own son Rock (Eddie Cibrian)
struts his stuff to the male staff like jailbait.

---

festing the conservative backlash against Vermont's progressive Civil Unions laws, which some conservative and Repub-
lican candidates attacked with homophobic zeal. "Take Back
Vermont" became the most visible signage of the season in
some corners of my native home state, though I'm happy to
say the candidates associated with that campaign were soundly
defeated.

The film's initial sassy tone and impeccable counter-cultural credentials promise more than the film delivers. Bud Cort (Harold of the 1971 cult classic *Harold and Maude*) and Mink Stole (co-star of every single John Waters movie!) are Megan's parents; RuPaul Charles sheds his usual drag attire to play camp counselor Mike (sporting a "Straight is Great" t-shirt and lending one of his tunes, *"Party Train,"* to the soundtrack); Melanie Lynskey, co-star of Peter Jackson's ravishing *Heavenly Creatures* (1994), co-stars as one of Megan's roommates; and Julie Delpy (*Killing Zoe, Before Sunrise*) has a saucy cameo. But the film isn't as subversive as it pretends to be; it abandons the tenor of its opening scenes and falls too 'in love' with its own love story and teen angst to maintain any real satiric edge. As the simmering emotions reach full boil, the comedy grinds to a halt for the earnest love scenes between Megan and Graham. Despite the presence of Mink Stole in the cast, forget the messy anarchism and ridiculous sexuality of John Waters; *But I'm a Cheerleader* is a rather sweet lesbian romantic comedy. There's nothing wrong with that, of course, but the passionate shift in gears away from comedy undermines the cartoony decor and flamboyant performances.

The rehab camp setting of the film is clearly intended *as* "camp." But many revered camp entertainments (the Steve Reeves *Hercules* movies, *Plan 9 From Outer Space*) are blithely unconscious of their subversive nature; it's essential to their charm. The repressed homoeroticism seething in the life-and-death frat horrors of *The Skulls*, *U-571*'s closeups of furtive glances between sweating sailors, or even the latest Abercrombie-Fitch catalog may remain in the "camp" cultural baggage of future generations long after *But I'm a Cheerleader*'s

arch dialogue and schematic visual design are long forgotten (the stark primary colors of the film's art direction and costumes are, of course, pink and blue). For the
immediate time, though, some viewers may find this
cheerfully non-violent love story a welcome balance to
the testosterone raging through the rest of this week's
new releases. *(Rated "R" for language, adult and sexual
situations, nudity.)*

October 12:

IF THESE WALLS COULD TALK 2 (2000) is the
made-for-cable sequel to the popular 1996 production,
composed of three tales. The original compendium feature related a trio of stories (set from the 1950s to present) in which women confronted unwanted pregnancies
and abortion issues; this follow up offers a similar trip-
tych set in the same house to probe the lives of three
generations of lesbian women.

Ever since the silent era, anthology features have
been problematic. Though there are notable exceptions
— from the British *Dead of Night* (1945) to the invigorating *Pulp Fiction* (1994) — anthology films usually
succumb to the variable quality of their respective installments; one bad apple can indeed spoil the viewing
experience, particularly if the rule of saving the best for
last is ignored. Sadly, *If These Walls Could Talk 2* fails
as a feature. Executive producer Ellen DeGeneres and
her former partner Anne Heche (writer-director of the
final episode, *"2000"*) do the film a gross disservice
with the third tale set here and now, in which a lesbian
couple (played by DeGeneres and Sharon Stone) hope to
sire their own child using current procreation technology. They fret and joke and yammer through their con-

cerns, breaking twice to make love; conceived and played with strident sitcom shallowness, it the weakest of the trio, ending the film on a sour note.

Don't let that misstep keep you away: the first story is an extraordinary piece, and the second is a charmer. The latter (set in 1972) charts telling rifts between young feminists and lesbians in the early years of the movement, and the friction intolerance and bigotry caused within gay ranks. As scripted by Sylvia and Alex Sichel and directed by Martha Coolidge (*Valley Girl, Rambling Rose*, etc.), this snapshot of a budding romance between a college activist (Michelle Williams) and motorcycle-riding "butch" townie (Chloe Sevigny) addresses its chosen issues without smothering its characters. Part of the fun here is watching Sevigny (*Kids, Trees Lounge, American Psycho*) playing the butch opposite of her role in *Boys Don't Cry* (1999), an opportunity this exceptional actress clearly savored.

But it's writer-director Jane Anderson's opening tale that merits attention and makes this new release most worthwhile. *"1961"* opens in a small-town movie theater showing the once-scandalous drama *The Children's Hour*. As older audience members leaves in disgust and teenagers jeer at Shirley MacLaine's onscreen confession of her love for Audrey Hepburn, elderly couple Edith (Vanessa Redgrave) and Abby (Marian Seldes) sob and hold hands in the dark, breaking their comforting touch when the jeers of the teens target them. That night, Edith's life is ravaged by Abby's sudden death. In the hospital, she is denied access to her partner because she is not family; days later, Abby's family and due legal process strips home and hearth, all they had built together.

Eschewing the romanticism and overt sex of its companion chapters, *"1961"* succinctly and eloquently confronts the very real human issues which prompted the adoption of Vermont's controversial civil union laws. Given the grace and power of this first story and the importance of the November elections, I heartily recommend this profoundly moving segment be sought out and seen by all Vermonters of voting age. Do what you will with the rest of the film — turn it off, if you must — but don't miss this heartbreaking short, which boasts a stellar performance by Vanessa Redgrave. *(Unrated, as it was made for television; the first episode, "1961," would probably be rated "PG" solely for its adult emotional content; the second and third episodes would be rated "R" for strong language, nudity, lovemaking, adult and sexual situations.)*

Don't pass on ***LOVE & BASKETBALL*** (2000): all in all, this marvelous film is what it says. Writer-director Gina Prince-Bythewood beautifully conveys the lifelong affection between Monica (Sanaa Lathan of *The Best Man, The Wood*, and *Blade*) and Quincy (Omar Epps of *In Too Deep, The Mod Squad*, and *The Wood*), a relationship forged and defined by their own love of basketball. Though the sport shapes their lives, this is hardly your traditional sports drama; it's much, much more than that, and for once, the final game's outcome really matters.

The story unfolds as game quarters: first quarter, eleven-year-old Monica (played by Kyla Pratt) upsets the neighborhood because she's a girl who outplays the boys, attracting and upsetting young Quincy (Glenndon Chatman) who's already groomed for stardom under the wing of his NBA basketball star father Zeke (Dennis

226

Haysbert). Monica and Q's first kiss and first fight are minutes apart, setting the stage for the second quarter, when their shared senior high school stretch finds Q chased by the girls as a local B-ball hero and easing into imminent Ivy League sports scholarships. Monica, however, struggles against her fiery temper, insecurities, and the gender strait-jacket while aching for the attention of college basketball recruiters. As their mutual affection for the game and each other blossoms, they are thrust into the more volatile adult arena of USC during the third quarter, culminating in the revelations of the fourth and final quarter, as Monica's globe-trotting basketball success and Q's personal and professional crisis threaten to forever keep them apart.

Any synopsis fails to convey *Love & Basketball*'s true nature. This is one of the year's best romances, and its marvelous use of the game is perfectly wed to its characters. The relations between son and father, daughter and mother (with Alfre Woodard delivering another fine performance as Monica's mother) are central to the tale, by turns anchoring and fraying the ebb and flow of Monica and Quincy's love for each other and their paths. With its story, people, and emotional landscape delineated in clear, bold strokes, this earnest film is as tough, tender, and tenacious as its protagonists. *Love & Basketball* is a gem, and Gina Prince-Bythewood is a talent to watch; kudos to producers Spike Lee and Sam Kitt for sheparding this modest masterpiece through the studio system without fouling out. Recommended! *(Rated "PG-13" for language, adult and sexual content.)*

Given the subject of **RULES OF ENGAGEMENT** (2000), let's follow strict protocol and cut to the chase.

The title refers to the U.S. military's self-defined parameters of combat on foreign soil; the film probes the validity of those rules in real battle situations. Though it opens with two harrowing action sequences — a flashback to Vietnam, and the contemporary (fictional) conflict at a Middle East U.S. Embassy — *Rules of Engagement* quickly settles into a sober, meditative drama that builds to its decisive "battle" in a military courtroom. Despite the promise of its premise and cast, the film doesn't deliver the heated rush of a contemporary war epic like *Three Kings* (1999), the intensive moral scrutiny of Brian DePalma's *Casualties of War* (1989) or Edward Zwick's *Courage Under Fire* (1996), or the satisfying courtroom theatrics of *The Caine Mutiny* (1954) and Rob Reiner's *A Few Good M*en (1992). This is a different beast altogether, a dissection of loyalty, friendship, and morality literally and figuratively under the gun, where cultural moors forcibly take a back seat to the hard realities of warfare and military law.

Under the command of Colonel Terry Childers (Samuel L. Jackson), the rescue of an American ambassador (Ben Kingsley) and his family from an embassy under siege in Yemen turns into a massacre. Seeking to divert responsibility away from the U.S., National Security Advisor Sokal (Bruce Greenwood, who played the unscrupulous husband of *Double Jeopardy*) targets Childers as the scapegoat in a rush to judgment; to ensure prompt saving of national "face," Sokal withholds crucial evidence from the savvy young Marine prosecutor assigned to the case (Guy Pearce of *L.A. Confidential, Ravenous*, and *Priscilla, Queen of the Desert*). For his defense, Childers turns to a reluctant Colonel Hodges (Tommy Lee Jones) on the eve of his retirement from the military. A mediocre military lawyer who is forced to rise above "the comfortable failure his life has been" (to quote Jones' own description of the role on one of the DVD extras), Hodges fights the clock and government's stacked deck to defend the soldier and friend who saved his life in Vietnam 28 years earlier by executing a prisoner... an incident that will play its role, too, in the court-martial trial and verdict.

Throughout the proceedings, Hodges squirms like a worm on a hook trying to defend the indefensible, while Childers stands firm, a seasoned vet vilified by the citizenry he defended and the non-combat officers and federal officials he despises. *Rules of Engagement* investigates military law on its own terms, and the schism between active warriors and peacetime warriors; as such, it demands to be taken on its own terms, though it remains caught between its aspirations as explorative drama and the commercial requirements of pop melodrama. Seasoned director William Friedkin (*The French Connection, The Exorcist, To Live and Die in L.A., 12 Angry Men*, etc.) helms a formidable veteran creative team, including military advisor Captain Dale Dye (*Platoon, Saving Private Ryan*, etc.), who also essays the role of General Perry. They effectively flesh out Stephen Gaghan's screen adaptation of a story by executive producer James Webb, who was himself a decorated Vietnam war veteran and former Secretary of the Navy under President Reagan (and during the Persian Gulf crisis), but the script is flawed. As melodrama, *Rules* falls short; after the heat of combat, the courtroom drama seems staid, the tension neither as urgent nor sustained as the opening acts, though a life remains at stake. But there's still plenty of meat on the bone: the climactic sparks between Jones, Jackson, and Pearce are riveting, and Friedkin and his collaborators hew to the narrative's core issues and follow them through to their difficult conclusions. Though they skirt the deeper moral concerns the situation evokes, their commitment to the material at the cost of delivering simplistic entertainment characterizes one of Friedkin's own "rules of engagement" — a laudable code that keeps this viewer watching his films through thick and thin. (*Rated "R" for language, war violence, and non-sexual adult content.*)

Note: The October 19, 2000 Brattleboro Reformer A&E *section featured two articles by yours truly,* "First Run Host 'My Mother's Early Lovers' Director," *referring to Vermont filmmaker Nora Jacobson and her debut narrative feature; and* "Skip Morrow: The art of love, life and humor," *about local cartoonist and good friend Skip Morrow. The former has already been reprinted, in revised and expanded form, in* Green Mountain Cinema I *(2004, Black Coat Press), and the latter will appear, also revised and expanded, in a forthcoming book on Vermont cartoonists. Thus, I have decided not to include them in this volume.*

October 26:

HALLOWEEN PIX & PASSES: THE BEST AND WORST HORRORS OF 2000

Sure enough, the hobgoblin season is upon us, and the video store new release wall is ripe with horror movies clamoring for your attention and vying for your rentals. But which of them will make — and which will break — your Halloween weekend fun? Here's a one-stop shopping list for the best and worst of the fall harvest.

TOP TEN TERRORS: Here's my recommendations; sadly, there's few strong independent contenders this year (a stark contrast to last year, when a low-budget wonder entitled *The Blair Witch Project* dominated the scene and sleepers like *Habit* and *The Ugly* brightened the shelves). The new release wall is also graced with an abundance of restored "Special Editions" of *Jaws, Interview With the Vampire, The Rocky Horror Picture Show, From Dusk to Dawn, Rosemary's Baby, Jurassic Park, The Lost World,* and Brian DePalma's *Sisters,* any or all of which are guaranteed to deliver the goods.

I hasten to add that most of the following titles are adult entertainments, *not* suitable for the preteen set (with the notable exception of *The Simpsons* trio, which is great fun for the whole family). In alphabetical order, they are: [59]

(1) ***AMERICAN PSYCHO*** (2000): Director Mary Harron (I Shot Andy Warhol) crafts a sly, savage black comedy from Bret Easton Ellis' notorious and almost unfilmable 1991 novel. Christian Bale lends his impossibly good looks and considerable thespian skills to the lead role, swimming like a shark through the upscale environs of 1980s Upper Manhattan. The only thing that sets him apart in his own mind from the emotional vacuum his peers, associates, fiance, and mistress flounder in is his sadistic appetite for misogynistic sadomasochism and murder. Cruel, chilling, harrowing, and often quite funny; stay with it to the bitter end, whatever you do!

---

[59] I am only footnoting the films reviewed in *Blur, Vol. 1,* since you've already read all the full reviews of those in this volume.

(2) ***THE BEYOND*** (1981): It's been a great year for European horror film fans, with a clutch of video and DVD labels resurrecting many choice treasures from the 1960s, '70s, and '80s in lustrous restored editions. Much as I would love to dwell on these marvels, I've selected the most recent and revelatory of the batch, Lucio Fulci's *The Beyond*, fresh from its 1999 theatrical "midnight movie" success. A remote Louisiana hotel harbors a portal to an unspeakable netherworld, but forget linear storytelling: with nightmarish precision, any and all conventional narrative expectations crumble beneath Fulci's intoxicating torrent of disorienting visions, horrific setpieces, and abundant gore. Not for the squeamish, as blood becomes an almost alchemical cinematic element in Fulci's universe, opening the doorway to a genuinely haunting, dreamlike finale.

(3) ***DEEP BLUE SEA*** (1999): When a tropical storm hits, mutant super-sharks display near-human predatory intelligence seeking freedom and stalking an oceanic research facility that cans its hapless cast like ready-to-eat fish food. Can't hold a torch to the original *Jaws*, but this by-the-numbers action-science fiction-horror hybrid boasts an engaging cast led by Samuel L. Jackson, taut direction by Renny Harlin, and a competent script that harbors a couple of effective surprises. Okay, it's a dumb monster movie, but I had a great time watching it. Some of you might prefer the equally silly-but-fun recent release *Lake Placid* (1999), which plopped a giant croc into a remote Maine lake with similar results; *Lake Placid* is much funnier, thanks to rib-tickling turns from Edward Platt as an eccentric croc-hunter and *Golden Girls* vet Betty White as a foul-

mouthed widow who prefers the reptiles to the trouble-some locals.[60]

(4) *FINAL DESTINATION* (2000): A lively teen-terror roller-coaster ride from *The X-Files* veterans Glen Morgan and James Wong. Freaked by his premonition of a mid-air explosion, Alex (Devon Sawa) gets himself and a handful of classmates tossed off the plane chartered to take them on their Paris class trip; the plane explodes seconds after lift-off. Now a town pariah, Alex struggles to save himself and his surviving classmates as Death incarnate seems intent on reclaiming them all. Though it flirts with compelling issues — contemporary teenage fears of mortality in the face of disaster — this is primarily a thrill-machine, and it delivers its share of shocks and surprises with engaging high spirits. Recommended co-features: Sawa's recent horror-comedy *Idle Hands*, or fellow *X-Files* vet David Nutter's directorial debut *Disturbing Behavior*, an underrated gem of its kind.

(5) *THE HOUSE ON HAUNTED HILL* (1999): Ever since Dino DeLaurentiis' insulting *King Kong* remake (for which Dino actually tried to buy up the rights to the 1933 original in order to *destroy* all prints and negatives!), shameless Hollywood hustlers have peddled substandard remakes while ignoring or insulting their source material. In the wake of Dreamworks' dreadful *The Haunting* travesty, this remake of *House on Haunted Hill* is a valentine for horror aficionados. Director Bill Malone's affectionate remake of William Castle's classic 1958 Vincent Price vehicle stands on its

---

[60] See *Blur, Vol. 1*, pp. 141-142.

own ectoplasmic tendrils as a shuddery revamp that pays its debts before carving out its own turf, led by Academy-Award-winner Geoffrey Rush's fruity spin on the central Price role. The DVD is especially recommended, packed with extras including an ode to 1950s horror mogul William Castle and scene-by-scene comparisons with the original. With its black heart firmly in the right place, this funhouse shocker scores.

(6) *PITCH BLACK* (2000): The long, influential shadow of *Alien* (1979) spreads over this film like a cloak — but unlike other recent *Alien* knock-offs (i.e., *Event Horizon, Supernova*, etc.), *Pitch Black* wears its colors with pride and an engaging grasp of its pulp-science fiction virtues. In a cacophonous opener, a spaceship crashes on a desolate desert planet that simmers beneath four suns; it's a knockabout shambles, but stay with the film, which soon settles into its proper groove. Unfortunately, the survivors have arrived on the eve of the planet's 22-year "daylight" cycle, culminating in an extended period of darkness during which hordes of subterranean, nocturnal creatures swarm and feed on the surface. Creature designer Patrick Tatopoulos (mastermind of the American *Godzilla*) breeds an eye-popping menagerie of wedge-headed monsters; director/co-author David Twohy (*Grand Tour: Disaster in Time* and *The Arrival*) crafts another solid, unpretentious science fiction entertainment; and the cast plays it for all it's worth, led by Vin Diesel's riveting lead as convicted killer Riddick, whose uncanny night-vision becomes crucial to their fight for survival. True to the spirit of 1940 and '50s pulp science fiction, *Pitch Black* economically sets up its premise, introduces its exotic horrors, then plays its narrative cards with straightforward

precision. For my money, this was the best science fiction film of the year.

(7) *THE SIMPSONS: TRICK OR TREEHOUSE, Volumes 1-3*: Trick or treat, indeed! This trilogy of tapes collects many of the best *Simpsons* Halloween shows, which always compacted the best of *The Simpsons* satire into tight, tidy tidbits. In fact, since every Halloween episode crams no less than *three* parodies into their half-hours, this collection has more bang-for-the-buck than any other video on the new release shelves! Includes *"The Shinning"* Stephen King parody and many other gems; great pumpkin-season fun, not to be missed.

(8) *THE SIXTH SENSE* (1999): Even if you've already seen this marvelous ghost film (or number among the few who saw through its climactic narrative twist), *The Sixth Sense* merits another viewing. Along with *The Blair Witch Project*, this atmospheric tale of a child psychologist (Bruce Willis) seeking redemption through his relationship with a traumatized little boy (Harley Joel Osment) who "sees dead people" embraces the "less is more" esthetic which characterized the work of 1940s producer Val Lewton (*The Cat People, I Walked With a Zombie*, etc.): in a refreshing shift from splashy gore and CGI-effects, it's what you *don't* see that chills. *The Sixth Sense* goes further, cumulatively plucking deep emotional chords to arrive at a profound, heart-breaking moment between mother (Toni Collette) and son that will leave you in tears. This is a modern masterpiece from writer-director M. Night Shyamalan, aided by re-

markable performances from Osment, Collette, and Willis.[61]

(9) **SLEEPY HOLLOW** (1999): Tim Burton's annual treat is a ghost tale of another sort altogether, building its homage to the horror films of Burton's youth on the bare bones of the classic Washington Irving short story about the Headless Horseman. Here, Ichabod Crane (Johnny Depp creating another spot-on eccentric) isn't the victimized schoolmaster; he's a timid detective wielding his curious forensic tools in hopes of finding natural causes for genuinely supernatural horrors personified by Christopher Walken's speechless Horseman (played in its "headless" mode by Ray Park, who starred as Darth Maul in *Star Wars: The Phantom Menace*). Most critics (who have little regard for horror films, a genre most of them despise) were quick to praise the lavish visuals, acknowledge Burton's debt to the classic Hammer Films, and bemoan the rest, but *Sleepy Hollow* is a grand entertainment. Yes, Burton consciously sought to recreate the aura of Hammer's glory days, peppering his cast with Hammer vets like Christopher Lee and Michael Gough, but the Roger Corman Edgar Allan Poe films were a wellspring, too, as were period illustrators like Arthur Rackham and Harry Clarke. The imaginative script, deft characterizations, and energetic direction more than live up to the lavish art direction and design. Boasting the most inventive plethora of decapitations in cinema history, *Sleepy Hollow* is an absolute delight. Ideal co-features: Roger Corman's *The Pit and the Pendulum* (1961) starring Vincent Price, and Walt Disney's *"Legend of Sleepy Hollow"* cartoon (available in a num-

---

[61] See *Blur, Vol. 1*, pp. 250-252.

ber of Disney videos, including *Ichabod and Mr. Toad*),
both of which inspired *Sleepy Hollow*.

(10) *A STIR OF ECHOES* (1999): This 'black
sheep' contender unfortunately suffered from the one-
two punch of its contemporaries *The Sixth Sense* and *The
Blair Witch Project*, but *A Stir of Echoes* is an effective
chiller. Working from a forgotten potboiler by genre
master Richard Matheson (*The Incredible Shrinking
Man, Somewhere in Time, I Am Legen*d, etc.), screenwriter-director David Koepp and producer-star Kevin
Bacon craft a convincing portrait of an ordinary blue-
collar suburban father (Bacon) whose reality unravels
when a party parlor-trick goes sour. After being hypno-
tized, Bacon is sensitized to the spirits haunting his
home and neighborhood, and plagued by premonitions
of disaster and death. Despite two unfortunate narrative
detours that were not in Matheson's novel (a black po-
liceman and his own son also see ghosts), this is a solid
chiller true to the tone and temper of Rod Serling's *The
Twilight Zone* — which, by the way, Matheson often
wrote for, creating some of its finest episodes and arguably among its prime architects.[62]

PUMPKIN SCRAPINGS: The pulp you don't need,
bad candy gone worse, a half-dozen rotten apples with
razor blades in 'em:

(1) *ANCIENT EVIL: SCREAM OF THE
MUMMY* (2000): Eye-catching box for a mind-numbing
cowpie of a movie. College nerd (Trent Latta) happens
to be the last in a long line of Aztec High Priests and

---

[62] See *Blur, Vol. 1*, pp. 192-194.

resurrects you-know-what (at one point referred to as "beef-jerky face") in this amateurish Aztec mummy romp from direct-to-video auteur David DeCoteau, who's only made *one* solid movie (*Skeletons*, 1996) in a decade of cheapjack filmmaking. Give me the original Mexican Aztec Mummy movies — they were wretched, but they were a lot more fun than this frat-boy flatulence.

(2) ***BATS*** (1999): Mutant vampire bats sweep into a New Mexican town, threatening to suck the local citizenry dry. The speed with which the opening scenes skip like a flat stone over narrative logic is enticing, but that giddy promise evaporates within the first half-hour. By the time our surviving heroes (Lou Diamond Phillips and Dina Meyer) are literally up to their nipples in bat guano, you realize you've been wading through the same for almost 90 minutes. By the time they're outrunning the titular menace — the way action heroes these days outrun lava, fireballs, explosions, and tsunamis (the lamest, least credible cliche of the past decade) — you realize you've been *eating* guano.[63]

(3) ***BLOODY MURDER*** (1999): Thanks to the success of *Scream*, the late 1990s have been just like the early 1980s all over again. Brrrrr; no wonder Bush is running for office. Camp Placid Pines harbors a hockey-masked killer wracking up yet-another teen body count. Could it be the legendary Trevor Moorehouse (who???), or Nelson Hammond (eh??), or a homicidal impostor, or — ah, who cares. Insipid *Friday the 13th* throwback is a moronic bore that squanders even its basest exploitation potential. Sample conversational snippets between the

---

[63] See *Blur, Vol. 1*, pp. 208-209.

two female leads: "Misery comes in a lot of forms — all miserable." "Do you ever feel cheated?" "Your toes are beautiful!" You've been *warned*...

(4) *THE HAUNTING* (1999): An insult to both the Shirley Jackson novel and the fine 1961 film adaptation directed by Robert Wise, which stayed true to Jackson's source material and raised hackles by keeping its ghosts wisely offscreen. This vapid remake is an utterly mechanical travesty, wasting fantastic sets, big bucks, solid special effects artisans, and a solid cast in a sterling example of "filmmaking-by-committee" dynamics. An abomination, to be avoided at all costs. Better yet, it won't cost you *anything* to just leave this sucker on the shelves.[64]

(5) *HELLRAISER: INFERNO* (2000): Another bummer for Clive Barker fans marks the continuing decline of the series that kicked off with Barker's 1987 directorial debut, which still packs quite a wallop. This woof-bag features Craig Sheffer (lead in Barker's *Nightbreed*, second-fiddle in the Sandra Bullock cheapie *Fire in the Amazon*) sweating, twitching, and sniveling as the unpleasant LAPD hero whose corruption, curiosity, and occasional depravities lead him to the Lament Configuration, Cenobites, severed fingers, and damnation. Pinhead has one, count it, *one* scene; some diverting hallucinatory horrors, but little else.

(6) *SCREAM 3* (1999): Thankfully, the concluding installment of a trilogy that has wandered far, far afield from all that made the original *Scream* of interest to its

---

[64] See *Blur, Vol. 1*, pp. 130-131.

target audience. The surviving high school and college grads of the prior two installments are caught in the vortex of a fresh spate of copy-cat murders amid tinseltown Hollywood settings and a bitchy clutch of new characters. You quickly come to hate them all, and hope for the worst, which doesn't happen soon enough in this shivering clam of a movie. Wes Craven's best work (*The Hills Have Eyes, A Nightmare on Elm Street, The People Under the Stairs*, and, yes, *Scream*) emerged from hunger during his lean times; now that he's a fat cat, he's lost his way again. I'm not wishing you into the poorhouse, Wes, but get a grip, man.

PUMPKIN PIX: HALLOWEEN VIDEOS FOR KIDS & FAMILIES by Maia and Danny Bissette [65]

Given the dearth of family-friendly titles in this year's crop of horror videos, I asked my teenagers, Maia Rose

---

[65] The original byline for this complete, two-part Halloween 2000 column read as follows: *Stephen R. Bissette is a co-manager and buyer at First Run Video, and regular columnist for the Reformer. He has his own crop of Halloween horrors in local bookstores, having illustrated Joe Citro's The Vermont Ghost Guide (University Press of New England), co-authored The Monster Book: Buffy the Vampire Slayer (Pocket Books), and his short story "Jigsaw" is featured in the anthology Hellboy: Odd Jobs (Dark Horse). Maia and Daniel Bissette are currently students at BUHS, ages seventeen and fourteen, respectively; Maia's first published short fiction appeared in VMag. All together, they've seen more horror movies than you can shake a stick at, though why you'd shake a stick at such a thing is beyond them.* At the time of this book's publication in 2008, Maia is 25 years old and an artist; Daniel is 22 and a musician and artist.

and Daniel, to put together their own list of 'suitable-for-all-ages' family-friendly Halloween movies they'd recommend. Since Danny just tossed titles into the mix from the back seat while Maia did all the actual writing, let's just say this is by Maia Bissette with an assist from her younger brother. Thanks! Okay, I'll shut up now, kids.

(1) ***MONSTER SQUAD*** (1987): Dracula, the Creature, the Mummy, the Wolfman, and Frankenstein vs. a treehouse full of kids. My personal favorite while growing up.

(2) ***THE NIGHTMARE BEFORE CHRISTMAS*** (1993): Tim Burton's visually-amazing stop-motion Halloween and/or Christmas film follows the tradition of the *Rudolph the Red-Nosed Reindeer* TV Christmas special — only it's better!

(3) ***IT'S THE GREAT PUMPKIN, CHARLIE BROWN!*** (1966): At this point, *It's the Great Pumpkin* is a Halloween tradition for most, and Linus' finest half-hour.

(4) ***E.T.*** (1982): A classic, as well as one of the few extra-terrestrial movies that portrays an alien creature as harmless. The story also takes place during the Halloween season, so it belongs here.

(5) ***GOONIES*** (1985): Just ask anyone who ever saw this movie as a kid and they'll probably tell you they loved it.

(6) ***THE WITCHES*** (1989): Produced by Jim Henson, this British film is one of the only live-action movies about witches that's aimed at a child audience. *[Hey, Maia, what about* The Wizard of Oz? *I know, "shut up, Dad" - Dad]* I was lucky enough to see it in the theater.

(7) ***ERNEST SCARED STUPID*** (1991): The ultimate battle against the Boogeyman with plenty of Ernest P. Worrel-esque humor.

(8) ***FRANKENWEENIE*** (1984): One of Tim Burton's earliest creations. It's a very cool little film with a silly title.

(9) ***BEETLEJUICE*** (1988): An incredibly off-the-wall ghost story with a great soundtrack and clever humor.

(10) ***KING KONG*** (1933): Most kids refuse to watch black-and-white movies in this day and age, but *King Kong* is an absolute classic that all should see.

(11) ***LITTLE MONSTERS*** (1989): Sure, this is Fred Savage's strangest role, worth seeing because there's nothing else like it.

(12) ***EXPLORERS*** (1985): From the creator of *Gremlins*, this has got to be one of the greatest sci-fi movies of my youth.

About the Author

Stephen R. Bissette is world renowned for his 30+ years of work in comics (*Saga of the Swamp Thing, Taboo, 1963, Tyrant*, etc.) and now savors life as an artist, writer, lecturer and instructor. His latest comic story appeared in the anthology *Secrets & Lies* (Magic Inkwell Press, 2008) and he recently co-authored *Prince of Stories: The Many Worlds of Neil Gaiman* with Hank Wagner and Christopher Golden for St. Martin's Press. He presently teaches at the Center for Cartoon Studies in White River Jct., VT, and lives in Windsor, VT with his wife Marjory. Visit his website at www.srbissette.com

S.R. Bissette's Blur, Volume 1 is also available from Black Coat Press.

CPSIA information can be obtained at www.ICGtesting.com
Printed in the USA
LVOW041736270712

291887LV00001B/17/P